The Quality of Police Education

A Critical Review with Recommendations for Improving Programs in Higher Education

A Report Prepared with the Support of the Police Foundation

Lawrence W. Sherman & the National Advisory Commission on Higher Education for Police Officers

Warren Bennis, Chair
Tom Bradley
Lee Brown
Hugo Masini
Stephen May
Norval Morris
Patrick V. Murphy
Robert M. O'Neil
Charles B. Saunders, Jr.

Richard A. Staufenberger, Project Officer
Maureen McLeod, Research Associate

The Quality of
Police Education

Jossey-Bass Publishers

San Francisco • Washington • London • 1978

THE QUALITY OF POLICE EDUCATION
*A Critical Review with Recommendations for Improving Programs
in Higher Education*
        by Lawrence W. Sherman and the National Advisory Commission
        on Higher Education for Police Officers

Copyright © 1978 by: Police Foundation
                       1909 K Street
                       Washington, D.C. 20006

                       Jossey-Bass, Inc., Publishers
                       433 California Street
                       San Francisco, California 94104

                       Jossey-Bass Limited
                       28 Banner Street
                       London EC1Y 8QE

Library of Congress Catalogue Card Number LC 78-62575

International Standard Book Number ISBN 0-87589-389-9

Manufactured in the United States of America

JACKET DESIGN BY WILLI BAUM

FIRST EDITION

Code 7830

*The Jossey-Bass Series
in Higher Education*

Preface

A decade ago the American police were in trouble. Conservatives criticized the police for failing to control crime. Liberals criticized them for brutality, corruption, racism, and failure to provide due process. The troubles of the police were a favorite topic of the news media, and several national commissions wrestled with the question of how to improve the police. One of the most popular of the many proposals was higher education for police. The idea that a college-educated police officer would be a better police officer gained wide support, and a federal program supporting police education was created that soon provided over forty million dollars a year. By one estimate, the number of college programs related to policing increased from 125 in 1965 to 1,245 in 1976 (Kobetz, 1975, p. 7), and the proportion of police officers with at least some college education increased from 20 percent in 1960 to 32 percent in 1970 and to 46 percent in 1975 (National Planning Association, 1976, p. V-138).

Today it is police education that is in trouble. The decade of rapid expansion has come to an abrupt halt, and the future of federal funding is growing more uncertain. Higher education for police has been torn by internal strife among police educators and attacked by police administrators, academics, and several national study groups. The central thrust of this criticism is that police education is generally low in quality.

Measured by traditional standards, there is substantial evidence that police education is often poor in quality. But as higher education increasingly serves nontraditional students with nontraditional programs, traditional standards of quality are rapidly breaking down. The troubles of police education are symptomatic of the troubles of higher education in general. Conflicts over the quality of police education are part of a larger conflict over the nature and purpose of all higher education.

Conflicts over the quality of police education are also linked to conflicts over the quality of policing. Both the police and their educators are subjected to diverse and conflicting public expectations. Some people expect higher education to make the police more efficient at performing their present tasks. Others would like to see education serve as a basis for changing the nature of police tasks, or even for changing the objectives of policing. The conflicting expectations of the police role in society have made it very difficult to define the objectives of higher education for the police. As Richard Myren (1976), a leading police educator, has put it, "How can we say what we want education to do for policing until the public can agree on what it wants policing to do for the community?"

The conflict and confusion over purpose in both higher education and policing have created problems in every aspect of police education: What subjects should be taught for police careers, where should they be taught, who should teach them, who should study them, and how should police department personnel policies take account of them? Some of these problems are the normal growing pains of any new field of professional education. Unlike higher education for other professions, however, those concerned with police education do not even agree that there should be a specialized course of study related to policing. A Twentieth Century Fund (1976) task force report, for example, has recommended that police students take only liberal arts courses, leaving specialized study in police-related topics to the police academies. Nonetheless, most higher education for police careers now takes place in specialized undergraduate programs of study in law enforcement and criminal justice subjects. And by even the most modern conceptions of quality, the quality of many of these programs is dismal.

The condition of police education in 1978 is much like the condition of medical education in 1908, when Abraham Flexner undertook a comprehensive study of every medical school in the United States and Canada. The Flexner report (1910), with the help of substantial foundation resources and the growing strength of the American Medical Association, had a major impact on medical education, forcing the diploma mills out of business and integrating medical education into the university. As Cheit (1975) has noted, similar results were achieved in engineering by the Mann (1918) and Grinter (American Society for Engineering Education, 1955) reports, in business education by the Carnegie (Pierson and others, 1959) and Ford (Gordon and Howell, 1959) reports, and in forestry by the National Academy of Sciences study (Graves and Guise, 1932). In hopes of producing a similar impact on police education, the Police Foundation decided in 1976 to sponsor this report.

The Police Foundation is a privately funded, independent organization established by the Ford Foundation in 1970 and dedicated to supporting innovation and improvement in policing. Concerned about the present condition of police education, the Police Foundation assembled the National Advisory Commission on Higher Education for Police Officers to examine this question: *How can the quality of police education be improved to make it a more effective force for changing the police?*

The commission sought answers to this question in a variety of ways. We began by meeting with faculty, students, and alumni of the police education programs at the University of Cincinnati, of which commission chair Warren Bennis was then president. We then wrote to over two hundred state and national organizations representing both law enforcement and higher education, soliciting their viewpoints on the key issues addressed in this book. We held regional public forums in San

Francisco, New York, and Chicago, at which police officers, city administrators, police union leaders, representatives of minority police officers, college administrators, and faculty members in police programs expressed their views. Several consultants prepared reports on selected topics requiring in-depth study, including five empirical research projects. The commission met with the academic association of faculty members in the police and criminal justice programs, the Academy of Criminal Justice Sciences, at the association's 1977 convention. The executive director of the commission addressed the Education and Training Section of the largest organization of police officials, the International Association of Chiefs of Police, at its 1977 convention. In addition, the commission received hundreds of letters from police officers, students, and faculty members all over the country.

The report draws heavily on the statistical portrait of police education assembled by the multimillion-dollar "Nationwide Survey of Law Enforcement Criminal Justice Personnel Needs and Resources," a study mandated by the Congress in 1973 and completed in 1976, which concluded that the quality of federally supported police education programs was "disappointingly low" (National Planning Association, 1976, p. V-181). In general, that survey confirmed the predictions made by commission member Charles B. Saunders in his 1970 Brookings Institution study, *Upgrading the American Police,* as well as the analysis offered by Charles Tenney in his 1971 Law Enforcement Assistance Administration study, *Higher Education Programs in Law Enforcement and Criminal Justice.* The report also draws upon the perspective on police education presented by Herman Goldstein in his 1977 treatise, *Policing a Free Society.* The new policy contribution this book makes is its action recommendations to a wide range of actors for changing police education. The new scientific contribution this book makes is its reported findings of a survey showing strong correlations between faculty characteristics and course content (as measured by the books assigned for the courses).

In preparing this report, the commission has drawn mainly on the police and higher education communities, where the greatest knowledge of the issues can be found. In publishing the report, however, the commission seeks to address a broader audience: members of Congress, Justice Department officials, state legislators, state higher education authorities, civil service commissions, city administrators, as well as police administrators, students, college and university boards of trustees, presidents, deans, and faculty members. Collectively, these groups make—or are empowered to make—the vital decisions that will shape the future purpose, character, and quality of higher education for police officers. It is to these decision makers that this report and its recommendations are addressed.

In examining the major policy issues in police education, the report attempts to present the evidence and arguments for all sides of the issues as a basis for the commission's recommendations. A summary of the recommendations and the rationale for each is presented before the main body of the text. Wherever possible, the recommendations are directed to specific decision makers.

Part One of the book, on the purpose of police education, reviews the problems of policing and the historical development of higher education as a strategy for dealing with those problems, as well as the recent debates over the objectives of educating the police. Arguing that a primary objective should be educating the police for change, we then trace the implications of that objective in Part Two, on the quality of police education, for the major academic issues in police education: the curriculums appropriate for police careers, the standards and commitment of colleges offering specialized police education programs, the qualifications of the faculty teaching in these programs, and the nature of student experiences in police education. Part Three, on police education and change, shows how both police and educational policies must be changed if education is to have a major impact on policing. The book concludes with a detailed strategy for changing police education.

Acknowledgments

We owe a great debt to the many people and organizations who contributed their ideas, their time, and their resources to our work. The students and faculty of the University of Cincinnati, especially Robert Mills and the late Gene E. Carte, provided our first close-up view of the problems of police education. Our Cincinnati session also profited from the insights of the Cincinnati Police Division and its chief, Myron J. Leistler.

The three regional forums would not have been possible without the hospitality of President Otto Butz of Golden Gate University, President Gerald W. Lynch of John Jay College, and Chancellor Donald H. Riddle of the University of Illinois at Chicago Circle. Lieutenant John Kerr of the Nassau County Police Department deserves our thanks for suggesting the idea of the forums to us. Terry Eisenberg deserves special thanks for his help in organizing the San Francisco forum, as do Richard H. Ward, Marie Rosen, and Denise Dwyer for (among many other things) the New York forum and James Osterburg and Seymour Raven for the Chicago forum. The most important people at the forums, though, were the many participants (listed in Appendix 2) who came great distances to spend what was never enough time in sharing their thoughts with the commission.

Mike Genz and Harold Wool spared considerable time from conducting the National Planning Association's survey of police education to explain it to us. Gordon Misner, J. Price Foster, Arthur Brandstatter, and Richard Myren all gave valuable counsel to the Police Foundation during its planning for the project. William P. Brown offered helpful comments on early drafts of several chapters. Eva F. Sherman read the first draft of every chapter with a sharp eye for organization and clarity.

Commission consultants Gene E. Carte, James B. Jacobs, Samuel Magdovitz, Richard Myren, Donald J. Newman, Bruce T. Olson, Elinor Ostrom, Gwynne Peirson, Thomas Reppetto, Donald H. Riddle, Richard Schick, Dennis C. Smith, David T. Stanley, and John Stead provided a wealth of insights to the commission, and we urge readers interested in their reports to request copies of them from the Police Foundation.

Jayne Parker and Karen Boston smoothed the way for the commission meeting arrangements from Washington. Maureen J. M. Ely got things organized in Albany and helped design the books survey. Harriet Spector exhibited her usual grace under pressure in getting the manuscript to press on time.

The School of Criminal Justice at the State University of New York at Albany provided office space, mailing facilities, and research assistance in support of the commission director's research activities, although it should not be held responsible for any aspect of the work of the organizationally autonomous commission. The school's dean, Donald J. Newman, and former dean (now president of the university), Vincent O'Leary, deserve particular thanks for both the resources and the ideas they contributed to the project.

We must also thank the hundreds of people who took the time to express their views in writing to the commission. Many of the letters we received in response to our request for viewpoints were lengthy and thoughtful essays, and only the limitation of space prevents us from incorporating more of them in the report. The almost 300 heads of police education programs who returned our questionnaire were crucial to a key element of our study, as were the many textbook publishers who provided us with copies of the books named in the survey responses.

Two people must be thanked in a special category for their personal qualities, qualities that meant a great deal to this effort. One is Clurie Bennis, whose hospitality at several commission meetings provided just the right atmosphere. The other is Richard Staufenberger, assistant director of the Police Foundation, whose coolheaded judgment kept the project on an even keel.

Albany, New York   Lawrence W. Sherman
June 1978

Contents

⟩━◯━◯━◯━◯━◯━◯━◯━◯━◯━◯⟨

Part Three: Change

The Authors

Lawrence W. Sherman is assistant professor in the Graduate School of Criminal Justice, State University of New York (SUNY) at Albany, director of the Project on Homicide by Police Officers at the Criminal Justice Research Center, and executive director of the National Advisory Commission on Higher Education for Police Officers.

A graduate of Denison University (B.A. degree in political science, 1970), the University of Chicago (M.A. degree in social science, 1970), and Cambridge University (Diploma in Criminology, 1973), Sherman received the Ph.D. degree in sociology from Yale University in 1976. A 1970-1971 Alfred P. Sloan Foundation Urban Fellow in the Office of the Mayor, New York City, he also served as a research analyst in the Office of the Police Commissioner in New York in 1971-1972 and an associate-in-research at Yale University in 1974-1976.

Sherman is the author of *Scandal and Reform: Controlling Police Corruption* (1978), coauthor of *Team Policing:*

Seven Case Studies (1973), and editor of *Police Corruption: A Sociological Perspective* (1974). He is a contributing editor of the *Criminal Law Bulletin* and has written over twenty-five articles, book chapters, and monographs on policing, organizations, and the sociology of law.

Lawrence Sherman and his wife, Eva, an assistant counsel of the SUNY system, live in Albany, New York.

Warren Bennis chairs the National Advisory Commission on Higher Education for Police Officers. Formerly president of the University of Cincinnati, Bennis has also served as provost of SUNY at Buffalo. A graduate of Antioch College, he received the Ph.D. degree from the Sloan School of Management at the Massachusetts Institute of Technology.

Tom Bradley has been mayor of Los Angeles since 1973. A former Los Angeles police lieutenant and city council member, Bradley has served on several advisory boards of colleges in the Los Angeles area, where he has also practiced law. He received the LL.B. degree from Southwestern University.

Lee Brown is public safety commissioner of Atlanta. The former sheriff and director of justice services for Multnomah County, Oregon, Brown has also taught at Howard University. A graduate of San Jose State University, he earned his Ph.D. degree in criminology from the University of California at Berkeley.

Hugo Masini is chief of police of Hartford, Connecticut, and president of the American Academy for Professional Law Enforcement, a national organization of college-educated police officers. Masini rose to the highest uniformed rank in the New York City police department during his career there. He is a graduate of Columbia College and the Baruch School of the City College of New York.

Stephen May is vice-chairman of the New York State Board of Elections and member of the Board of Directors of the Police Foundation. A graduate of Wesleyan University and the Georgetown University Law School, he was mayor of Rochester from 1970 to 1974.

Norval Morris is dean of the University of Chicago Law School. An internationally known criminologist, he earned the LL.B. degree and LL.M. degree from the University of Melbourne and a Ph.D. degree in criminology from the London School of Economics.

Patrick V. Murphy is president of the Police Foundation and former chief police executive in New York City, Detroit, Washington, D.C., and Syracuse. Murphy served as dean of what is now the John Jay College of Criminal Justice, City University of New York. He earned the B.A. degree at St. John's University and the M.P.A. degree from the Baruch School of the City College of New York.

Robert M. O'Neil is vice-president of Indiana University for Bloomington and member of the Carnegie Council on Policy Studies in Higher Education. He has taught at Tufts, the University of California at Berkeley, and SUNY at Buffalo. A former law clerk to Justice William J. Brennan, O'Neil is a graduate of Harvard College and Harvard Law School.

Charles B. Saunders, Jr., is vice-president for Governmental Relations, American Council on Education. A Princeton graduate, he served as Deputy Assistant Secretary for Education of the Department of Health, Education, and Welfare.

Richard A. Staufenberger has been assistant director of the Police Foundation since 1973. He has taught at the University of Nebraska, Howard University, and the Univer-

sity of Maryland, where he earned the Ph.D. degree in
political science.

Maureen McLeod is a doctoral student at the Graduate School
of Criminal Justice, SUNY at Albany. A 1975 graduate of
Mundelein College, she served as research associate of the
National Advisory Commission on Higher Education for
Police Officers from 1977 to 1978.

The Quality of Police Education

A Critical Review with Recommendations for Improving Programs in Higher Education

A Report Prepared with the Support of the Police Foundation

Summary
of Recommendations

Part One: Purposes

This report addresses one of the most important objectives of police education, one that in recent years has received too little attention: fostering basic change in policing. Higher education for police officers was first proposed fifty years ago as a strategy for changing the police role in society, and the same objective was implicit in the federal legislation enacted ten years ago to support police education. Yet the present structure of police education often results in little more than tacking credentials on to police personnel, serving the status quo in policing rather than stimulating change. Police education will have to do much more if it is to help the police find new methods, new organizational structure, and a more effective role in society for coping with crime and providing social justice.

The commission believes that the best way to educate the police institution for change is to develop the capacity of the police to use knowledge to solve problems. The art of using knowledge includes the habits of working with written and spoken ideas, computational tools, and information gathered from many sources to produce and test new conclusions. Much of the college education that present and future police officers now receive develops those essential habits. But much of it—particularly the courses offered in specialized police education

1

programs—does not. In order to improve the quality of many of these programs, major changes must be made in their curriculums, the level of resource support they receive from their colleges, the qualifications of their faculty, and the nature of their students' educational experiences.

The commission's recommendations rest on the premise that more and better higher education may be the key to producing the personal qualities necessary for police officers to create a new role for the police institution. Our review of the scant empirical evidence about this premise was inconclusive, but it did suggest that the recent dramatic increase in the educational levels of police personnel has had little impact on police performance. Given the many complex factors shaping police behavior, as well as the often poor quality of police education, the absence of any impact—if true—is not surprising. No matter how high the quality of police education, education alone cannot change the police. New organizational designs, better management, and community leadership are also necessary conditions of change. The potential contribution of higher education to police work will not be realized until police department policies generally treat education as a resource rather than a threat.

The problems of police education are the fault of systems, not individuals. There are many conscientious police educators who should not be blamed for providing an education whose nature and content is shaped by forces beyond their control. Accordingly, we direct our recommendations for changing police education to the major institutional actors who now control it.

Part Two: Quality

Curriculum. Many police officers have been educated in traditional liberal arts and science fields, from history and literature to mathematics and physics. Others have graduated from professional education programs in such fields as business administration and teacher education. In recent years, however, present and future police officers have most often majored in specialized criminal justice or police science programs. Although we lump these programs together in this report under the common label of "police education programs," there are three very different types of specialized programs. One type is an interdisciplinary liberal arts and science curriculum in criminal justice and criminology, which stresses the explanation and understanding of crime and social control. Another type is a professional education curriculum in criminal justice, which stresses the description of the complex issues and operations of the entire criminal justice system. A third type is a paraprofessional or vocational training curriculum in police "science" or "technology," which stresses the prescription of the techniques used to perform basic police tasks.

In one respect or another, all three types of specialized police education programs are too narrow. The commission believes that police officers should be educated in a wide variety of disciplines, including but not limited to the police education programs. Given the great concentration of resources and enrollments in these programs, however, it is most important that their curriculums be changed.*

3-1. *All college programs focusing on issues in policing and criminal justice should provide a broad education that is useful for many careers and for living through an uncertain future,* if only because half of all "preservice" graduates of these programs do not enter police employment.

3-2. *The required number of specialized courses in police and criminal justice in any police education program should not exceed one fourth of the total course work for a degree.* Courses on urban planning, family relations, and psychology are just as relevant to police work as courses on crime, law, and police organization. Students should be counseled out of taking all the criminal justice courses available, in favor of taking related courses in other fields.

3-3. *Police education programs that offer vocational training courses (courses that train students to perform specific*

---

*The recommendations are numbered according to the chapters in which they appear.

police tasks) should replace those courses with more analytical and conceptual courses on issues related to those tasks. Courses on how to use firearms, for example, should be replaced with courses covering the law, ethics, and social science research on police use of force. In geographical areas that lack an adequate police training academy, colleges filling the training gap should keep the training program separate from the academic curriculum.

3-4. *Police education programs at the undergraduate level should give greater emphasis to the major issues in doing police work and less emphasis to issues of police management and supervision.* Very few police officers will become managers or supervisors, and a specialized curriculum should reflect that fact by stressing the enormous complexity, power, and importance of the police officer's job.

3-5. *Every police education program should include in its required curriculum a thorough consideration of the value choices and ethical dilemmas of police work.* Because there are no adequate texts and materials presently available in this important area, either the U.S. Law Enforcement Assistance Administration, under section 406(e) of the Safe Streets Act,* or private foundations should support the development of curricular materials on police ethics.

3-6. *Police education programs using a "criminal justice system" framework for their required curriculum should also include comprehensive treatment of the most commonly performed police work, which falls outside of the criminal justice system.* Many studies have shown that little of what the police do is connected with the criminal justice system. Much police work is linked to health care, social service, and other systems, and much is separate from any broader system. Even the most liberal interdisciplinary criminal justice curriculum will be too narrow as a police education program if it is confined to the police role in the criminal justice system.

*Or its equivalent section in any new authorization or reorganization bill for the Law Enforcement Assistance Administration.

3-7. *College courses on policing should be continually revised to reflect and incorporate the rapidly growing body of research findings on police behavior.* The commission's review of the textbooks used in courses on policing disclosed that few of them discuss recent (or any) empirical research on the police. Until more research-oriented textbooks become available, instructors should assign reading materials other than texts, such as the inexpensive research monographs published by the U.S. Law Enforcement Assistance Administration and the Police Foundation.

3-8. *The U.S. Law Enforcement Assistance Administration (or any successor organization) should establish a research program on the relationships between different college curriculums and both the individual performance of college-educated police officers and the organizational performance of the departments they serve.* Our recommendations about the curriculum, although supported by extensive research on the general impact of college on students, rest more on faith than on fact in their focus on police education. A long-term program of research following cohorts of officers throughout their careers is needed to provide a better knowledge base for determining the curriculum most effective for changing the police, as well as for answering the more basic question of whether education can make a difference in police behavior.

Colleges. Most of the 1,070 police education programs the commission identified have been created in the past ten years, often in a rather hasty manner. There is some evidence—although it is far from conclusive—that many of the programs were created because the availability of federal funds provided a potential revenue surplus from police education. There is better evidence that some colleges have failed to commit sufficient resources to their police education programs. About one quarter of them, for example, failed to provide even one full-time faculty member for police education in 1975-76, even though some of them had hundreds of students. Predominantly off-campus teaching, loose practices for granting credit, and other indications can be found to support the claim that some colleges are more interested in high enrollments than in quality police education. Improving the quality of police education will require these colleges to provide greater resources and to enforce higher standards.

4-1. *Colleges should offer a police education program only as a long-term commitment demonstrated by institutional support commensurate with that provided to comparable programs.* Where part-time faculty and other forms of short-term commitment are justified on the basis that the demand for the program is only temporary, the program should not be offered at all.

4-2. *Colleges should rely on a core of full-time faculty to staff their police education programs and should rely much less on part-time faculty. In no case should part-time faculty be employed for more than 25 percent of a program's annual credit hour production.* Although some part-time faculty can make valuable contributions to a police education program (see recommendation 5-4), an overreliance on part-time faculty produces inadequate faculty participation in institutional governance and advisement and counseling of students.

4-3. *College libraries should engage in retroactive acquisition programs, as needed, in order to bring library resources for police education up to the present level for other programs in the college.* Many colleges reportedly have less adequate library resources for police education than they do for the more established programs. This situation must be corrected if police education students are to develop the habits of seeking and using written knowledge to solve problems.

4-4. *Colleges should grant no academic credit for attendance at police agency training programs.* Very few police academy training programs contain sufficient conceptual content to justify college credit. If a valuable learning experience is gained in this fashion, it should be carefully evaluated for life experience credit, not granted automatically as a means of attracting students to enroll in a program.

4-5. *Life experience credit for police service should be awarded only after careful review consistent with the guidelines recommended by the American Council on Education and endorsed by the Council on Postsecondary Accreditation.* Some colleges have offered up to three years of college credit for police experience, but their evaluation procedures have often been quite loose. Experience in itself is an inadequate basis for awarding credit. Colleges offering such credit in police education programs should devote greater attention to the documentation and evaluation of the learning acquired from police experience.

4-6. *Classroom instruction in police education programs should take place on college campuses in order to encourage greater student interaction with diverse kinds of people.* Off-campus teaching in police education programs, often done in police station houses, can suffer from excessive homogeneity among the students. On-campus instruction has a greater chance of providing a mix of students of differing values and backgrounds. Where off-campus instruction is offered, however, the colleges should provide easy access to library and other educational resources.

In general, a high-quality police education program can be provided in any organizational context of higher education. The one exception to this rule is the industrial or vocational education units in community and junior colleges providing terminal two-year degrees, often called the Associate of Applied Science. Since we believe that every police officer should complete a baccalaureate degree (see recommendation 7-3), since many of the credits from the terminal two-year degrees are not accepted as credit toward a four-year degree, and since police work is far more complex than the other occupations (such as auto mechanics and cosmetology) for which training is provided in these units, we recommend that no police education be offered in this context (see also recommendation 8-8).

4-7. *Community colleges should phase out their terminal two-year degree programs in police education. Meanwhile, special efforts should be made to increase opportunities for*

*community college students by ensuring articulation be-
tween two- and four-year programs.* These changes are
necessary for community colleges to serve more to draw
students into a full four-year college education and less to
"cool them out" of their four-year aspirations. (See also
recommendations 7-3 and 8-8.)

Faculty. The faculty members in police education programs are generally less qualified academically than faculty
members in other fields. Most of them have extensive criminal
justice experience but little graduate education. Almost none of
them have made major scholarly contributions to the field, and
many have never conducted any research. There is accordingly a
great need for intensive upgrading of the faculty in police education programs.

5-1. *Faculty members in police education programs at any level
should be required to have completed at least two full
years of postgraduate education.* Although this modest
standard cannot ensure a high-quality faculty, it can probably increase the likelihood that each faculty member will
be a thoughtful and well-prepared teacher. And since almost one quarter of all criminal justice faculty have no
graduate degrees, this standard would represent a major
upgrading of the faculty.

5-2. *Police education programs should actively seek out Ph.D.s
in arts and science disciplines to serve as faculty members.
The Law Enforcement Assistance Administration (or any
successor organization) should fund programs for "retooling" these Ph.D.s into criminal justice scholars and teachers.* The usual justification for the low educational level of
police education faculty members is that there are not
enough people with graduate degrees in criminal justice to
fill the available positions. At its best, however, criminal
justice is an interdisciplinary field, and there are more than
enough qualified Ph.D.s in arts and sciences to staff police
education programs. Within relatively short periods of
time, they could be trained to apply their own disciplines
to issues in policing.

5-3. *Educational background, teaching ability, research, and commitment—rather than prior employment in a criminal justice agency—should be the most important criteria of faculty selection in police education programs. Prior criminal justice employment should be neither a requirement nor a handicap for faculty selection.* The most likely reason for the low educational level of police education faculty is that police experience has often been the primary criterion used in faculty selection. Police experience may enrich an instructor's ability to teach, but it is not usually sufficient preparation in itself. Moreover, some of the best teachers of police have never been police officers, just as some of the greatest law professors have never practiced law.

5-4. *Part-time faculty appointments in police education programs should be limited to people with unique practical expertise. Such appointments should be distinguished by the title of clinical professor.* Many police education programs are staffed by police academy instructors and police middle managers. While some of these part-time instructors may make contributions to a program that no full-time faculty member could make, most are probably hired because they cost less per course than full-time faculty members. By limiting part-time practitioner-faculty to the very best, and by distinguishing clinical from academic instruction, colleges can strengthen instruction in both areas.

5-5. *Both the Law Enforcement Assistance Administration (or any successor organization) and private foundations should consider developing a program of one- or two-year fellowships for full-time faculty in police education programs to pursue their graduate education or to engage in research or the development of new courses.* A program of off-campus faculty development would give those faculty members who would be excluded under recommendation 5-1 the opportunity to upgrade themselves. Better-educated faculty members could use the program to make contributions to the field.

5-6. *Expanded opportunities should be provided on the campus for the continuing improvement and development of the teaching skills of faculty members in police education programs.* On-campus programs of faculty development do not necessarily require outside funding and could provide an immediate improvement in the quality of teaching in police education.

5-7. *Private foundations should consider the possible creation of named chairs in criminal justice or police administration at colleges or universities with a long-term commitment to police education.* Chairs could attract first-rank scholars to research and teaching on police issues and lend academic respectability to a new' and developing field. Chairs at colleges deeply committed to police education would be best for teaching purposes.

Student Experiences. The prevailing educational experiences of students learning for police careers are of lesser quality than they could be. There is a great need to strengthen police education by intensifying student experiences. Most students now attend classes as part-time commuters; and part-time education, as several studies have found, is generally less beneficial than full-time residential education. The student experiences in police education are partly a result of federal policies for supporting police education and partly a result of the modern structure of American higher education. While both the federal support of police education and the near universal access to nonresidential education have made higher education possible for many who would not otherwise have acquired it, both of these influences can be modified to improve the educational quality of student experiences.

6-1. *Congress should continue to fund the Law Enforcement Education Program (LEEP) at its present level, provided the program is restructured in the ways suggested here.* The many criticisms of LEEP are directed at its structure and operations, not its goals. Despite its generally poor administration and the poor quality of police education it has supported, LEEP remains the only federal program with the potential for changing the police through higher education.

6-2. *Congress should amend the statutory authorization of LEEP* to allow more intensive educational experiences through more extensive support of individual students than the present authorization for grants and loans allows. The limits on the support of each student should be high enough to cover all costs of full-time residential education.* The present structure of LEEP restricts student support to small grants for employees of criminal justice agencies (up to $400 a semester) and forgivable loans for "preservice" students (up to $2,200 a year). These limitations virtually preclude full-time residential educational experiences. While not all of LEEP should be allocated to the support of residential education, its authorization should provide enough flexibility for at least some funds to be used for that purpose.

6-3. *Federal, state, and local governments should devote greater resources to supporting one-year residential educational fellowships for both police officers and potential police managers. These fellowships should be offered in a diverse range of disciplines.* (See also recommendation 7-6.) More residential full-time education could be made available to in-service students by a combination of LEEP support and leaves with pay from police departments. The few efforts made in this area so far have largely been confined to potential police managers, but the importance of line police work merits giving equal attention to quality education for officers who may never be promoted out of doing police work.

6-4. *The administrators of LEAA's educational assistance programs should develop a program for sending potential police executives to the highest-quality schools of management to earn graduate degrees.* Many urban police departments are larger and more complex than many large cor-

---

*Title I, Part D, Section 406 (a-d), 42 U.S.C. Sec. 3701 and the following (Public Law 90-351) as amended by Public Laws 91-644 and 93-83.

porations. The study of management, and not of criminal justice or police administration, should be the best guarantee that police executives will take a sophisticated approach to managing their complex organizations.

6-5. *The Congress and the administrators of LEEP should give equal priority to supporting the education of both inservice police officers and other students planning to pursue police careers. Government policies at all levels should give highest priority to encouraging college education of officers before they begin their careers.* The commission believes that higher education can have the greatest impact on policing if students are educated before they enter police work. But since 1973 almost no LEEP support has been allocated to "preservice" students. Since the early need to upgrade the educational level of incumbent police personnel has largely been met, it is now appropriate to move toward greater emphasis on preservice education. (See also recommendation 7-3.)

6-6. *The Congress and the administrators of LEEP, in order to support the pursuit of a wide range of academic majors and courses by students participating in both LEEP and the Law Enforcement Internship Program should remove any requirements that course work be "directly related" to law enforcement and criminal justice. In-service students, presumably already familiar with the basic issues of policing, should be encouraged to study relevant subjects other than police science and criminal justice.* (See also recommendation 7-4.) Until the body of systematic, applied knowledge about policing is comparable to that in such fields as medicine or engineering, there is no reason for all police officers to study a common curriculum. The diverse and complex problems of policing can best be coped with collectively by personnel educated in a variety of disciplines.

6-7. *Every nonresidential police education program should provide and require brief, intensive residential periods of study at least once each semester or quarter.* The educational experiences of both in-service and preservice com-

muter students can be enhanced at very low cost by week-
end seminars or other programs for replicating the kind of
intellectual contact with other students routinely enjoyed
by residential college students.

Part Three: Change

Changing the Police. Many police departments have effectively prevented higher education from becoming an agent of
change. Their policies toward educated personnel have artfully
managed to produce the appearance of "better" personnel while
ensuring that even educated officers remain loyal to the values
and norms of the traditional police subculture. No matter how
high the quality of police education may be, it can have little
impact until certain widespread police department policies are
changed.

7-1. *Police departments should place less emphasis on educating the recruited and more emphasis on recruiting the educated. The organization, policies, and practices of police
departments should be modified to make better use of
educated personnel.* By failing to recruit college graduates
more extensively, police departments ensure that their
educated personnel will acquire an education filtered by
the occupational perspective of full-time police work,
which probably reduces the impact of college on the students. Those college graduates who are recruited often
leave police work early, possibly out of dislike for the current authoritarian atmosphere of most police departments.
The chicken-and-egg dilemma of designing police departments to make good use of educated personnel and of attracting more college graduates can be solved only when
both are done simultaneously.

7-2. *Police departments should conduct properly evaluated experiments with new organizational designs more appropriate for college-educated personnel.* Police organizational
designs have, in most important respects, remained unchanged since the early part of this century, when many

police officers were illiterate. More appropriate designs should be sought out—not with intuitive judgment but with careful research.

7-3. *All police departments should move now to require new recruits to have earned a baccalaureate degree and no police department should require two years of college as the minimum qualification for police recruits. Vigorous recruitment of qualified minority-group members should be undertaken in order to alleviate any possible exclusionary impact of this requirement upon minorities.* There now appear to be sufficient numbers of college graduates interested in police careers to fill most new recruit classes. Compromising on educational requirements at the two-year level might define police work as unsuitable for college graduates, and there is no need for such compromise from the standpoint of filling police positions. The now substantial numbers of minority college students and graduates provide a large enough pool for recruitment efforts to draw on in order to increase minority representation at the same time that educational requirements are increased.

7-4. *No major field of study should be specified in any college degree requirements for police positions.* (See also recommendation 6-6.) For the foreseeable future, any requirements that candidates for police positions hold degrees in criminal justice, police science, or other "directly related" fields would have the effect of excluding large numbers of highly capable and broadly educated people from making contributions to policing.

7-5. *No police salary increments should be awarded on a credit-by-credit basis.* While police departments should reward educational achievement, and while salary increments may be appropriate for the completion of a degree, a credit-by-credit system of salary increments can encourage such abuses as taking easy courses and attending college only for financial reasons.

7-6. *Police departments should regularly grant and encourage educational leaves of absence.* (See also recommendation 6-3.) Leaves afford the opportunity for full-time immersion in study that can help develop new perspectives and fresh insights on a police department's problems.

Changing Police Education. Perhaps more than other fields, police education programs have been vulnerable to a wide variety of influences external to the colleges in which they are offered. The interest of many police departments in maintaining their status quo has influenced police educational policies at almost every level, from Congress to the advisory boards of local police education programs. If police education can be sheltered from those interests, then it may be more likely to develop in the directions we recommend.

We are reluctant to create yet another kind of professional school in this era of contracting academic resources; however, a separate organizational identity for departments of criminal justice may often be the best way to strengthen the best programs and to build stronger ties to other disciplines. If a specialized program in police or criminal justice education is offered at all, it should be given the kind of autonomy that other professional education programs have used to flourish intellectually. At the same time, autonomy should not be allowed to perpetuate the currently widespread low standards. What is needed is a balance between increased external pressure for high quality and increased internal pressure for making policy decisions on the basis of academic judgments.

8-1. *Police education faculty members should seek more control over academic decisions in order to promote the objective of educating the police institution for change.* This recommendation is premised on the assumption that faculty standards will be improved and that faculty concerns will therefore increasingly shift from training students to do police work as it is presently done to educating them broadly, so that they may be better equipped to create a new kind of police work.

8-2. *College administrators should strengthen police education as a force for change, especially by protecting police education programs from the pressures of local agencies.* At many colleges deans and vice-presidents make the vital decisions about resource commitments, faculty selection, and even curriculum content. By adopting our recommendations despite the possible opposition of local police constituencies, college administrators can greatly improve the quality of police education.

8-3. *Police officials and other members of police education program advisory boards should avoid direct participation in such academic decisions as faculty selection or promotion and curriculum content.* While police officials can contribute valuable ideas and perspectives on matters of academic policy, there is no more reason for them to make academic decisions than there is for academics to make operational decisions in a police department.

8-4. *Accreditation of criminal justice programs should be explored as a possible strategy for changing police education, but neither the U.S. commissioner of education nor the Council on Postsecondary Accreditation should recognize any single organization as the accrediting authority for higher education programs in criminal justice. A more broadly based consortium, such as the Joint Commission on Criminology and Criminal Justice Education and Standards and the organizational members of its advisory group, is required to ensure that diverse curricular approaches are maintained.* The adoption of nationally recognized standards formulated by faculty associations may be the most effective way for colleges to improve the quality of police education, but great care must be taken to ensure that the professional education model of police education does not drive out the liberal arts model. The several faculty associations representing the diverse curriculums should all be represented in any accreditation process.

8-5. *State education agencies, and not state law enforcement training councils, should ensure that colleges provide their police education programs with adequate resources and otherwise guarantee their quality.* Where state agencies have the authority to regulate higher education programs, they should use that authority to pay special attention to police education in its still early stages of development. Law enforcement training councils, however, should be barred from prescribing standards for faculty selection and curriculum content in college programs, since the purpose of college programs is education, not training.

8-6. *State and federal agencies influencing the distribution of LEEP funds should give lowest priority to narrowly technical police education programs and highest priority to programs with a broader curriculum and better-educated faculty.* The process of selecting colleges for participation in LEEP has too often been guided by other than academic concerns. LEEP participation decisions should be used more aggressively by the agencies concerned to encourage the changes recommended here.

8-7. *Congress should keep the current programs of the Law Enforcement Assistance Administration's Office of Criminal Justice Education and Training intact under one administrative unit at the Department of Justice.* The administration of programs for improving the quality of police education should not be divorced from the administration of LEEP, as the Office of Management and Budget has proposed (as of this writing). Faculty and curriculum development efforts have only recently been linked to the policy decisions for distributing LEEP funds, and that linkage should be maintained. The proposed transfer of LEEP to a new Department of Education would threaten the present program for raising the standards of LEEP-funded education.

8-8. *Congress should amend the statutory authorization of the vocational education program to exclude police and criminal justice programs from eligibility.* The current curriculum guidelines of LEEP and the vocational education program are in direct opposition, one requiring education and the other requiring training. By taking police education out of the vocational education program, Congress would both remove the conflict and lend symbolic recognition to the complexity of police work. (See also recommendation 4-7.)

1

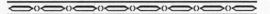

Higher Education and Police Reform

It has yet to be recognized that the work of the modern policeman requires professional training comparable to that for the most skilled profession.

Vollmer, [1936] 1971, p. 231

For over fifty years, the problems of policing have been blamed on the poor quality of police personnel. National study commissions, scholars, and police administrators have consistently argued that many of the problems of policing could be solved if more qualified people, particularly college graduates, were recruited to serve as police officers. The idea that police officers should be college educated has become a cornerstone of the movement to professionalize the police. The faith that better people can provide better policing has produced a vision of police reform through higher education.

Yet higher education alone cannot produce substantial changes in the nature and quality of police services in this country. The problems of policing have many causes other than the quality and education of police personnel. The major problems —conflicting public expectations for police behavior, inadequate methods for achieving police objectives, police violations of the

18

law, and poor relations between the police and the public—are caused more by the structure of our society and polity than they are by the people who do police work. Higher education for police officers may have little effect on those problems as long as the underlying causes remain. A broad strategy for dealing with those problems should include college-educated police personnel, but only as one element among many. In failing to recognize that higher education is only one of the many conditions necessary for changing the police, some police reformers have probably expected too much of higher education.

Whatever the potential value of higher education for changing the police, police education is now falling short of that potential. The early vision of police reform through higher education assumed that police education would be intellectually rigorous, conceptually broad, and provided by a scholarly faculty. Yet much police education today is intellectually shallow, conceptually narrow, and provided by a faculty that is far from scholarly. Rather than helping to change the police, police education appears to support the status quo, teaching what the police do now instead of inquiring what they could do differently. This chapter reviews the problems of policing and the reformers' vision of the kind of police education that could help solve those problems. The later chapters will show how different from the reformers' vision of police education the reality has become.

Problems of Policing

Ever since they were first created in the mid-nineteenth century (Lane, 1967; Fogelson, 1977), American police departments have suffered four basic problems. One problem is that different interest groups have expected the police to accomplish different and often conflicting objectives. Another is that the police never had adequate methods for meeting some of their most important objectives. A third problem is that some police officers have worked against police objectives by committing crimes themselves. Fourth, although general public esteem for the police has been gradually improving for a half century, the

American police have always encountered a great deal of hostility in their contacts with individual citizens.

Conflicting Objectives. In contrast to more homogeneous nations, Americans have never agreed on what they want their police to do—which laws the police should enforce and with what priorities. Police officers and administrators have been caught in the conflicts of class, ethnicity, and religion that have shaped our local politics. The police frequently have been under the control of one or another of the major interest groups but have rarely satisfied all groups.

The question of which laws to enforce is particularly intense in the area of personal morality. In the late nineteenth century, the efforts of the New York police to prohibit drinking on Sunday provoked beer-loving German immigrants to riot (Richardson, 1970). Modern police are under similar pressure to ignore laws against smoking marijuana. And even while the traditional laws regarding personal morality are slowly being rendered inactive by courts and legislatures, the police mandate is being extended to enforcing a new morality of public life-style: prohibitions on smoking in public places, for example, or against allowing dogs to defecate on the streets (Sherman, 1978b). Citizens often disagree with such laws, but they seem more likely to tell their police officers than to tell their legislators.

The conflicts over the role of the police extend well beyond their law enforcement responsibilities. Their legislative mandate to enforce all violations of all laws competes with their administrative mandate to perform a wide range of community services not directly related to law enforcement. All the recent research on how the police spend their time has found that very little of it is devoted to law enforcement. As virtually the only governmental agency available to citizens twenty-four hours a day, seven days a week, the police are asked to deal with all kinds of problems that citizens cannot handle themselves. One study of telephone calls to a metropolitan police department, for example, found that over half of the calls appeared to be requests for help with personal or interpersonal problems, seeking police assistance as "philosopher, friend, and guide" (Cumming, Cumming, and Edell, 1965). A study of calls made to the

Syracuse Police Department found that only 10 percent of them afforded a potential opportunity to enforce the law (Wilson, 1968, p. 20). Other studies have concluded that similarly low proportions of police tasks in both large and small police departments are related to crime (Bercal, 1970; Webster, 1973). As Goldstein (1977) observes, many of these studies fail to recognize the potential for crime in such "personal problem" calls as domestic disputes. But it is undeniable that police spend much of their time handling problems like accidents, illness, and stray or injured animals.

The requests by individual citizens for emergency services divert police resources from meeting the demands of citizens in general for reducing crime. The conflict between crime control and the other objectives of policing is not just a matter of which situations deserve police attention. The conflict also arises in many situations that the police confront. In responding to a robbery, for example, a police officer must often choose between rendering assistance to the victim or pursuing the fleeing offender (Goldstein, 1977). Value choices in policing arise on a regular basis; yet there is no public consensus to help police officers choose among the competing values.

The American Bar Association (1973) has recommended that each community explicitly identify its objectives for its police department and set priorities among those objectives. But few local police agencies in this country receive such guidance. Most communities seem reluctant to acknowledge the multiple and competing objectives of the police, let alone set priorities among them. Nor have police administrators attempted to obtain such guidance from their communities, preferring to leave the police mission stated in such vague terms as "to serve and protect."

Goldstein (1977, p. 35) has identified eight principal objectives of the police:

1. To prevent and control conduct widely recognized as threatening to life and property (serious crime).
2. To aid individuals who are in danger of physical harm, such as the victim of a criminal attack.

3. To protect constitutional guarantees, such as the right of free speech and assembly.
4. To facilitate the movement of people and vehicles.
5. To assist those who cannot care for themselves: the intoxicated, the addicted, the mentally ill, the physically disabled, the old, and the young.
6. To resolve conflict, whether it be between individuals, groups of individuals, or individuals and their government.
7. To identify problems that have the potential for becoming more serious problems for the individual citizen, for the police, or for government.
8. To create and maintain a feeling of security in the community.

Police departments are more different than they are alike (Gallas, 1977), and they vary widely in the frequency with which they are called upon to meet these various objectives. Yet all of them face the potential for public disagreement about the objectives. When they act unilaterally to emphasize one objective over another, they are often sharply criticized. For example, when police departments that dealt with antiwar protest marches decided that facilitating the movement of people and vehicles (objective 4) was more important than protecting the constitutional guarantees of free speech (objective 3), they were praised by conservatives and vilified by liberals. In this situation, as in many others, the police are the focal point of our conflicts over what kind of society we want to be.

Inadequate Methods for Meeting Objectives. Two of the most important objectives of policing are the control of serious crime and the resolution of conflict. American police departments, in general, have failed to accomplish these objectives. Police efforts seem to have had little impact on the rising crime rates of recent years (National Planning Association, 1976), although the statistical evidence is admittedly ambiguous on this point. The mismanagement of group conflict by the police helped spark the race riots of the 1960s (National Advisory Commission on Civil Disorders, 1968), and the police failure to help resolve interpersonal conflicts continues to result in domestic homicides in the 1970s (Police Foundation, 1977). Yet these failures of policing are not due to incompetence or laziness. Rather, they reflect the inadequacy of the methods available to the police for accomplishing their objectives.

Blaming the police for failing to control crime, of course, is like blaming doctors for failing to control cancer. In both cases the "failure" is premised on a public expectation that something should be done, despite the fact that adequate methods have not been found. And in both cases adequate methods may never be found. As one police executive argues, "American policing . . . cannot possibly wipe out crime, because the causes of the problem are huge, profound, and possibly beyond the capacity of any set of democratic institutions to eliminate" (Murphy and Plate, 1977, p. 25). Yet because of the public mythology—fostered by the police themselves—that the police do know how to control crime, they take most of the blame when the crime rate goes up—as well as most of the credit when it goes down (J. Q. Wilson, 1975).

The basic method the American police use to prevent crime is "preventive patrol," the visible presence of uniformed police officers on the streets at all times. The theory of preventive patrol was first proposed in eighteenth-century London (Colquhoun, [1806] 1969) and has been translated to the automobile age by the leading textbook on police administration: "Patrol in conspicuous automobiles . . . has a deterrent effect on criminals seeking a chance to attack and on opportunists who violate regulations when they think the police are not around. . . . The impression of police omnipresence created by conspicuous patrol thus . . . deters the potential offender" (Wilson, [1950] 1963, p. 245). Preventive patrol consumes the greatest portion of police resources and is the most expensive item in the criminal justice budget. One study of the Chicago Police Department found that uniformed patrol officers spent only 15 percent of their time performing any specific tasks; the other 85 percent theoretically was devoted to driving up and down the streets (Reiss, 1971b, p. 95).

The value of preventive patrol for deterring crime has seemed so obvious to police administrators and public officials that for almost two centuries no one tested the theory on which it was based. An experimental test of the theory was finally conducted by the Kansas City, Missouri, Police Department in 1972, with assistance from the Police Foundation. The findings raise disturbing questions about the adequacy of traditional patrol methods for deterring crime.

The Kansas City experiment randomly divided fifteen highly similar patrol areas (beats) into three groups. One group received the same amount of preventive patrol as it had before the experiment. Another group of patrol beats received a substantial increase in the number of police cars performing preventive patrol. Preventive patrol was withdrawn altogether from the third group of patrol beats, although police cars entered those areas to respond to citizen requests for police service. After one year of these arrangements, little difference was found among the three groups of patrol beats in either the level of crime (measured before and after the experiment in several different ways, including both official reports and surveys of local residents and business proprietors to see how often they had been victimized by crime) or the citizens' perception of police presence (Kelling and others, 1974). Despite some methodological weaknesses (see, for example, Larson, 1975), the study provides important evidence that "police time spent driving the streets waiting for something to happen is not time well spent" (J. Q. Wilson, 1975, p. 97).

How, then, should the police spend their time? What other methods can they use to prevent at least some of the serious crime in our communities? While a few answers have been suggested (J. Q. Wilson, 1975; Goldstein, 1977), most police departments have failed even to address this question. One reason the police do not have adequate methods for accomplishing their objectives is that they have not sought them out. Admittedly, the police generally have been quite innovative in recent years (Caiden, 1977), possibly even more so than any other municipal agency or component of the criminal justice system. Nevertheless, they have failed to weave research and experimentation into their institutional fabric (Bittner, 1970). Unlike the medical establishment, for example, they are not constantly testing and refining new methods for meeting their objectives.

The failure to seek adequate methods for meeting police objectives is even clearer in their attempts to resolve conflict. The most common police response to the wave of demonstrations and riots in the late 1960s seemed to have been the purchase of more sophisticated armament and weaponry for crowd control (Navasky, 1976). Some police departments sought out special training in techniques for conflict management (Broomfield, 1974), but most relied on the traditional "show of force" that does little to prevent violence (Goldstein, 1977). Few departments have experimented with alternative methods of crowd control or conducted systematic research on the effectiveness of various approaches.

Police methods for dealing with interpersonal conflict, a far more common task than dealing with large crowds, are barely more adequate. Experiments with different methods of quelling domestic disturbances began in the late 1960s (Bard, 1970, 1974), and a large number of police departments have undertaken training programs in family crisis intervention techniques (Leibman and Schwartz, 1973). Few of these programs, however, have been properly evaluated, and some of them seem to be more concerned with the appearance of improved techniques than with the substance. Of those that do change the methods of police response, the absence of proper evaluation prevents police administrators from knowing whether the new methods are more effective than the old ones.

Police Violations of Law. Both the conflicts over police objectives and the inadequacy of the available methods for accomplishing them have fostered widespread police violations of the law. These violations take three basic forms: excessive force, violation of constitutional rights and due process guarantees in criminal investigations, and corruption—the misuse of police authority for the personal gain of police officers or others, such as politicians.

Police brutality has probably declined in recent years, but it has certainly not disappeared. A century ago police routinely assaulted strikers and other protesters, and a police hero was given the affectionate nickname of "Clubber" (Steffens, 1931). A national crime commission reported in 1931 that the police routinely beat suspects until they signed confessions (Chafee,

Pollack, and Stern, 1931), and the Supreme Court soon barred the use of confessions coerced by the famous "third degree" (*Brown* v. *Mississippi,* 297 U.S. 278 [1936]). A study of police practices in Boston, Chicago, and Washington for seven weeks in the summer of 1966 found almost no violence in interrogations per se (Reiss and Black, 1967), but it documented unnecessary assaults on 3.2 percent of all criminal suspects that the police encountered, both on the street and in the station house (computed from Reiss, 1971a, p. 303). An analysis of public surveys on police practices in fifteen cities in the 1960s produced an estimate that over two million people had been beaten unnecessarily by the police (Stark, 1972, p. 78). As recently as 1978, the U.S. Civil Rights Commission named police misconduct as one of the major civil rights problems in the South (King, 1978).

The pattern of police brutality found by these and other studies (Chevigny, 1969; Westley, 1970; Toch, 1977) suggests that the police frequently are unable to accomplish their objective of resolving conflict. The causes of police brutality are complex, but as a problem of policing it is clearly linked to the inadequacy of the methods available to the police. With more effective techniques for coping with conflict situations, the police might use less force against their fellow citizens.

Police brutality is also linked to the diverse public expectations for policing. Some citizens clearly want the police to "break heads," perhaps hoping that violent policing will be a deterrent to crime (Gamson and McEvoy, 1970). One out of five respondents to a 1968 Harris poll, for example, approved of a "policeman striking an adult male citizen if he had said vulgar and obscene things to the policeman." In the same survey, however, almost three quarters of the respondents (73 percent) could not imagine *any* situation where they would "approve of a policeman striking an adult male citizen" (Stark, 1972, p. 221). The American public is clearly divided over how much violence the police should use.

The diverse conceptions of proper police conduct also foster police violations of due process. The 1966 field observation study found that police frequently failed to conform to the requirements of Supreme Court decisions regarding interrogations, confessions, and searches of citizens and their property (Reiss, 1971a). Skolnick (1966) has explained illegal practices in enforcing the law as a result of the tension *between* law and order—between the objectives of guaranteeing constitutional rights and of maintaining order. Legal restraints reduce the capacity of the police to coerce citizens and punish criminals. The right not to be searched without proper cause, for example, can be a right to avoid detection of criminality and subsequent punishment. Police occupational values often emphasize order over law, so that police may even lie in court to obtain a search warrant or a conviction (Manning, 1974).

Of all the problems of policing, however, none is potentially more serious than corruption. Other police violations of· the law occur at least partly to help accomplish police objectives, but corruption undermines the accomplishment of all legitimate police objectives. Corruption not only contradicts the objective of controlling crime; it also drains police resources from the accomplishment of their other objectives. Police organizations in which corruption is widespread tend to be inefficient in providing basic police services (Goldstein, 1977). The question of personal gain comes to influence a wide range of police activity, even to the point where officers will pay each other bribes to have routine paperwork processed (Knapp and others, 1972).

Born in the period when police departments were controlled by the big-city "machines" (Fogelson, 1977), police corruption now benefits police officers more than politicians (Sherman, 1978c). Corruption scandals continue to plague police departments, both large and small (Murphy, 1973), including— just since 1970—New York, Baltimore, Louisville, New Orleans, Cincinnati, Indianapolis, and Seattle, to name only a few (Williams, 1973). Corrupt police officers once confined themselves to "clean money" from gamblers and other purveyors of minor vices (Skolnick, 1966), but in recent years they have increasingly taken "dirty money" from drug pushers and murderers (Knapp and others, 1972; Sherman, 1978c).

Perhaps the most damaging consequence of corruption is

its effect on public attitudes and behavior toward the police. Revelations of corruption clearly undermine public respect for the police (Gardiner, 1970) and may even undermine public respect for the law itself. The way that the public treats the police clearly affects the ability of the police to accomplish their objectives. Corruption and the other major problems of policing have made the public image of the police a problem in itself.

Public Behavior Toward Police. Police officers tend to think that the public is generally hostile toward them (Skolnick, 1966; Westley, 1970). As Fogelson (1977) found from a historical analysis of big-city police, the police have long suffered from "occupational paranoia." Yet this perception of hostility does not reflect the true attitudes of the general public. While police officers consistently report that public respect for them has declined in recent years, national surveys of public opinion indicate that the occupational prestige of police work has been increasing. The prestige of the police, in fact, has been rising faster than that of almost any other occupation (Hodge, Siegel, and Rossi, 1964; Fogelson, 1977). Moreover, public surveys consistently show that a majority of the public, both black and white, thinks that the police behave properly (J. Q. Wilson, 1975).

Police officers, however, have little contact with the majority of the public. Their experience is largely with the minority of the public who are troubled enough to call the police—or to have the police called about them. The people that the police actually deal with are often rude, antagonistic, and disrespectful. In Reiss' study (1971b, p. 146) of police encounters with 13,939 citizens, 1,149 of the citizens—almost one in ten—were openly antagonistic toward the police. The frequency of disrespectful behavior toward police may well explain the "occupational paranoia" of the police. As Reiss points out, a civil police may well depend upon a civil citizenry.

Yet citizen disrespect for police authority may be caused by the police themselves. As Reiss (1971b, p. 144) also found, "There is a striking lack of reciprocity in incivility" between citizens and police, and "officers are somewhat more likely to be uncivil toward citizens than are citizens toward officers." Past experience and assumptions on both sides of police-citizen encounters may lead to a mutually self-fulfilling prophecy of antagonism and violence. The history of police violence toward citizens, as well as corruption and other police failures to accomplish their objectives, cannot be overlooked as a possible cause of the antagonism of some citizens toward the police.

In addition to the problems posed by the citizens whom the police encounter, the general public also poses problems for the police. While the general public may approve of police conduct, it seems to have grave reservations about the competence of the police. Research on criminal victimization has consistently found that many citizens, up to half in some surveys, do not even bother to tell the police about the crimes committed against them (Ennis, 1967; Crosby and Snyder, 1976; Hindelang, 1976)—often because they believe that there is little the police can do (Hindelang and Gottfredson, 1976). The public seems to be well aware of the inadequacy of police methods for dealing with crime. It is little wonder that, in one study, the police ranked well into the bottom half of the public's assessment of the *competence* of twenty selected occupations (Rotter and Stein, 1971). The public's reservations about the competence of the police is another self-fulfilling prophecy. The police depend on information from citizens in order to detect crime and to identify criminals (Reiss and Bordua, 1967; Manning, 1977). By denying the police their assistance, the public ensures that the police will be unable to accomplish their objectives.

Finally, public attitudes and behavior toward the police are affected by the conflicting public demands on the police, especially in the enforcement of norms regarding life-style and personal morality. What has been described as the overreach of the criminal law (Morris and Hawkins, 1970) undermines the legitimacy of police power and authority. No one questions, for example, the right of the police to conduct searches for a murder weapon, but many citizens are outraged by police searches for marijuana. For the many people who violate the laws governing personal morality, the police "are seen to be more intrusive than protective" (Packer, 1969, p. 283).

The Reformers' Vision

Solving, or even coping with, the major problems of policing requires nothing less than creating a new police role in the
community. Creating a new role was the objective of many
police reformers in the first half of this century. Their vision for
how a new role could be created was the professionalization of
police personnel. The central element of that vision was recruiting college graduates to serve as police officers. The premise of
that vision was that the major cause of the problems of police
work was the kind of people who were then doing it. While this
assumption appears in retrospect to have been overly simplistic,
there was good reason to be concerned with the quality of police personnel.

Almost sixty years ago, the first scholarly treatise on the
American police concluded that "the heart of the police problem is one of personnel" (Fosdick, [1920] 1969, p. 270). Even
before then, police reformers were trying to change the police
personnel situation: "Pointing out that most policemen did not
finish high school, scored below average on intelligence tests, received little or no training, earned inadequate salaries, and continued working into their sixties, seventies, and eighties, these
reformers argued that the rank and file were largely unqualified
at the outset and remained so thereafter" (Fogelson, 1977, p.
51). Most police officers obtained their appointments through
political patronage rather than through merit selection and were
protected by their ward boss or patron from being punished for
misconduct. The informal personnel system made central control of police departments almost impossible and seemed to be
the major stumbling block to any other organizational strategies
of reform.

The reformers' plans for police personnel were not confined to removing politics from the appointment process. Their
ultimate objective was to turn police officers into professionals
on a par with doctors and lawyers. They were so certain of the
value of this strategy for solving the problems of policing that
one of the proponents of police professionalization, August
Vollmer, claimed: "When we have reached a point where the

best people in society are selected for police service, there will be little confusion regarding [their] duties" (in Carte and Carte, 1975, p. 84). As Vollmer's biographers observed, his search for the "perfect man" led him away from the social conflicts over the content of policing, throwing the burden of change on the policeman rather than on society (Carte and Carte, 1975). Vollmer and his followers had great faith that the problems of policing would disappear if society could obtain "truly exceptional men" to serve as police officers, men who were of "superior intellectual endowment, physically sound, and free from mental and nervous disorders; they must have character traits which will ensure integrity, honesty, and efficiency; their personality must command the respect and liking of their associates and of the general public (Vollmer, [1936] 1971, pp. 222-223).

Vollmer was himself a truly exceptional man. An eighth-grade graduate, he became a professor at the University of Chicago and the University of California at Berkeley. From his small-town base as Berkeley's police chief from 1905 to 1932, he served as interim police chief or consultant in major cities from Los Angeles to Havana. The most prominent police reformer in the country, he inspired scores of Berkeley police recruits to carry out his reform program in their later careers as police administrators in other cities. A prolific writer, he invented dozens of new methods for criminal investigation and other police operations. And at a time when 75 percent of all policemen could not pass an army intelligence test (U.S. National Commission on Law Observance and Enforcement, 1931, p. 61), Vollmer proposed that police officers should be college graduates.

Vollmer was the first to suggest higher education as the central element for professionalizing the police, for giving them dignity and raising their social status (Carte and Carte, 1975). The existence of police-related teaching in established colleges and universities would, he believed, support his claim that the police profession has a specialized body of knowledge as the basis for its practice (Fogelson, 1977). Given the historical role of higher education in the professionalization of engineering, business (Cheit, 1975), and even medicine and law (Rudolph,

1977), Vollmer was probably quite correct in his assessment that "the university is indispensable" to professionalizing the police (Carte and Carte, 1975, p. 95).

What sort of education did Vollmer have in mind for police careers? What was his position on the major issues now confronting higher education for police officers? These questions are clearly answered in his publications and private letters. His objectives for police education included both a change in the police role and an improvement in the social status of the police officer. The curriculum he envisioned for college study for police careers was "a general education in academic subjects relevant to the field. It was not meant to be a technical police school within a university setting" (Carte and Carte, 1975, p. 69). Vollmer believed that state colleges should play a key role in police education, using their established faculty to teach psychology and other social, biological, and natural sciences (Vollmer, 1971). He also wanted university faculties to devote research efforts to the "literally thousands of police problems that need to be studied," to writing "police treatises on every conceivable subject," and to developing new techniques of police work (in Carte and Carte, 1975, p. 95). Vollmer's ultimate objective for police policies toward higher education was that every police department should require a B.A. degree for its recruits, since "the ideal police officer would be one who had already received academic training before he was recruited and who could be trained in the technical aspects of police work after joining the force" (Carte and Carte, 1975, p. 42).

Vollmer and his fellow reformers, of course, had no evidence that this model of higher education for police officers would be any more effective at accomplishing its objectives than other models or, for that matter, that higher education of any sort could help solve the problems of policing. Their faith in this approach was derived from its success with other alliances between occupations and universities. Vollmer merely borrowed the model prevailing at that time in most of the occupations for which a college degree was then a fairly common minimum standard of education. Vollmer's statements on curriculum even showed the ambivalence found in other fields between emphasizing liberal arts courses or topics more directly relevant to work. At a time when only a small fraction of the population was college educated, Vollmer wanted the police to be part of that elite. In short, Vollmer wanted to make policing a profession appropriate for gentlemen, in every sense of the word.

The irony of his objective was that the idea of having gentlemen serve as police officers had been explicitly rejected by the creators of the first modern civilian police force in London a century before Vollmer's heyday. The rank-and-file constables were chosen to be as much like the lower classes they were intended to police as possible (Critchley, 1972). Yet Vollmer saw that policing was rapidly becoming more democratic and that the advent of the automobile required police officers to deal with all classes in society, not just the lower classes. The brutality and violations of due process that the lower classes had tolerated from the police would not be tolerated by the middle and upper classes (Carte and Carte, 1975). It was no accident that the vision of police officers as professional gentlemen originated in the period of rapid social change following World War I, a period when class barriers were fast breaking down.

Vollmer created the first college program for in-service police officers: a noncredit summer institute at the University of California at Berkeley in 1916 (Vollmer and Schneider, 1917; Phelps, 1977). In 1917 he hired University of California undergraduates as part-time Berkeley police officers. By 1933 the university program had become a full-fledged major within the Department of Political Science, and Vollmer had returned from organizing similar programs at the University of Chicago and San Jose State College in order to help design Berkeley's interdisciplinary curriculum. While Northwestern, Wisconsin, and Harvard had established research and training programs for police in the 1920s, most of them became victims of the Depression (Mathias, 1976). Despite the Depression, the University of Southern California, Michigan State, Indiana University, and Washington State all created programs in criminology or police administration that have survived to the present day. Police education programs increased slowly after World War II, particularly at the two-year or community college level. But Vollmer's idea of higher education for police officers did not take hold generally in either colleges or police departments until the late 1960s.

The social conflicts and rising crime of the 1960s threw the police into the national spotlight. Their long-standing problems were rediscovered by several presidential commissions, whose empirical research on policing provided many new insights about the causes of police behavior. The research provided little information about the solutions to police problems, however, and most of the recommendations of the various commissions were old ideas that had yet to be tested. Among these ideas was Vollmer's vision of a college-educated police service.

The most influential proponent of this idea was the President's Commission on Law Enforcement and Administration of Justice. In its main report, the commission (1967a, p. 279) recommended that "the ultimate aim of all police departments should be that all personnel with general enforcement powers have baccalaureate degrees" and that immediate steps should be taken to begin a gradual increase in educational requirements for entry and promotion. In its task force report on the police, the commission (1967b, p. 126) supported the recommendation by arguing that "the complexity of the police task is as great as that of any other profession" and that higher educational requirements were necessary—if not sufficient—for improving the quality of police service.

The idea of higher education for police officers was also supported in either the staff reports or the recommendations of the National Commission on the Causes and Prevention of Violence, the President's Commission on Campus Unrest, and the National Advisory Commission on Criminal Justice Standards and Goals—which even set a timetable for implementing a nationwide baccalaureate requirement for police recruits by 1983 (National Advisory Commission, 1973, p. 121). None of these reports, however, were very specific about the objectives they thought higher education would accomplish or about the kind of college education that should be provided for police careers. Only the President's Commission on Law Enforcement and Administration of Justice even addressed the issue of curriculum, but in doing so it adhered to Vollmer's vision of a *general* education: "There is a current and rapidly growing movement among colleges and especially junior colleges to develop degree programs for potential and existing law enforcement personnel. . . . The commission's examination of these programs discloses that many of them are highly vocational in nature and are primarily intended to provide technical skills necessary in performing police work. College credit is given, for example, for such courses as traffic control, defensive tactics, and patrol procedures. Although there is a need for vocational training, it is not and cannot be a substitute for a liberal arts education" (President's Commission on Law Enforcement and Administration of Justice, 1967b, p. 127).

In support of this position, the commission cited the argument by the executive director of the International Association of Chiefs of Police that police work is too complex to be "done best by those unencumbered by a study of the liberal arts" (Tamm, 1962, p. 5). But the commission did not say why it thought that a liberal education was superior to a vocational curriculum. The 1973 report of the American Bar Association's Advisory Committee on the Urban Police Function, however, was quite explicit about its reasons for supporting a broad liberal arts education for police careers. Citing Saunders' (1970) observation that law enforcement leaders claim to look for the same personal qualities in recruits that a liberal education is believed to nurture, the ABA endorsed the view that a broadly based education would give police officers a knowledge of changing social conditions, an understanding of human behavior, an ability to communicate, and the moral values needed for a commitment to public service.

The *idea* of higher education for police officers became accepted so rapidly that the Congress created a Law Enforcement Education Program (LEEP) in 1968 to provide small grants to in-service employees of criminal justice agencies and forgivable loans to potential ("preservice") employees. Since the creation of LEEP, the quantity of higher education for police officers has grown almost geometrically. A 1967 survey by

the International Association of Chiefs of Police (IACP)
counted 184 institutions offering "degree programs" (majors) in
law enforcement and criminal justice (see Table 1). By 1977 we

Table 1. Higher Education Programs in Law Enforcement and
Criminal Justice Identified by IACP Surveys

Year	Associate	Bacca-laureate	Master's	Doctorate	Number of Institutions
1966-67	152	39	14	4	184
1968-69	199	44	13	5	234
1970-71	257	55	21	7	292
1972-73	505	211	41	9	515
1974-75	729	376	121	19	664

Source: Kobetz, 1975, p. 3.

were able to count 1,070 institutions offering undergraduate
programs oriented to police careers,* a fivefold increase. The
number of schools receiving LEEP funds (Table 2) only doubled

Table 2. The Growth of LEEP

Fiscal Year	Appropriation (in millions)	Number of Schools	Preservice Students	In-Service Students	Total Students
1969	6.50	485	1,248	19,354	20,602
1970	18.00	735	7,909	46,869	54,778
1971	21.25	890	13,437	60,516	73,953
1972	29.00	962	16,564	70,436	87,000
1973	40.00	993	16,367	79,233	95,600
1974	40.00	1,036	9,800	86,700	96,500
1975	40.00	1,065	11,000	89,000	100,000
1976	40.00	1,031	6,800	76,200	83,000
1977	40.00	993	5,100	70,986	76,086

Source: National LEEP participant summary, Office of Criminal Justice Education and Training, U.S. Law Enforcement Assistance Administration.

*We derived this figure by combining all institutions listed in two
surveys of colleges (Bruns, 1975; Kobetz, 1975) and from the U.S. Justice
Department's list of institutions receiving LEEP funds in 1975-77, excluding institutions whose program orientation is exclusively nonpolice (for
example, "Correctional Administration").

in the period from 1969 to 1974, suggesting that the IACP either undercounted the programs in 1968 or that 250 colleges (485 LEEP colleges minus 234 IACP colleges) created programs in 1968-1969 alone (which other reports suggest may have been the case). The number of police officers with some college education increased during the same period by almost 100,000, from 31.8 percent of all sworn police personnel in 1970 to 46.2 percent in 1974 (Table 3).

Table 3. Educational Attainment of Sworn Police Personnel, 1960-1974

Educational Attainment	1960		1970		1974	
	Number	Percent	Number	Percent	Number	Percent
Totals	271,000	100.0%	392,000	100.0%	444,100	100.0%
Less than high school	100,000	36.9	73,300	18.7	45,740	10.3
High school graduate	116,300	42.9	193,600	49.4	193,180	43.5
College:						
Less than 2 years	27,100	10.0	67,400	17.2	70,170	15.8
2-3 years	19,800	7.3	42,700	10.9	95,480	21.5
4 years or more	7,300	2.7	14,500	3.7	39,520	8.9
Subtotal: some college	54,200	20.0	124,600	31.8	205,170	46.2

Note: Detail may not add to totals because of rounding.
Source: National Planning Association, 1976, p. V-138.

In addition to the availability of new funding from LEEP at the beginning of a "new depression" in higher education (Cheit, 1971), several forces probably combined to produce the boom in police education at existing colleges and universities:

- The strong shift of student interest to career education generally (Carnegie Foundation, 1977) and criminal justice in particular.
- The availability of veterans' educational benefits (GI Bill money) to many young police officers who had served during the war in Vietnam (National Planning Association, 1976);
- The lowering of admissions barriers in many publicly supported institutions (National Planning Association, 1976),

which enabled many police officers who could not meet the former admissions standards to attend college.

Yet another source of the rapid expansion in higher education programs for police careers is the growth in the number of community colleges. Of the 531 community colleges we identified in 1977 as having police education programs, 284 of the colleges—over half (54 percent)—did not even exist in 1968. The newly created community colleges thus account for over one fourth of all institutions now offering police education programs.

In recent years the boom in police education has subsided, and some contraction seems almost inevitable. The 40-million-dollar LEEP budget has been slashed by presidential budgets (but restored by Congress) every year since 1975, and the number of colleges participating in LEEP has declined by about 4 percent since 1974. The veterans' educational benefits supporting many students in police education programs have expired, and so has their interest in going to college. The quantity of police education, however, seems to be leveling off rather than declining. The more pressing problem is its quality.

The idea of higher education for police officers has become firmly established. But the reformers' vision of the kind of education needed to change the police has been all but forgotten. In the rapid expansion of police education programs, the objectives and content that Vollmer and others proposed for police education have been left behind in favor of more parochial concerns. The realities of police education are now a far cry from the vision.

2

Objectives

College and university programs must be
prepared to pave the way for innovations and
changes in the police system. . . . [They] have
a moral obligation to produce change agents
. . . capable of challenging all of the existing
assumptions held by the police and, where
necessary, implementing radical changes. This
is the challenge of higher education.
                                Brown, 1974, p. 123

The quality of higher education can be measured only in reference to a set of objectives. Since the time of Aristotle, however, opinions have differed on the objectives of higher education. In modern times educational philosophers have proposed the objectives of preserving old knowledge and moral values (Newman, 1873), furthering democracy (Dewey, 1916), pursuing knowledge and truth purely for their own sake (Veblen, 1918; Hutchins, 1936), discovering new knowledge and solving problems (Flexner, 1930), preparing students for careers (Marland, 1974), and accomplishing all these goals simultaneously (Kerr, 1964).

Similar differences of opinion can be found in police education. One major study concluded that specialized police education programs lack "a clearly defined set of goals" and that "program quality has suffered because of the lack of definition" (National Planning Association, 1976, p. V-48). Another found that "in law enforcement higher education no . . . common agreement on goals yet exists, and indeed considerable difference of opinion exists as to whether higher education for criminal justice should focus on simply *improving* the performance of what is currently being done, or whether it should focus on *changing* what is being done" (Tenney, 1971, p. 5). In the many letters the commission received and in the testimony presented at the commission's three regional public forums, there was a striking lack of consensus on the objectives of higher education for police officers, particularly on the issue of changing the police versus merely making them more efficient. Moreover, the differences of opinion did not appear to be consistent among such groups as police chiefs, educators, and criminal justice planners. Each group appeared to be equally divided in its views.

Three types of objectives are offered for police education, with considerable disagreement within each type. The most frequently debated type consists of the different objectives for the impact of college on individual students. A second type consists of objectives for the impact of higher education on the performance of policing as an institution. A third type of objective for police education concerns its role in the movement to professionalize the police and enhance their prestige.

In examining the many objectives proposed for higher education for police officers, we are as concerned with what is *possible* as with what is desirable. This country tends to expect far too much of higher education (Spaeth and Greeley, 1970), just as it expects too much of the police. Objectives must be realistic as well as challenging. Consequently, we devote considerable attention to the available empirical research on the effects of higher education. While this research is generally far from conclusive, it does provide some basis for assessing the possibility of accomplishing certain objectives.

Impact on Students

Among those who locate the objectives of police education in its impact on students, the commission found proponents of several distinct viewpoints. One view is that the objectives of higher education for police officers should be the same as the objectives of higher education for anyone else, developing certain general skills and values in students. Another view is that higher education should equip students with specific skills required for competent performance of police work as it is presently structured.and defined. A third view is that the objective of higher education should be to mold students into change agents who can work within police departments to create a new police role.

Develop General Qualities. The classical ideal that all students should derive the same benefits from higher education has been challenged by many forces since the classical curriculum was abandoned in the late nineteenth century (Rudolph, 1977). But while the idea of a general education *curriculum* has fallen into some distress (Carnegie Foundation, 1977), the idea of general *objectives* of education, regardless of variations in the curriculum, seems to be alive and well, even in an area as seemingly specialized as police education.

The Education Committee of the Georgia Association of Chiefs of Police, for example, adopted this position in a 1977 communication to the commission: "The objectives of higher education for police should be the same as for any other career group: development of a broad-based knowledge of many disciplines, including basic science courses, history, languages (particularly the development of communications skills), sociology/psychology for improved understanding of people and groups, and mathematics." In an independent communication, the Academic Committee on Criminal Justice of the Board of Regents of the University System of Georgia adopted a similar position: "The majority favors a broad liberal understanding of behavior built around social and behavioral sciences, with objectives being no different from objectives of higher education in general."

Most of the comments the commission received did not distinguish the objectives of higher education from its content —its outcomes from its subject matter. Yet in saying that "the general objectives of higher education for police should be very similar to those of other participants in postsecondary education" (as the Illinois Board of Higher Education put it), the proponents of this position are linked to the growing discussion of what those common objectives should be. The Carnegie Commission on Higher Education (1973b); the dean of Harvard College, Henry Rosovsky (1976); the president of Western Washington University, Paul J. Olscamp (1977); and others have recently developed lists of goals for the personal development of students (Carnegie Foundation, 1977). Perhaps the most comprehensive list is Bowen's (1977) empirical analysis of more than 1,500 goal statements for the impact of higher education on individual students offered by past and present educational philosophers, commissions, faculty committees, and institutional reports, which yielded the catalog of objectives presented in Table 4. Bowen also reviewed the available empirical research on the degree to which colleges achieve these goals, the results of which are also presented in Table 4.

It should be stressed that the studies Bowen examined measured only the *average* change in each quality in groups of students and did not examine the effects of education on all these qualities in individual students. As the president of Immaculate Heart College in Los Angeles recently suggested, anyone who actually acquired all these traits would be rather awesome (Kelley, 1977; cited in Carnegie Foundation, 1977). Indeed, that seems to have been just what August Vollmer had in mind. And the idea of having "truly exceptional men" serve as police officers did not die with Vollmer, as the testimony at a commission public forum by Anthony V. Bouza, deputy police chief of the New York City Transit Authority, suggests: "The proper role of the educational system, in terms of the police, is to turn out the Renaissance man . . . a man of thought and action, a man at home in the world of ideas, who would nevertheless actively confront, on the basis of these ideas, the situations on the streets of the cities" (Bouza, 1977).

These characteristics may well be worth striving for—not only as ultimate purposes for higher education but also as life goals in general. Yet it is unrealistic to expect higher education to accomplish all these things in all students. Education is only one of the many forces shaping human behavior. The recently documented failures of many graduates of the Harvard College classes of 1938 through 1942 to develop many or even most of

Table 4. Goals for College Students and Empirical Evidence on Their Achievement

Goals	Average Effects of College Education
A. *Cognitive Learning*	
1. Verbal skills	Moderate increase
2. Quantitative skills	Small increase
3. Substantive knowledge	Large increase
4. Rationality	Small increase
5. Intellectual tolerance	Moderate increase
6. Esthetic sensibility	Moderate increase
7. Creativeness	Small increase
8. Intellectual integrity	Not ascertainable
9. Wisdom	Not ascertainable
10. Lifelong learning	Moderate increase
B. *Emotional and Moral Development*	
1. Personal and self discovery	Large increase
2. Psychological well-being	Moderate increase
3. Human sympathy	Moderate increase toward groups in the abstract; no change toward individuals
4. Morality	Not ascertainable
5. Religious interest	Moderate decrease
6. Refinement of taste, conduct, manner	Small increase
C. *Practical Competence*	
1. Traits of value in practical affairs generally	
a. Need for achievement	Not ascertainable
b. Future orientation	Strong correlation
c. Adaptability	Strong correlation
d. Leadership	Not ascertainable
2. Citizenship	Moderate qualitative gain
3. Economic productivity	Moderate increase
4. Sound family life	Large qualitative gain
5. Consumer efficiency	Small qualitative gain
6. Fruitful leisure	Small qualitative gain
7. Health	Moderate improvement

Adapted from Bowen, 1977, pp. 98, 134, 138-143, 218.

these traits (Vaillant, 1977) suggests that even a high-quality education is no guarantee of a successful life. However, as Bowen found, there is considerable evidence suggesting that many students do develop many of these traits over the course of a college education.

Bowen's findings confirmed those of an earlier review

(Feldman and Newcomb, 1969) of almost 1,500 empirical studies of the impact of college on students. These studies almost always show that students' intellectual aptitudes, including the ability to think critically and independently, increase as they progress through college. They also show that students increase in their factual knowledge of various content areas. Moreover, students in many different types of colleges have been found in recent decades to become more open-minded during their college careers, declining in their measured authoritarianism, dogmatism, and prejudice. They generally become less conservative with regard to public issues, less committed to religion, more sensitive to aesthetic experiences, and more self-confident. For the most part, the attitudes held by college graduates tend to persist after they leave college, particularly if their postcollege environment supports those attitudes.

How does the impact of college relate to the qualities required of a good police officer? Once again, a lack of consensus makes this question difficult to answer. The attempts to identify the qualities of a good police officer on the basis of supervisor's performance ratings (Baehr, Furcon, and Froemel, 1968) or empirical task analyses (American Justice Institute, 1976) have been attacked for failing to look beyond the present state of police work to how it ought to be. A relatively modest list of ideal qualities offered by one observer, however, is hard to quarrel with (Goldstein, 1977, p. 263): intelligence sufficient for making complex decisions, tolerance and understanding of differences between cultures, values supporting the controls on police conduct, self-discipline, and the ability to control one's emotions.

Despite some important methodological questions about the evidence on the impact of college on students, it does suggest that higher education can help develop these ideal qualities of individual police officers. The most important question, perhaps, is not *whether* higher education can develop these qualities but rather *what kind* of education is most likely to develop these qualities. "American colleges," as Feldman and Newcomb (1969, p. 5) point out, "are diverse, and so are their students—even within a single institution; no generalizations could be expected to apply equally to all colleges, nor, *a fortiori*, to all individual students. The more interesting questions . . . are more specific—what kinds of students change in what kinds of ways, following what kinds of experiences, mediated by what kinds of institutional arrangements?"

The many studies (producing scant evidence) of the impact of higher education on police attitudes and performance generally suffer from the failure to separate different kinds of education. Although these studies generally have not found that more education is associated with "better" police performance, the available studies are all so weak methodologically that no conclusions can be drawn from them (Smith, 1978). Moreover, even if the studies were more rigorously designed, there is no theoretical reason to believe that educated police officers would behave differently if the only aspect of their police department that is different is their own education. If education is only one of the many forces shaping police behavior, then it makes little sense to expect educated officers to behave differently in otherwise traditional police agencies.

Until the impact of educational changes can be studied in conjunction with the impact of other changes in police departments, it is safer to base the objectives of police education on the empirical evidence about the impact of college on students in general. Yet even those studies are of limited value. Most of the research on the impact of college on students has examined full-time residential study during late adolescence at institutions stressing general education (but see Astin, 1977, for a more diverse sample). Whether part-time adult learning at institutions stressing career education can produce the same impact is by no means clear. Yet that is the most common form of higher education for police careers.

Train Students for Police Careers. A second viewpoint on the objectives of college for individual students is that they should learn the practical skills and knowledge required for functioning as a police officer. The distinction between the "qualities" identified in the first viewpoint and the "skills" identified by this viewpoint is largely one of breadth. The qualities that education should develop for a police career, according to the first viewpoint, are broadly applicable to many careers. The skills that education should develop, according to this second viewpoint, are limited to a career in law enforcement and are of little use in other occupations.

The Research and Evaluation Office of the Rochester, New York, Police Department, for example, wrote the commission that an objective of police education should be "to provide technical expertise in the skills of the trade; that is, to provide the necessary training to develop the skills required to perform the duties of patrol and investigation in a comprehensive and efficient manner." This viewpoint is the basis for the state of California's long-standing practice of certifying graduates of a two-year college program in police science for immediate entry into police work without their having to attend a police training academy (Myren, 1970). Two-year colleges in most states have adopted a mission of providing career training in specific skills (Harris and Grede, 1977), and the published guidelines for police education programs at the two-year level clearly imply this objective (Crockett and Stinchcomb, 1968; Pace, Stinchcomb, and Styles, 1970; Stinchcomb, 1975), with one recent exception (Hoover and Lund, 1977). The objective of educating for specific careers has even been endorsed by a U.S. commissioner of education (Marland, 1974).

The growth of support for the objective of educating for specific careers has intensified the ancient conflict in education between the "useful" and the "liberal." Aristotle described the conflict over two thousand years ago: "Should the useful in life, or should virtue, or should the higher knowledge be the aim of our training?" (Quoted in Cheit, 1975, p. 3.) Plato's academy was devoted to the search for truth; the Pythagoreans were concerned with mathematical precision; the Sophists taught the useful skills required for material success; and these "three cultures" of the humanists, the scientists, and the professionals are still at odds over the objectives of higher education (Kerr, 1964).

To a large extent, however, the career education movement has underestimated the practical utility of the more general objectives of higher education. A major history of the undergraduate curriculum, for example, concluded that, even when the seven classical liberal arts dominated college curriculums, "the course of study had always to some degree . . . been relevant to the practical affairs of men, intentionally oriented to social utility" (Rudolph, 1977, p. 14). As a nineteenth-century Harvard student responded to Henry Adams' question of why the student was at Harvard, "The degree of Harvard College is worth money to me in Chicago" (Adams, [1906] 1961; in Rudolph, 1977, p. 14). American colleges were founded as training institutes for the clergy and have steadily added more and more vocations to their list of "clients" (Bledstein, 1976). The question has never been whether to educate for specific careers but, rather, how specifically or generally to educate and for *which* careers (Cheit, 1975).

The career education movement has recently been attacked on its own grounds, not for holding the wrong objectives but for failing to accomplish the objectives it articulates. The greatest failure is the widespread unemployment of many students educated for specific careers: "Vocationally trained students have been consistently unable to obtain work in the fields for which they were trained" (Grubb and Lazerson, 1975, p. 461). Among "preservice" college students majoring in law enforcement or criminal justice, studies conducted in 1967 and 1974 both found that over half failed to find work in law enforcement (Newman and Hunter, 1968; U.S. Comptroller General, 1975). Even those who advocate career training for police education criticize it on these grounds. For example, the Sheriff's Department of Arapahoe County, Colorado, in its statement to the commission, noted: "Too often the academic community has been guilty of overpopulating the employment field with educated people with no jobs for them to go to. We feel it is incumbent upon the academic community to survey the field to make sure their programs do not turn out an inordinate amount of graduates which the field of law enforcement could not possibly absorb. We feel this type of fraud perpetrated upon the students is one which cheapens the profession and degrades the academic community."

One educational researcher believes that this kind of

attack is encouraged by academic adherence to the objective of educating people for specific jobs (Solmon, 1977). Even if jobs were readily available for every college graduate, however, it is by no means clear that a "career education" would actually have prepared them for their career. Relatively little is known about the extent to which any education provides the knowledge and skills required for any occupation (Bird, 1975; but see Bisconti and Solmon, 1976, for some evidence that college education in some subjects is used on the job), and no research on this question has been conducted in the area of policing. Even so, one may wonder whether a college education in report writing, traffic control, and firearms—the typical content of many "career education" courses on policing—can possibly prepare a student for the wide diversity of tasks and problems faced during the course of a police career. One may also wonder how much a college education of that nature contributes to developing the qualities that police officers should possess—qualities such as intelligence, tolerance, self-discipline, and respect for constitutional values. The goals of career education may well conflict with the more general goals of higher education.

The most serious criticism of the objective of teaching students the specific skills of police work is that this objective is inimical to change. Teaching a student how to perform police work as it is now done may discourage broader inquiry into how it might be done differently. Several critics have voiced the fear that career education in policing will serve "only to reinforce the most parochial concepts prevalent in the police field" (American Bar Association, 1973, p. 218). Career education emphasizes making the student acceptable to the employer, rather than making the student the kind of person who can change the employer. Many critics of this viewpoint on police education have recommended that colleges teach students how to change police work rather than how to do it in its present form.

Create Change Agents. The third viewpoint on the objectives for police education's impact on individual students falls somewhere between the first two. The objective of creating change agents can be seen as consistent with the general objectives of all higher education, or it can be seen as providing a specific career skill. In either case, the objective is to make students imaginative, critical, and, to a certain extent, rebellious: the "antiorganization man," in contrast to career education's implied model of the well-adapted "organization man" (compare Whyte, 1956; and Berkeley, 1971).

Despite a number of·published statements of this objective (Tenney, 1971; Brown, 1974; K. W. Johnson, 1977; Mills, 1977), only one of the several hundred statements of objectives received by the commission adopted this position. Texas Christian University professor Joseph L. Schott, a former FBI agent and president of the Southwestern Association of Criminal Justice Educators, acknowledged the influence of Tenney's (1971) work in formulating his own position: "I personally favor a change-agent role for higher education, but again must bow to a Tenney restraint which holds that . . . ‘no system . . . can ever be changed or improved until there are substantial numbers of individuals, both within and without, who recognize the need for change and have the competence to bring it about.’ "

Goldstein (1977, p. 296) expresses "the hope that higher education will result in the police having in their ranks a greater number of people who have the breadth of understanding, the creativity, and the motivation to bring about changes in the orientation, policies, and operations of the typical police organization, and resolve the many conflicting pressures that currently hamper their effectiveness. This objective must be made explicit."

Commission member Hugo Masini (1977, p. 21) proposes a somewhat different conception of the change agent that higher education should produce, one who can effect change not in the police department but in the community: "We have to have officers skilled enough to get out there in the community, identify those groups that are representative of the community, be able to bring them together in meetings, be able to sit down with them and talk about problems, and then be able to do something. If we can use the skills that are being taught (namely, problem identification, analysis, and development of alternatives), that's what the term *change agent* means."

In the various statements of this objective, three individual qualities of a change agent are noted. One is the ability to determine what needs to be changed, or the analytical capacity to define a problem. Another quality is the imagination and foresight required for solving a problem—for accomplishing change. A third quality of a change agent is a value system that supports both the content of particular changes and the preference for accomplishing change over maintaining career security and advancement.

How realistic is the hope that higher education can develop these qualities in many or even any students oriented to police careers? And even if these qualities are developed in college, will they persist throughout a police career? There is some reason to believe that a college education can improve the analytical ability necessary to identify a problem and its causes, but there is little evidence that education can improve one's ability to solve a problem once it has been identified. And whatever the effect of higher education on values and attitudes regarding the content of change, it is unclear whether higher education increases one's propensity to challenge accepted practices at the risk of one's career.

The lack of systematic evidence, of course, does not mean that the objective of developing these qualities is unrealistic. Indeed, some isolated cases are quite encouraging in this regard. In the recent wave of police officers leaking information to the news media about institutionalized police misconduct (Sherman, 1978a), many of the "whistle-blowing" officers have been college graduates, possibly in disproportion to the number of college graduates on the force. These instances, however, all involved serious police violations of the law, from selling narcotics to committing homicide. The more important question may be whether educated officers are more likely to do anything about the routine, daily practices of policing that need to be changed—from time poorly spent on patrol to unnecessary public danger created by high-speed chases of traffic offenders.

In most police departments, there may be little that any individual officer can do to change present practices. A rigid, quasi-military hierarchy commonly inhibits the upward flow of information and suggestions from the rank and file. While indi-

vidual officers have wide discretion over important decisions
they make in specific cases, they are usually excluded from any
participation in making decisions about general policies. Some
alternative models of police organization have been proposed
that would give more policymaking power to individual officers
(Murphy and Bloch, 1970; Angell, 1971), and some experiments in participatory management have been attempted (Kansas City Police Department, 1973; Sherman, Milton, and Kelley,
1973), but there is still very little that an individual officer can
do to change most police department policies and practices.

Some officers do obtain the power to effect change by
rising in the rank structure. Yet with a few remarkable exceptions, the kind of person who rises to the top of police departments is less interested in "rocking the boat" than in "survival"
(Murphy and Plate, 1977). The personality attributes associated
with advancement to high police rank are typically not those of
the change agent. Moreover, the power of the socialization
process in the police subculture (Westley, 1970; Harris, 1973;
Van Maanen, 1974) may eliminate any effects of higher education in the early years of any officer's career. Thus, even though
education is associated with less "authoritarianism" in police
officers (Smith, Locke, and Walker, 1967, 1968; Smith, Locke,
and Fenster, 1970), there is evidence that a college education
presently makes little difference in police officers' attitudes
toward due process guarantees and toward certain proposals for
changing the police (Smith and Ostrom, 1974; Watts, 1978).

The problem with the objective of educating individuals
to be change agents is that police behavior is probably determined more by the police organization and the character of
police work than by the background of police officers. Even if
higher education can produce graduates with the qualities of a
change agent, there is good reason to doubt that these qualities
will persist in individuals working in our present police organizations. In the absence of any other changes in policing, educating
students to be change agents may be a futile endeavor. At its
most successful, it may merely result in educated officers' leaving police work in frustration (Marsh, 1962; Levy, 1967; Stoddard, 1973). Yet an educated police service may be a necessary

condition for effecting other changes in policing. The dilemma is the chicken-or-egg question of which comes first, educated police officers or the organizational environment they will work in? Which must change first, police personnel or police organizations? In real life the objectives for the impact of police education on individual students cannot be separated from the objectives for its impact on policing as a social institution.

Impact on Policing

The second category of objectives defines higher education as a social force that should have an impact on police behavior in the aggregate. Rather than arguing that an educated officer should be a better officer, this viewpoint argues that higher levels of education, in general, should improve the performance of police departments and of policing as an occupation. Some proponents of this viewpoint even reject the individual-level objectives as meaningful. McNamara (1977, p. 27), for example, observes that "university education for the police officer might deepen his understanding, . . . make him more self-confident, . . . prepare him for a second career; it might do a large number of things, and yet it might not have an affirmative social impact on the problems which the police forces of this nation are accountable for to the society."

The problem of crime, for example, was the major rationale for the creation of the federal Law Enforcement Education Program (LEEP) in 1968. While Congress did not list specific objectives for LEEP, it was instituted as part of the Omnibus Crime Control and Safe Streets Act. The general objective of this act was "to assist state and local governments in reducing the incidence of crime"; concern for the problem of police misconduct, however, also was expressed: "to increase the effectiveness, *fairness*, and coordination of law enforcement and criminal justice systems at all levels of government" (P.L. 90-351). The administrative guidelines for LEEP in 1969 adopted the vague objective of improving law enforcement, but by 1975 they were more specifically stated as developing the human resources needed by the criminal justice system for reducing crime and delinquency (Jacobs and Magdovitz, 1977).

More often, however, the objectives for the impact of higher education on policing are expressed in terms of the police themselves as the social problem, rather than in terms of their ability to solve social problems. A staff report to the National Commission on the Causes and Prevention of Violence, for example, hypothesized that higher education will help police understand the constructive role of dissent in a democratic society, thereby reducing collective police violence in response to protest demonstrations (Skolnick, 1969). Similarly, the President's Commission on Campus Unrest (1971) argued that higher education for the police might reduce collective conflicts between police and citizens. And a leading police educator (Lynch, 1976) has suggested that higher education can contribute to ethical behavior in law enforcement generally.

To the extent that some police educators define their objectives at the aggregate level, they seem to forget the police problems of the 1960s and to return to the less controversial concerns of the 1950s. The 1976 report of the Task Force on Law Enforcement Education of the Ohio Council of Higher Education in Criminal Justice, for example, defines the objective of police education as "improving police efficiency" (Todd, 1976, p. 36). The report is a prime example of police educators' preference for "improving" the status quo of policing, using empirical task analyses of what the police do now as the basis for teaching future police how to do it. Such "improvement" is unlikely to do much to change the police (Mills, 1977).

It is one thing to propose aggregate-level objectives and quite another thing to accomplish them, whatever their content. The problems of policing, as we have repeatedly observed, probably cannot be solved by personnel changes alone. As Balch (1972, p. 119) points out, "Attracting better people to the same job is not necessarily an improvement." The result may simply be that college graduates rather than high school dropouts "will be busting heads." The proper question may be whether changes in the average educational levels of police departments would interact with other changes in police organizational and environmental characteristics to produce changes in the problems of policing. If higher education for police is a necessary condition for changing police performance, what other conditions would provide a sufficient basis for change? This question is central to determining whether changing police institutional or organizational performance is a realistic objective for higher education. Given the assumption that education alone cannot change police performance, it is difficult to assess empirically the soundness of this objective. Studies comparing the aggregate educational levels of police departments to various measures of their organizational performance (Smith and Ostrom, 1974; Smith, 1976), for example, can say little about what difference educational levels might make in combination with such other factors as better leadership, a decentralized organizational structure, or better accountability to the public. The fact that such studies find little difference among more and less educated police departments—with very little variation in educational levels from one department to the next—does not mean that education cannot be a force for change. It only suggests that average educational levels alone might make little difference in police organizational performance.

Perhaps the strongest empirical argument for assuming that education can change police institutional performance is the role of higher education in the development of several other occupational fields (Cheit, 1975). Professional education in business, agriculture, and engineering has provided new knowledge about how to practice those "useful arts"—knowledge which, in turn, has changed the practice. College-educated farmers and engineers apparently did not need the qualities of the change agent described above to have their suggestions influence their colleagues' work. A combination of research and teaching on police matters in the major universities might accomplish the same result in police practices (Bittner, 1970). It might also help accomplish a third major type of objective for higher education: achieving professional status.

Impact on Police Professionalization

The objective of police education as a means of professionalizing has two distinct elements: providing professional behavior and professional prestige. Of the two, prestige has been of much greater concern to police reformers and others. Raising the social status of police work, in fact, has been described as the "overriding objective" of the police reform movement since World War II (Fogelson, 1977). The commission found that prestige is still a major concern of police officials and police educators. Thomas Carroll, a former New York City police officer who became a community college instructor after his retirement, provided a frank statement of this concern to the commission, which suggested that police "occupational paranoia" (Fogelson, 1977) is still quite strong. Carroll (1977) argued that education will help reduce "the contempt of the general public toward the policeman's background. Most people don't like us. . . . The average businessman has no use for a policeman. [Education] will lead to less contempt and superiority . . . by judges, the district attorneys and lawyers toward the police. . . . Better education will lessen the hate by the pressure groups, civil rights and political groups."

Other opinions presented to the commission seemed to stress professional police behavior more than professional prestige, although the definition of "professionalism" in such statements was rarely explicit. Police Chief Robert Watson of Junction City, Kansas, whose officers attend both a local community college and Kansas State University, provided this statement: "Obviously, from a police standpoint, the principal objective of higher education for police is the coveted goal of professionalism. While many already refer to law enforcement as a profession, it unfortunately will not stand the test. The law enforcement community, as a whole, does not possess all the basic characteristics of a professional group and is lacking primarily in educational and competency standards for admission to the field. . . . There are, of course, other objectives to be achieved through advanced education of police officers. However, all lesser objectives are really fragmentations of the prime goal: Professionalism."

The concept of police professionalism is so vague that unions and management, conservatives and liberals, J. Edgar Hoover and Ramsey Clark have all supported it (Fogelson, 1977). For some people in policing, professionalism is simply a

matter of prestige and dignity for the members of the profession, which can be achieved by high standards for entry. For
others, police professionalism means adopting the ideal social
structure of the established professions: practice based on complex formal knowledge, autonomy from lay interference in decision making, collegial discipline and peer accountability, and a
value system placing public service higher than selfish concerns.
Regardless of how professionalism is defined, however, the proponents of professionalism have generally failed to specify how
it would change police behavior, other than saying that a professional police would be more ethical (White, 1972). Without a
more explicit conception of how a professionalized police
would behave, it is difficult to assess the ability of higher education to help professionalize the police.

Nonetheless, there is some evidence that higher education
might at least raise the prestige of the police. The correlation
between the general educational level of an occupation and its
prestige has been quite high for centuries (Ben-David, 1977) and
persists in modern times around the world (Treiman, 1977).
The historical development of crafts into professions has always
included higher education (Kerr, 1964; Rudolph, 1977), not
necessarily for improving the practical skills but for increasing
the social status of the occupation (Bledstein, 1976; Collins,
1977). For as Becker (1964), Coleman (1966), Bird (1975), and
others have pointed out, higher education can teach status-
reflective behavioral "style" as much as it teaches substantive
knowledge.

The relationship of prestige to performance, however, is
not at all clear (Fogelson, 1977). On the one hand, there is
some evidence that the prestige of the police is higher in those
countries where the police are less repressive and more re-
strained by constitutional safeguards (Treiman, 1977). On the
other hand, the status of the American police increased substantially from 1947 to 1963 (Hodge, Siegel, and Rossi, 1964), as
did their education, despite a later survey finding that the public rates the police very low on competence (Rotter and Stein,
1971). It may be quite possible for education to improve the
social status of police work without police behavior's changing
at all.

If the only purpose of higher education is to make the police feel better by giving them more prestige, then it should probably not be supported as a national priority. If the police deserve such special treatment, why not garbage collectors or engineers? Police prestige for its own sake would do little good for the public interest. The consequences of greater prestige, however, might well justify public support for its attainment. Greater public respect might increase the level of civility in police-citizen encounters (see Reiss, 1971b) and reduce the level of force that police use to accomplish their tasks and maintain their authority. Greater prestige might also attract more individuals to police work who have the personal qualities necessary for good police performance. An acknowledged policy of furthering class and status stratification in American life, however, is not a wise position for higher education to adopt in a society that pays homage to an ideal of equality. Whatever the effects of higher education on the prestige of police work, they should probably be treated as by-products rather than as a primary objective. The public relations value of police education must not be allowed to obscure the basic need for dealing with the problems of policing, especially since the public relations value of professionalization is declining.

There is a growing disenchantment with both the professional model and its use of higher education to restrict access to the profession as a strategy for dealing with the problems of policing. Some of the disenchantment with police professionalism stems from the problems of the established professions. There is some question about whether the established professions actually adhere to the ideal professional model (see Freidson, 1975), and an even greater questioning of the competence of the established professions. The growth of malpractice litigation in law, medicine, and architecture; Chief Justice Burger's assessment that about half of all trial lawyers are incompetent (Goldstein, 1978a); and President Carter's attacks on the legal and medical professions (Tolchin, 1978; Goldstein, 1978b) are but a few of the indications of the troubles of the established professions. Ironically, just as the police reach the point at which they could realistically achieve some of the elements of professionalization, the professional model is becoming bankrupt.

The ability of professionalization to improve police performance has often been questioned on the basis of the performance of police departments that have adopted some aspects of the professional model (see Wilson, 1971). Autonomy from lay control, in particular, has been attacked as inappropriate for policing in a free society. Much of police work involves value judgments, and the technical expertise of police officers is irrelevant to making those judgments. Legitimate political influences on police policymaking, while contradicting the autonomous professional model, are essential for a democratic police (American Bar Association, 1973).

There is also a question about the extent to which the police actually have professional expertise of a formal and systematic nature. While experienced officers have the intuitive knowledge of a craftsman (Wilson, 1968), there is little scientific or theoretical basis for that knowledge (Tenney, 1971). In contrast to medicine, for example, the number of empirically established principles of practice in policing is very small. Higher education cannot offer an applied body of knowledge about police work that is comparable to what it can offer about engineering or even agriculture. It can prescribe how to fix broken bones, build bridges, and grow crops, but it cannot prescribe the proper method for handling a family fight, at least not with the same degree of certainty.

Given the absence of a professional body of knowledge that can be acquired through higher education, the propriety of requiring a college education of police recruits has been increasingly attacked. The college requirement has been challenged in court as irrelevant to the skills needed to do police work and as discriminating against educationally disadvantaged minority groups. Any attempt to raise entry standards in police work will necessarily alter the historical function of the police institution in providing upward mobility to recent urban immigrants (Fogelson, 1977). One response to this critique, which will be dealt with in depth in Chapter Seven, is that the mission of the police is to provide high-quality services and not to provide upward mobility (Murphy and Plate, 1977).

It should be stressed, however, that the absence of a formal body of knowledge did not deter other occupations from establishing professional education. More often than not, the development of empirically derived applied knowledge for the practice of other occupations was a *result* of creating professional schools, not a prerequisite for their creation. A conscious policy of directing academic research toward the development of applied knowledge for policing might well succeed. If a body of applied knowledge is the central element of professionalization, then it would seem that a *long-term* objective of professionalizing the police is realistic for higher education. It is also reasonable to assume that more applied knowledge can improve the quality of police performance.

Educating for Change

Most of the objectives offered for police education are compatible with the primary concern of this commission: educating the police for institutional change. Like the early police reformers, we would direct the aims of police education to solving, or at least coping with, the problems of policing. As Whitehead ([1929] 1967, p. 4) observed, "Education is the acquisition of the art of the utilization of knowledge." We believe that an educated police institution would have a greater capacity to use knowledge to solve problems and to change itself.

Educating the police institution to use knowledge will first require that individual police officers develop the general qualities of educated persons: the habits of using written and spoken ideas, computational tools, and information gathered from many sources to produce new conclusions and observations and to test the validity of conclusions (see Carnegie Foundation, 1977). It may also require that some officers learn or adopt a change-agent role to overcome some of the police institution's resistance to the use of certain kinds of knowledge. The institutional conditions needed to support the use of knowledge may include the major elements of a profession, such as professional schools and their research enterprises associated with policing (Bittner, 1970).

What is *not* required for educating the police institution

for change is to train individual students in performing basic police skills or to increase the "systems efficiency" of policing as an institution. A narrow focus on the status quo in either individual or institutional objectives for police education is incompatible with educating for change. An education designed to achieve those narrow objectives may only reinforce the most parochial and conservative tendencies of the police. While these objectives may be far more palatable to present police departments than the others, they could result in mere credentialing of existing police knowledge without contributing anything new to policing. The purpose of police education should not be to make students as attractive as possible to police department employers. The purpose should be making the police the kind of institution that actively recruits people with the qualities higher education can foster, qualities that an educated police institution should know how to use.

Higher education, however, should not be held institutionally accountable for its impact on police performance. The proper role of higher education is limited to providing the knowledge and skills that might enable the police to change, as well as the research, criticism, and analysis that can map out alternatives for what should be changed and how change might be accomplished. The responsibility for implementing change lies with the police and the society they serve. The responsibility of higher education is to provide the highest-quality education its resources allow.

3

Curriculum

*In exploring the substance of the curriculum,
the stuff of which the learning and teaching
is made, we are in the presence of quality,
whether good or bad.*
                              Rudolph, 1977, p. 2

Perhaps the most important element of the quality of higher education for police officers is the curriculum. Judgments about the quality of the curriculum clearly vary with the different viewpoints on what the curriculum is expected to do. If judgment is based on the objective of educating the police institution for change, the quality of the specialized police education curriculum in many colleges is extremely low. The curriculum in most programs does little more than provide atheoretical training in basic police skills. Unless the prevailing curriculum is changed, it will not succeed in educating the police institution for change.

Despite the prevalence of the training curriculum, there are several other models of the college curriculum for present and potential police officers. One model that many police officers have selected is majoring in subjects other than specialized police or criminal justice studies, from the traditional arts and science disciplines to professional education programs in other fields such as business and teaching. Among the more directly related police education curriculums, two alternative models to

61

the training curriculum are available. One is an interdisciplinary arts and science program on criminal justice topics, consisting mostly of social science. The other is a professional education program in police administration or criminal justice, which gives greater emphasis to legal and management issues than either the liberal criminal justice curriculum or the basic vocational (or "paraprofessional") training curriculum.

Each of the four models—general education, criminal justice as an interdisciplinary liberal arts field, criminal justice as a professional education, and police technology as paraprofessional vocational training—provides different positions on a number of issues in the content and purpose of police education. This chapter describes those issues, analyzes the arguments for and against each model, presents some data on their relative frequency among colleges and police officers, and assesses the implications of each model for achieving the objective of educating the police institution for change.

Issues

Should the curriculum offer training or education? The most frequently debated issue in police education is where to draw the boundary between the curriculums of police training academies and college programs (O'Neill and Lance, 1970; Santarelli, 1974). A great deal of overlap now exists, most often in the direction of training courses in educational programs. To be sure, the definitions of training and education are by no means clear. Stanley (1978) describes the boundary between them as more of a swamp than a fence (but see Kreml, 1966, for a sharper distinction). Nonetheless, there is a growing sentiment that colleges should not teach "basic agency skills" (Academy of Criminal Justice Sciences, 1976). At the same time, a number of states have moved in the direction of accepting a two-year college level police education program as the basic training required for officers to be certified by the state to practice policing (Myren, 1970, 1978). The absence of adequate academy training in many areas has made the community college, in particular, an economical substitute. In other places, however, the college curriculum clearly duplicates the content of police academy training (Saunders, 1970; Wachtel, 1977). In one survey of police science graduates, for example, 64 percent of the respondents said that their college course work duplicated their recruit training (Tenney, 1971, p. 64).

Should education be specialized or general? Regardless of the boundaries between college and police academy curriculums, there is a major question of whether a professional education on topics directly related to policing is more valuable than a general education in preparing students for police careers. Fifty-eight percent of all American undergraduates are now enrolled in professional education programs, most of which demand that over half of all college courses be taken in the major subject (Carnegie Foundation, 1977, p. 103). At the same time, there is growing interest among educators in a return to some form of distribution requirements to guarantee that all students receive a "core of learning" (Boyer and Kaplan, 1977; Maeroff, 1977; Scully, 1977; Fiske, 1978c, 1978d). The questions for police education are twofold: whether to offer and encourage students to take a professional education curriculum; and, if so, how much of their total course work should be in the major field.

Is there a sufficient knowledge base for specialized education? If a specialized police education curriculum is the preferred alternative, there is some question about the adequacy of the materials available for such a curriculum. A decade ago college programs for the police could draw on little research on police problems (Saunders, 1970). As one observer commented, the programs suffered from a "lack of nourishment" (Brown, 1965). In the past decade there has been an explosion of research on police problems (Manning, 1976), much of it supported by federal funds. The commission's review of the textbooks used in many college programs for the police, however, revealed that most of them fail to incorporate research findings. The research has not advanced the state of systematic knowledge about policing to anything like that of the established professions, but it is probably a sufficient basis for a specialized undergraduate program. The prevailing practice of using dogmatic texts written by practitioners, however, does not seem to provide an adequate knowledge base for a college curriculum.

   Which skills should be taught? A related issue in specialized curriculums is whether they should encompass all aspects of police work. Should a professional (or even a liberal arts) curriculum require that students take forensic science, as à number of academic criminalists urged in letters to the commission? Or should a specialized curriculum be limited to more general issues about the role of the police in society, as the American Bar Association (1973) recommends? Much depends on how the skills are taught. The investigative process can be taught as a form of historiography (Osterburg, 1968). However, a course in police report writing (Cox, 1977) seems less appropriate for a college curriculum than a basic English composition course.

   Should police work or police management topics dominate? Another issue in specialized police education curriculums is whether they should prepare people to do police work or to manage it. Much of what is now taught in college programs for the police concerns the management of police organizations. The management content is both too much and too little for the needs of the police. It is probably too much for the vast majority of police officers, who will never rise to any supervisory rank, and may lead them to view as second best the line police work that will be their career. It is too little for those who will become police managers, because it gives inadequate treatment to such managerial tasks as budgeting, goal definition, and press relations. The present effort is comparable to a program that attempts to educate medical doctors and hospital administrators simultaneously, with a guarantee that the administrators will always earn higher salaries than the doctors.

   How should values be treated? Another consideration in choosing between a general and a specialized curriculum for police education is the effectiveness of each in teaching students to comprehend the complex moral dilemmas of police work. The general education curriculum was once heavily slanted toward the teaching of morality, but in recent times values have been replaced, in many areas of teaching, with purely cognitive and rational concerns (Murchland, 1976). Specialized programs in police administration have been dominated by a value-neutral conception of government administration based on technical expertise. In the wake of Watergate, there has been renewed interest in moral values in general education curriculums and in several professional education fields (Carnegie Foundation, 1977; Fiske, 1978b), but this trend seems to have missed specialized police education programs. Much of the material taught in police edcuation programs implies value positions, but our examination of the textbooks shows that these positions are rarely made explicit or analyzed in relation to competing values. There is some scattered sentiment among police administrators (for example, Bouza, 1977) that police education places too much emphasis on how to do things and not enough on whether it is right to do them, but this viewpoint is far from widespread. Indeed, some of the most "progressive" police administrators often look to the law as their sole source of moral guidance, denying the wide range of value choices the police make that the law does not resolve for them (Wilson, 1968).

Is "criminal justice" the most useful disciplinary framework for police education? If a specialized course of study is preferred to general education, there is some question about whether police issues should be studied in the context of a curriculum examining the entire criminal justice system. Since 1968 many college programs in police science and administration have changed their names to "Criminal Justice." This change in name is said to represent both a change in content and a change in product. The change in content is that the curriculum of a criminal justice program is supposed to cover the workings of the entire criminal justice system, not just the police (Newman, 1978). The change in product is that such programs are supposed to produce criminal justice "generalists" capable of working in any agency in the system (Lejins, 1976). One purpose of this change is that higher education is expected to "act as a unifying force, bringing together the police and the other components of the administration of justice" (Shanahan, 1977). But it is unclear what benefits would be gained by "unifying" the criminal justice system, especially since much of what the police do has no connection at all with the other agencies of criminal justice.

What level of conceptual abstraction is most appropriate? Another major consideration has to do with how concrete or theoretical the courses should be: Should the content of the courses emphasize how to do things, how things work, or why things work the way they do? The history of police education programs has been "characterized by continuous tension between the nuts-and-bolts approach and the ivory tower crew" (Misner, 1977, p. 14). Courses on topics directly related to policing are most often taught with an emphasis on prescribing police practices, less often taught by describing the policy issues surrounding police practices, and least often taught by explaining crime and crime control with social science theory (Sherman and McLeod, 1978). The current balance in specialized police education is heavily weighted toward concrete prescriptions for practice.

Should students be educated for present or future jobs? Another important consideration in designing any college curriculum is whether it is useful only for jobs as they are presently structured or for adapting to new kinds of jobs that have not yet been invented. One argument against a specialized program of police education is that it provides students with less security and adaptability for the possible future changes in the structure of employment. "The economic organization of our country is being transformed at such a rapid rate that it is no longer wise for students to elect a course that is too narrowly vocational," as a 1944 Allegheny College catalogue put it (Rudolph, 1977). Balanced against the possible changes of the future is the student's immediate concern for employment upon graduation. But employment conditions can change rapidly even during the course of a college career, and colleges cannot guarantee a high demand for the graduates of any professional education program. The many letters the commission received from unemployed graduates of college programs in law enforcement and criminal justice demonstrate that pursuing an education for a specific job can increase as well as decrease the risk of unemployment.

Should decisions be based on consumer demand or educational judgment? The overriding question in all these issues is the basis on which they should be decided. On some campuses many of the issues have been resolved more on the basis of course enrollments than on the basis of academic policy considerations. "If in the nineteenth century the curriculum defined the market for higher learning," as Rudolph (1977, pp. 247-248) observes, "in the twentieth the market defined the curriculum." The curriculum has become highly responsive to a new consumerism in recent years, especially at the kinds of colleges that offer police education programs (community colleges, the less highly selective liberal arts colleges, and the comprehensive colleges and universities), because faculties and administrators have "fewer convictions than in earlier times about what is right and what is proper, about what they will and will not do" (Carnegie Foundation, 1977, p. 5). In the face of this strong trend, the Carnegie Foundation has recommended that "the curriculum of the future should be less the result of pressures and more the consequences of sustained thought" (1977, p. 18). As Tom Bradley suggested to one police educator who told the commission that his program gave police students what they wanted, such "responsiveness" may be "just reinforcing the worst attitudes, the worst practices, the worst habits that we find in law enforcement already, . . . developing highly trained bigots."

Models

Police education varies from one college to the next on each of the major issues in curriculum content. In general, the positions on the issues vary consistently among the four models of the curriculum: general education, criminal justice as a liberal art, criminal justice as a professional education, and police technology as paraprofessional vocational training. The models are presented as a continuum from less to more direct relevance to police work.

General Education. The first college-educated police administrators, men like Theodore Roosevelt and Arthur Woods, were Ivy League graduates with a general education. The first college-educated police officers, the University of California students whom August Vollmer recruited to the Berkeley Police Department, were also educated in the liberal arts, or in business or other professional education fields. And even today some police officers pursue an education as general as the "Great Books" program at St. John's College ("New York Policeman to Seek SJC's Master's," 1977). But the recent boom in specialized police education programs seems to have pushed the general education model of higher education for police into the background. As early as 1972, almost half of the police recruits in four states who had attended college had majored in law enforcement or criminal justice (Table 5), and the percentage is probably even greater by now. The trend in curricular preferences, in turn, has prompted a backlash of criticism.

Table 5. Major Field of Collegiate Study of 1972-73
Police Recruits in Four States

Field	Number	Percent
Law Enforcement/Criminal Justice	834	46%
Social Science	297	17
Education	73	4
Arts and Letters	31	2
Business/Management	232	13
Natural Sciences	90	5
Nonpreference	108	6
Other	131	7
Total	1,796	100

Source: Hoover, 1975, p. 30.

There is a clear and growing sentiment that police officers should not be educated in college programs directly related to policing. A Twentieth Century Fund (1976) task force report, for example, considered the college programs receiving LEEP funds and concluded that the participants in the programs "do not really get the benefits of either a college education or a learning experience in a context that might broaden their intellectual perspectives and alert them to concerns not generally associated with the law enforcement community" (p. 17). The Twentieth Century Fund report also argued that "special education in criminal justice is best left to the regular training programs of criminal justice agencies and that the purpose of sending people to college should be to provide them with the education that they desire," recommending that "LEEP's provisions be revised so that payments are made directly to individuals instead of to institutions, enabling those individuals to attend the college and pursue *the curriculum of their choice*" (p. 17; original italicized).

A report of the American Bar Association (1973) on *Standards Relating to the Urban Police Function* was less strongly opposed to special college programs for the police, but it clearly preferred a general education: "The need is for individuals with a broad liberal arts education. . . . Police officers should follow a general course of study, taking courses that cover such areas as social disorganization, abnormal psychology, urban affairs, constitutional law, politics, and American history. . . . It is not essential that the college program provide a special course of study concerned with policing" (p. 218).

Some police educators also support the view that police students should major in other programs. Gordon Misner (1977, pp. 14-15), a former president of the Academy of Criminal Justice Sciences, has observed that "the police world could profit from having people with degrees or with college credits in electrical engineering, mathematics, computational sciences, philosophy, history. . . . We should not cast our net so narrowly to exclude those majoring in some academic subjects other than police administration or the administration of justice" (see also Trubitt, 1967).

Even some police administrators, who generally might be expected to prefer a vocational curriculum, have expressed a preference for a liberal arts curriculum. Almost ten years ago a group of police administrators attending a seminar at LEAA attacked many LEEP-supported college programs as too narrowly vocational (and the behavioral sciences as "irrelevant") and agreed on the position "that a liberal education is *directly related* to the needs of law enforcement. Therefore, law enforce-

ment education is not to be limited to specialized fields but is
to encompass all those subjects considered general education
courses" (quoted in Tenney, 1971, p. 82).

More recently a number of police administrators expressed similar views to this commission. David C. Couper,
police chief of Madison, Wisconsin, told the commission that he
had abolished his department's requirement that all new recruits
have two years of college credits, because it limited his manpower pool largely to the graduates of community college
police science programs, people he found to be too narrow in
outlook. William Kolender, police chief of San Diego, California, also expressed a preference for traditional liberal arts majors over criminal justice majors to serve as police officers. And
former New York City police commissioner Michael Codd expressed strong support for police officers' studying the
humanities.

The arguments in favor of police officers majoring in traditional liberal arts disciplines generally assert the superiority of
this model in developing the general qualities of educated people described in Chapter Two, qualities that are deemed important for police officers to have. Another argument in support of
a general education is that it will give students more options for
employment after they leave police service (Salten, 1977). Yet
it is just for this reason that Edward J. Kiernan, president of the
largest police labor organization in the country, the International Conference of Police Associations, opposed a liberal
arts education in his testimony before the commission: "I can't
for the life of me see us educating police officers in other than
police sciences, so that after we get all done educating these
guys . . . within six months they are no longer cops" (Kiernan,
1977).

A survey of all the police recruits in four states in
1972-73 has been interpreted as supporting this argument
against a traditional liberal arts education for police (Hoover,
1975, p. 31). Recruits who had majored in a field other than
law enforcement or criminal justice were less likely than criminal justice majors to say that they anticipated serving out their
entire careers in criminal justice work. Yet the majors in "un-

related" fields in this sample were also much more likely than the criminal justice majors to have completed four years of college (Hoover, 1975, p. 30), and all those who had completed four years of college were more likely to anticipate a shorter tenure (p. 29)—a finding consistent with the findings of several other studies (Levy, 1967; Cohen and Chaiken, 1972; but see Weber, 1973). The association between major field and anticipated tenure, then, may well be spurious; if level of education is held constant, the correlation of major field and tenure might disappear. These data cannot be used as evidence that students pursuing a more general major have less commitment to police work than those majoring in police education programs. But the finding does suggest that a full career in our presently structured police departments is less attractive to college graduates, regardless of their major.

Perhaps the strongest argument against a traditional liberal arts major is that the basic training provided by most police agencies is inadequate for providing a full conception of the complex role of the police in a democratic society. While history or philosophy majors may acquire cognitive skills and values that are desirable for police officers to have, they may be unaware of the major issues in policing until they attend a police academy or, worse yet, begin doing police work, where they are unlikely to be taught to consider all sides of the issues. The proposed remedy to this problem is a curriculum applying the methods and theories of arts and science disciplines to substantive issues in policing and criminal justice.

Criminal Justice as a Liberal Art. The proponents of a "liberal" criminal justice (or criminology, or a number of other related names—see Foster, 1974) curriculum for police education seek the best aspects of both liberal arts and career education. On the one hand, they argue that a broad, multidisciplinary approach to the problems of crime and crime control can serve just as well as traditional majors to develop the general qualities of educated persons, qualities which can help them contribute to educating the police institution. On the other hand, they argue that students will be better prepared for police careers by studying the subject matter of criminal justice. The graduates of a liberal criminal justice program are not expected to be fully prepared for police work, but they are expected to be able to understand police work in relation to their understanding of self and society (Brown, 1974; Vanagunas, 1976).

The specific components of a criminal justice major have been debated at great length (Adams, 1976; Kuykendall, 1977), although relatively little attention has been given to distinguishing a liberal arts curriculum in criminal justice from a professional or training curriculum. More attention has been paid to the issues of teaching about the entire criminal justice system rather than only one or two of its parts (Newman, 1974), of teaching on a more theoretical and less prescriptive level of abstraction (Hoover, 1975), and whether or not criminal justice is a discipline (Adams, 1976; Olson, 1978). These issues are also addressed in the commission's consultant reports by Donald Newman, Donald Riddle, and Bruce Olson.

The liberal arts model of a criminal justice major for police is usually described as having a strong behavioral and social science component (Brown, 1974; Streib, 1977) and as primarily concerned with explanation and understanding of human behavior. Tenney's (1971) study of college programs for police found that a social science criminal justice curriculum typically included such courses as criminology (the causes of crime); the development of police systems in society; criminal gangs, organized crime, and the political process; and criminal justice and the social structure. Others have argued that humanities courses should also be offered in criminal justice curriculums, especially those that build an understanding of value systems, natural law, and jurisprudence. Few courses of this nature appear to be offered in even the most liberal criminal justice programs. But, as the head of one of the leading doctoral programs in the field has observed, "Without doubt, the field is loaded with enough epistemological and ontological questions to warrant some broader approaches beyond the ambiguous limits of social science" (Czajkoski, n.d.).

A well-rounded conceptual education organized around criminal justice topics could encompass almost every traditional discipline. Literature, for example, could be taught with the

great novels of crime and punishment. Philosophy could be
taught with an emphasis on the morality of punishment. Chem-
istry could be (and is now) taught with an emphasis on its
forensic applications. And history could be organized around
the changes over time in social norms, deviance, and social control. The material that could be covered in this fashion would
easily occupy an entire undergraduate curriculum as well as a
doctoral program. An important aspect of the liberal arts model
of criminal justice, however, is the position that the proportion
of courses taken in the major should be strictly limited at the
undergraduate level (Myren, 1970). The Forensic Studies Department at Indiana University (Bloomington) follows this principle in urging its majors to take more courses in other fields.
The accreditation standards for criminal justice programs proposed by the Academy of Criminal Justice Sciences (1976) also
endorse this principle: "Since criminal justice education is multidisciplinary, overspecialization should be avoided on the
undergraduate level."

Two major arguments have been made against a liberal
criminal justice major as an appropriate college curriculum for
police officers. One argument holds that a criminal justice major, no matter how it is taught, is too narrow a framework for
developing a sophisticated perspective on the police. The other
argument holds that a liberal approach to criminal justice is too
broad to provide adequate preparation for police careers.

Herman Goldstein (1977, pp. 32-33), a proponent of a
traditional liberal arts curriculum for police education, argues
that an emphasis on criminal justice is unduly restrictive in
studying the totality of police functioning and the police as an
institution: "The bulk of police business . . . takes place *before*
invoking the criminal justice system (for example, checking suspicious circumstances, stopping and questioning people, maintaining surveillance), makes use of the system for purposes
other than prosecution (to provide safekeeping or to investigate), or occurs in its entirety *outside* the system (resolving conflict, handling crowds, protecting demonstrators). . . . In order
to gain a better understanding of these issues, we need a conceptual framework for viewing the police function that is suffi-

ciently broad to encompass all that the police do." Majoring in criminal justice might reinforce the unfortunate tendency of many police officers to define tasks unrelated to criminal justice as unimportant, bothersome distractions. An alternative model implied by this critique is a liberal program in police studies, with courses built around the problems the police encounter: family relations (for understanding domestic disturbances) or urban sociology (for understanding changing neighborhoods). As far as we know, however, no programs of this nature are now offered.

The second criticism of the liberal arts approach to criminal justice is based on the objective of teaching students the skills required to function competently as police officers. The liberal arts approach clearly fails to prescribe applied principles of police practice, leaving that task to police training academies. Criminal justice as a liberal art may also be too broad to provide a legitimate basis for using educational requirements in licensing students for the practice of policing, an element of the police professionalization movement that has already been partly achieved in a number of states. The two alternatives that would justify education as a basis for licensing are criminal justice (or police administration) as a professional education and police technology as paraprofessional career training.

Criminal Justice as a Professional Education. This model of the curriculum for police education is borrowed from undergraduate education in engineering, architecture, journalism, and business administration, rather than from the liberal arts and sciences. In contrast to criminal justice as a liberal art, criminal justice as a professional education emphasizes descriptions of professional and policy issues rather than theoretical explanations of deviance and social control. Courses in this model are organized around more concrete topics than in criminal justice as a liberal art, but their treatment is more abstract and complex than in the courses on related topics in the paraprofessional training curriculum.

The professional education model of police education predates the emergence of the academic field of criminal justice, and some institutions have resisted the trend toward the "total system" curriculum. Thus, while Michigan State University's School of Police Administration (founded in 1935) recently changed its name to the School of Criminal Justice, the University of Louisville has maintained its long-standing School of Police Administration, and Eastern Kentucky University has recently established a College of Law Enforcement. Tenney's study of the professional model in the late 1960s found courses reflecting this fairly exclusive emphasis on the police (1971, p. 12):

- Introduction to Law Enforcement
- Police Patrol and Services
- Principles of Criminal Investigation
- Police-Community Relations
- Substantive Criminal Law
- Criminal Procedure
- Police Management Systems
- Police Administration
- Police Supervision
- Juvenile Delinquency
- Prevention and Control of Crime

The more recent emphasis on the criminal justice system (Kuykendall, 1977) is evident in a set of guidelines for two-year programs in criminal justice that follows the professional model (Hoover and Lund, 1977). The guidelines recommend several core courses to be taken by all students (Introduction to Criminal Justice, Introduction to Criminology, Concepts of Criminal Law and Legal Procedures, Social Values and the Criminal Justice Process) and options for several different components of the criminal justice system, including law enforcement (Concepts of Police Operations, Police Organization Theory, Criminal Investigation, Criminal Justice Internship, Dynamics of Substance Abuse).

The combination of core courses in criminal justice and subsequent options for careers in different agencies resolves a major argument against a professional education model: that there is no such thing as a "profession of criminal justice" for which to provide professional education. Despite some recommendations that higher education should create a profession of criminal justice generalists (Lejins, 1976), the obstacles to lateral movement from one type of criminal justice agency to another (except at the very highest levels) make such an objective rather pointless. A better argument for criminal justice as a professional education for police officers is that police should be aware of the issues affecting the criminal justice system as a whole, but even that argument may be hard to justify in terms of the impact of such awareness on police behavior.

The debate over "systemic" versus "component" professional education in criminal justice may be of little consequence. The primary argument for a professional education curriculum for police officers is that, no matter what its specific content may be, it will help to professionalize the police. Sociologist Egon Bittner (1970, p. 81), writing before the emergence of criminal justice as an academic field, observed: "The main purpose of having professional schools of police work . . . is not to produce educated policemen but to make *specific education*, and the range of meaning associated with it, part of the conception of the occupation. This can only be achieved by independent degree-granting institutions functioning within the framework of existing universities, in the maintenance of which the practicing profession will have a realistic interest." Bittner rejected both a traditional general education and a curriculum oriented to policing within existing social science departments, arguing that neither the application of scientific knowledge to police work nor the prestige of having college-educated officers is as important to professionalizing the police as the *symbolic* significance of creating professional schools of police work. He even ventured to recommend "the formation of postgraduate professional schools of police work— graduation from which will ultimately be a condition of employment for all licensed policemen" (Bittner, 1970, p. 79).

This conception of professional education is implied by the effort of the Academy of Criminal Justice Sciences to obtain recognition as an accreditation authority for college programs in criminal justice. While motivated by other purposes

(Misner, 1975; Bassi and Rogers, 1976), the specialized accreditation of criminal justice programs would be required "to provide some assurance to the public of the quality of the education and training of future practitioners" (Selden, 1976, p. 7). All the professional schools to which Bittner refers as analogs are accredited by professional associations of either educators or practitioners, and in some cases by both (Orlans, 1975). Specialized accreditation is not found in the liberal arts and sciences, since they are not held accountable for the occupational competence of their graduates—nor could they be, given the wide range of occupations their graduates enter. The movement toward accreditation is clearly a rejection of the liberal arts conception of criminal justice. It is not necessarily a rejection of the paraprofessional training model, however, given the existence of specialized accreditation in such fields as practical nursing and cosmetology (Orlans, 1975).

Another argument made for professional education in general is that the liberal arts have become an anachronism because of the new realities of higher education: the large numbers of diverse students and the massive explosion of knowledge (Newman and others, 1974; Clecak, 1977). Carl Kaysen (1974), former director of the Institute for Advanced Study at Princeton, argues that professional training can adapt to these changes by meeting students' needs for economic security, higher occupational status, and more interesting work. At the same time, Kaysen sees "professional training as the central means toward securing the results that we seek: the creation of the critical, inquiring, and informed mind" (1974; quoted in Clecak, 1977, p. 421). Or, as McGrath (1959) has argued, training in the skills of logical reasoning can be done just as well in a professional education curriculum as it can in the liberal arts.

This position suggests a professional curriculum that fuses liberal and technical learning. The fusionist position was first suggested by Alfred North Whitehead ([1929] 1967, p. 48): "The antithesis between a technical and liberal education is fallacious. There can be no adequate technical education which is not liberal, and no liberal education which is not technical: that is, no education which does not impart both technique and intellectual vision." Meyerson's (1974; quoted in Clecak, 1977, p. 423) argument for the "creative tension between the concrete and the theoretical" and O'Toole's (1977) proposal for fusing liberal and technical learning indiqate the growing popularity of this position. It avoids atheoretical vocational training at the same time that it raises the place of vocation and service in the value system of higher education. The trend toward this position in higher education generally seems so strong that the Carnegie Foundation for the Advancement of Teaching (1977, p. 119) was moved to ask, "Must one plan to become a professional in order to acquire a good undergraduate education?"

The fusionist position is commonly articulated in discussions of the professional education model for police education. Gerald Lynch (1977), president of the John Jay College of Criminal Justice of the City University of New York, recommended that the commission "support a strong liberal arts-based curriculum with a mix of professional courses. But those professional courses should be approached from a liberal arts perspective. That is, they should not be 'how-to' courses but should encourage critical analysis of the issues." At a symposium on higher education for police sponsored by the American Academy for Professional Law Enforcement, a national organization of college-educated police officers, a great deal of discussion was devoted to finding an "ideal mix" of liberal arts and professional courses (Loughrey, 1977; McNamara, 1977). One speaker even paraphrased Whitehead in declaring that "professional education is as sterile without liberal arts as liberal arts is without utility in today's society" (Shanahan, 1977).

In its extreme form, the fusionist conception of a professional education for police officers is difficult to distinguish from criminal justice as a liberal art. Aside from the organizational accoutrements of separate schools, accreditation, and licensing, a broad professional education is indistinguishable from a multidisciplinary arts and science offering on the same topics. Some professional schools almost openly acknowledge that fact. The Yale Law School, for example, is said to teach everything but the law (Orlans, 1975), in sharp contrast to the many local law schools that cram state law into the heads of students whose sole concern is passing the bar examination. Most professional education curriculums for police officers probably resemble those of the local law schools rather than those of the national law schools. The many proponents of the fusionist position notwithstanding, there are few police education programs that actually adopt Robert M. Hutchins' conception of professional education: "I don't think a law school should be engaged in training lawyers to be successful at the bar. It should be educating young men and women to understand the legal institutions of the world and how they can be improved" ("The Hutchins View . . . ," 1977).

Whatever the current state of the professional curriculum for police education, there is good reason to believe that it may grow more liberal over time. The history of professional education in other fields shows a distinct trend away from atheoretical training to more abstract forms of teaching (Cheit, 1975). Some engineering schools, for example, are now trying to train "technological humanists" ("Training Humanists . . . ," 1978). The assumption that a field of practice is complicated enough to merit scholarly attention in a professional school tends to generate broader and more sophisticated conceptions of the profession's tasks (Bittner, 1970). In the long run, there may be little substantive difference between criminal justice (or police studies) as a liberal art and as a professional curriculum. The difference between these two models and the *para*professional career training model, however, will probably continue to widen.

Police Technology as Paraprofessional Vocational Training. Most two-year and many four-year specialized police education programs offer courses on policing that are little different from what is taught in police academies. These courses are taught at an extremely concrete level, prescribing how to perform police tasks without analyzing the rationale for those tasks. Not every course in the programs following this model is completely prescriptive, but the courses on policing generally seem to be (at least according to our study of textbooks reported in those programs). Despite the fact that this curriculum is offered for credit in colleges, there is considerable opinion that it does not qualify as higher education. The police technology (or police science, or law enforcement technology, or many other related names) curriculum is the target of most of the criticism of police education.

The intellectual aridity of this curriculum is evident in the guidelines published by the Office of Education in 1975 for two-year programs in law enforcement technology (Stinchcomb, 1975). The guidelines provide detailed course outlines (up to eight pages per course) and three or four possible textbooks to be used with each course. The mere fact that the field can be packaged in this manner suggests a rather low level of complexity. The recommended courses provide even more evidence on this point (p. 31):

First Semester: Introduction to Psychology
                         National Government
                         Introduction to Law Enforcement
                         Communications Skills
                         Police Organization and Administration
                         First Aid I and II

Second Semester: Technical Report Writing
                         State and Local Government
                         Introduction to Sociology
                         Police Role in Crime and Delinquency
                         Patrol Operations
                         Police Defense Tactics

Third Semester: Criminal Law
                         Criminal Investigation
                         Social Problems
                         Police Community Relations
                         Police Arsenal and Weapons (Firearms)
                         Elective

Fourth Semester: Basic Mathematics
                         Criminal Evidence and Procedure
                         Introduction to Criminalistics
                         Organized Crime and Vice Control
                         Elective

Out of the 64 credit hours of recommended courses, all but 24 hours (37 percent) are about police work. Although this figure is comparable to national norms of course concentration in undergraduate professional education programs (Carnegie Foundation, 1977, p. 115), the recommended curriculum clearly violates an accreditation standard of the Academy of Criminal Justice Sciences (1976), which proscribes overspecialization on the undergraduate level. Putting aside the question of balance, the inclusion of courses in firearms, defensive tactics, first aid, and report writing also violates the standard of the Academy of Criminal Justice Sciences that "basic agency skill training for criminal justice practitioners which is not designed to develop logical, analytical, or cognitive skills or develop the reasoning capabilities of the student is clearly not a part of the academic collegiate degree program mission." Although some of these courses can be taught analytically, the course outlines in the guidelines hardly encourage such an approach.

The police technology guidelines, then, appear to be more highly vocational than the other models. However, they once represented a major step toward liberalizing the prevailing two-year curriculum. As recently as the late 1960s, some colleges were actually teaching courses in handcuffing and the use of the nightstick. In publishing the first version of these guidelines a decade ago (Crockett and Stinchcomb, 1968), the American Association of Community and Junior Colleges performed an important act of leadership.

We do not oppose this model of the curriculum merely because it includes training in basic skills. Courses in self-defense for the police are no less appropriate than courses in legal research methods for lawyers. The source of our concern is the apparent failure of this model to connect skill training to more general moral and intellectual issues. As Dewey and Whitehead argued, acquiring a specific skill without understanding its background is not learning, because knowledge acquired in this manner cannot be used later when a problem arises in a different context (O'Toole, 1977). Training courses devoid of theoretical or analytical content are inadequate for preparing students for anything besides doing police work as it is presently done.

In the name of professionalizing the police, many police managers have actively sought to develop a training curriculum at local colleges. Ironically, their efforts have aided the view that police work is merely paraprofessional, a "middle-manpower" job requiring equal amounts of cognitive and manual skill (Harris and Grede, 1977). Instead of making police officers comparable to doctors and engineers, the paraprofessional training curriculum defines police officers as comparable to practical nurses and technicians. Teaching courses about the police at such a low level of complexity does a gross injustice to the true complexity of the police task.

The only possible arguments for this curriculum are that its graduates will be more efficient police officers and that they can obtain employment more readily than graduates of more liberal programs. Indeed, the Office of Education guidelines assert that "the quality of a law enforcement education program may be judged upon the final employability and performance of its graduates" (Stinchcomb, 1975, p. 11). Unfortunately, employability may be conditioned on the acceptance of the status quo in policing. Career education seeks to build "positive" attitudes toward work, with the goal of producing "contented technicians rather than perceptive social critics" (Rudolph, 1977, p. 288). Policing needs the critics much more than it needs the technicians.

Frequency

It is one thing to describe the different models of the curriculum and quite another to measure the relative frequency with which colleges offer them. Previous attempts to study the prevalence of the models have been hindered by poor methodology, although the results of some studies are suggestive. The commission's attempt to study the frequency of the models provides somewhat stronger findings about the course content of the specialized police education programs.

The most recent attempt to measure the frequency of the three models of specialized police education programs (Pearson and others, 1978) illustrates the two major problems of methodology: sampling and measurement. This study interviewed 250 program heads, faculty members, and college administrators attending "seven national and regional meetings of major professional associations related to criminal justice education" (Pearson and others, 1978, p. 34). The respondents, who represented only 146 different programs, were asked to describe the curriculum in their program. Only one sixth said that their program had a "technical-vocational" curriculum, one fifth said that their curriculum was "professional-managerial," and the remaining majority claimed that their programs had a "humanistic-social" curriculum. The authors conclude that "the criticism of excessive vocationalism is less valid today than it was, say, five years ago." The study actually provides scant basis for the conclusion, however. By sampling (on an apparently haphazard basis) the respondents from among those with both the interest and the funding to attend a conference, the study may have been drawing from a stacked deck: conference participants may be more likely to come from the more "humanistic-social" programs. And even if the sampling was representative of all police education programs, there is still no assurance that each respondent defined the three curriculum models in the same way. One respondent's vocational curriculum may have been what another thought of as professional. Finally, since more than one respondent was interviewed about some programs, the multiple responses should have been (but apparently were not) collapsed into one where they agreed and discarded where they did not. These flaws are serious enough to make the finding totally inconclusive.

Two earlier studies provide more suggestive results. Both studies used course titles listed in federal funding applications as an indicator of course content in police education programs. Tenney (1971) found that half of the twenty-eight programs he examined followed the training model, but it is inappropriate to generalize from that small sample, observed a decade ago, to all the present college programs for police. More recently the National Planning Association (1976, p. V-152) examined the titles of all 14,640 courses listed on the funding applications of all programs receiving LEEP funds in 1975-76, classifying 14.6

percent of all the courses and 34.9 percent of the law enforcement courses as "training-type" courses. Although the sample
used in that study was probably quite representative, the use of
course titles to indicate course content has been criticized because courses with the same titles can be taught in many different ways. A course on traffic, for example, might be confined
to traffic-directing techniques, or it might consider transporta-
tion planning and automotive engineering.

As a more direct indicator of course content, the commission examined the textbooks assigned in courses on policing in
college programs for the police. After identifying 1,070 undergraduate programs on policing or some broader field including
the police (such as criminal justice or criminology) from three
different lists of such programs (Bruns, 1975; Kobetz, 1975; list
of LEEP-participating institutions, fiscal years 1975-1977, U.S.
Law Enforcement Assistance Administration), commission staff
mailed questionnaires to the heads of every program. We received responses from 261 program heads, listing 606 different
books. Commission staff obtained copies of four fifths (80.9
percent) of the books and assessed their conceptual level of abstraction as either prescriptive, descriptive, or explanatory. The
categories for classifying the books roughly correspond to the
training, professional, and liberal arts models of the specialized
police education curriculums.

The books were classified on a scale of 1 to 6:

1. Textbooks prescribing how to do police tasks. Examples include *Police Patrol: Tactics and Techniques* (Adams, 1971),
   Basic Police Report Writing (Gammage, 1974), and *Fundamentals of Criminal Investigation* (O'Hara, 1973).
2. Books prescribing police administrative policies. Examples
   include *Police Administration* (Wilson and McLaren, 1972),
   Police Personnel Administration (Bopp, 1974), and *The Police Traffic Control Function* (Weston, 1975).
3. Textbooks describing policy issues and police behavior from
   multiple points of view. Examples include *Introduction to
   Law Enforcement and Criminal Justice* (Germann, Day, and
   Gallati, 1975), *Municipal Police Administration* (Eastman and

Eastman, 1969), and *Introduction to Criminal Justice* (Newman, 1975).

4. Research reports describing policy issues and police behavior. Examples include *Police Community Relations* (Cohn and Viano, 1976) and *City Police* (Rubinstein, 1973).
5. Textbooks emphasizing theoretical explanations of police behavior. Examples include *The Police Community* (Goldsmith and Goldsmith, 1974), *Police in America* (Skolnick and Gray, 1975), and *The Juvenile Offender and the Law* (Hahn, 1971).
6. Research reports explaining police behavior. Examples include *Justice Without Trial* (Skolnick, 1966), *Varieties of Police Behavior* (Wilson, 1968), and *The Police and the Public* (Reiss, 1971b).

All the books reported by each program were assigned the appropriate score, and the mean abstraction score of all the books in each program was computed. As Table 6 shows, over

Table 6. Mean Abstraction Level of Books Assigned in Police-Related Courses in College Programs for Police Officers

Mean Abstraction Level	Number of Programs	Percent
Task-Prescriptive Text	11	4.2%
Policy-Prescriptive Text	147	56.3
Descriptive Text	77	29.5
Descriptive Research Report	18	6.9
Explanatory Text	7	2.7
Explanatory Research Report	1	0.4
Totals	261	100.0

60 percent of the responding programs used predominantly prescriptive texts, suggesting that the reported death of excessive vocationalism (Pearson and others, 1978) may have been somewhat exaggerated. Unfortunately, the low response rate (27 percent, but with little variation across different types of colleges) lends much uncertainty to any conclusions about the general state of the curriculum in specialized college programs for the police. At the very least, however, the findings demonstrate that

a minimum of 15 percent of all these programs (158 responding, compared to 1,070 identified) approximate the training model.

Many factors account for the content of the curriculum. The Carnegie Foundation for the Advancement of Teaching (1977) lists no fewer than seventeen external and six internal forces that generally shape an undergraduate curriculum. The next three chapters examine the impact of several of those forces on police education curricula: institutional characteristics, faculty background, and student orientation. The purpose of analyzing the forces shaping the curriculum is to determine how best to implement the recommendations offered below.

Recommendations

Each of the curricular issues and models has important implications for achieving the objectives of higher education for police officers. In offering the following recommendations, the commission is guided by its central objective of educating the police institution for change. We believe that the likelihood of change will be increased if police officers are educated in a wide variety of disciplines and curriculums. We therefore oppose any attempts to encourage or require all college-educated officers to pursue any of the three models of the specialized police education programs. A broad general education should provide just as sound a preparation for police work as majoring in criminal justice (as either a liberal art or a professional education) and perhaps an even better basis for institutional change, since general education may do a better job of teaching students how to use knowledge to solve problems. We encourage students oriented to police careers to consider majoring in traditional arts and science disciplines as well as in other professional fields. For the near future, however, most police education will probably be provided in the specialized, "directly related" programs. Accordingly, we address our recommendations to the content of those programs, which is presently far too narrow.

Our first concern with the overspecialization of police education programs is that they may be restricting students' career options. Since almost half of the preservice students in these programs do not find criminal justice employment, it is important that their education be useful to them in other kinds of work. Even those who enter police work should be able to fall back on their education as a resource for adapting to changing times. John Dewey observed that education should prepare students for an *un*predictable rather than a predictable and steady-state future (O'Toole, 1977). Police education should do no less in that regard than any other kind of college education:

> 3-1 *All college programs focusing on issues in policing and criminal justice should provide a broad education that is useful for many careers and for living through an uncertain future.*

Courses on policing and criminal justice, of course, can be taught quite broadly, and it might even be possible to present most substantive areas of knowledge in terms of their applications to police-related issues. But to ensure breadth of content, faculty and administrators should counsel students out of their frequent inclination to take all the courses they can in the police education program. Similarly, students should not be forced to spend too much time in directly related courses:

> 3-2 *The required number of specialized courses in police and criminal justice in any police education program should not exceed one fourth of the total course work for a degree.*

In many programs the courses on policing are not taught broadly or conceptually. The programs employing the paraprofessional vocational training model of the curriculum seem most unlikely to accomplish the objective of educating for change. By merely teaching basic and routine police skills, these programs do little to develop the student's capacity to use knowledge to solve problems. In addition, because these programs are closely affiliated with paraprofessional training in other fields, they are counterproductive to the goal of professionalizing the police. This model of the curriculum must be replaced with a broader approach:

> 3-3 *Police education programs that offer voca-*
> *tional training courses (courses that train stu-*
> *dents to perform specific police tasks) should*
> *replace those courses with more analytical and*
> *conceptual courses on issues related to those*
> *tasks.*

An extreme form of overspecialization without any benefit for most students is the common emphasis on police management topics in police education programs. The present emphasis on management is inappropriate for the vast majority of students who will never become police managers. A curriculum stressing the complexity and importance of the police officer's role would be far more useful at the undergraduate level, and possibly even at the graduate level. For those who become police managers, additional education at the graduate level in general public management would be of much greater value than the parochial treatments of police management now found in undergraduate courses:

> 3-4 *Police education programs at the undergrad-*
> *uate level should give greater emphasis to the*
> *major issues in doing police work and less em-*
> *phasis to issues of police management and*
> *supervision.*

One of the most important and complex aspects of doing police work is making difficult value choices, often on a split-second basis. The police serve competing value systems in almost all their tasks, but few indications of this fact were found in any of the statements the commission received on the nature of the curriculum. The textbooks we examined tend to present ethics in a simplistic, didactic fashion, listing obvious things that police officers should not do (for example, taking bribes). Not one book is available on the applied ethical dilemmas of police work, showing that police officers must often choose between two wrongs or two rights rather than between right and wrong. Course materials should be developed so that our recommendation can be made realistic:

> 3-5 *Every police education program should include in its required curriculum a thorough consideration of the value choices and ethical dilemmas of police work.*

In many respects, criminal justice as a liberal art is the model least likely to be guilty of overspecialization. In its use of the "criminal justice" framework, however, it may provide too narrow a conception of the police function. Very little of the police role is connected to the criminal justice system. By ignoring those other aspects of policing, the criminal justice framework can reinforce the television stereotype that police work is all crime fighting. Students should be given a more complete and realistic portrayal of policing:

> 3-6 *Police education programs using a "criminal justice system" framework for their required curriculum should also include comprehensive treatment of the most commonly performed police work, which falls outside of the criminal justice system.*

A sophisticated portrayal of the nature of police work should include a discussion of the major findings of the rapidly growing scientific knowledge about policing. Neither the authors nor the publishers of most textbooks for courses on policing, however, have tried to incorporate the available research findings (Conley, 1977; but see National Planning Association, 1976, p. V-59, for some findings of improvement). Nor have instructors sought out the few books that are up to date. The four most frequently reported books in a 1968 survey of associate degree programs (Tenney, 1971) were also the four most frequently reported books in the commission's 1977 survey of undergraduate programs. Although some of them had been re-

vised in the intervening decade, they generally failed to keep up
with social science research findings. This pattern reflects an un-
healthy intellectual stagnation:

> 3-7 *College courses on policing should be continu-
> ally revised to reflect and incorporate the rap-
> idly growing body of research findings on po-
> lice behavior.*

One area of research on policing that remains largely un-
explored is the subject of this chapter: the effects of different
college curriculums on the performance of educated police officers. In the absence of research, curricular recommendations
must rest on judgments, not proof (Carnegie Foundation,
1977). There is enough evidence that the impact of college on
students varies significantly by major field (Feldman and Newcomb, 1969, p. 179), however, to warrant a national investment
in research on the subject of curricular differences in police performance, at both the individual and organizational level. To be
conclusive, research on this issue should be designed to follow
cohorts of officers over a lengthy period of time and to compare a large number of police departments with varying percentages of officers with different kinds of curricular experiences in
college:

> 3-8 *The U.S. Law Enforcement Assistance Admin-
> istration (or any successor organization)
> should establish a research program on the re-
> lationships between different college curricu-
> lums and both the individual performance of
> college-educated police officers and the organi-
> zational performance of the departments they
> serve.*

As Bittner (1970) has observed, discussions of the proper
college curriculum for police officers can go on endlessly. We
believe that this is exactly what should happen. The curriculum
should be continually examined, not just for its relevance to
changing conditions and knowledge but for its adherence to

such basic principles of education as breadth and intellectual challenge. Many people representing many different interests should engage in these ongoing discussions. And for the near future, the locus of discussions of the curriculum will be the colleges educating the police.

4

Colleges

A lot of colleges, I must say, are in it for the money.

Schembri, 1977

Much of what is wrong with police education can be blamed on the colleges that educate the police. Many of the 1,070 colleges and universities offering specialized undergraduate programs in police education have failed to make long-term commitments of resources to the programs, defining them as a temporary response to a short-term demand. Some critics have charged these colleges with being more interested in the profitability than in the quality of police education. The colleges often justify their practices on the grounds of providing greater access to higher education, implying that there must be a tradeoff between quality and access. This argument is particularly powerful in the community colleges, which provide almost half of all police education programs. But greater access is no justification for lower quality. Nor is it an excuse for failing to make long-term institutional commitments to educating the police.

This chapter examines the evidence of insufficient commitment of resources to police education programs. It describes some questionable educational practices—justified in the name of greater student access—which we believe should be modified. Finally, it considers the important role of the community colleges in police education and how that role must be changed.

Resources and Commitment

Many colleges seemed to have created police education programs only because federal funds were available for their support, and not because of any long-range plans to make police education a part of their mission. Their commitment to police education may be no more lasting than the funding. As the Twentieth Century Fund (1976, p. 16) has observed, "Given this opportunity to obtain federal funds in a time of fiscal crisis, many educational institutions have hurriedly established a series of jerry-built programs 'related to law enforcement and criminal justice,' " the criterion of eligibility for LEEP support of pre-service students. Just how hurriedly the programs were established is suggested by a 1970 survey of 237 police education programs, three fourths of which had been established since 1965. The study found that 82 percent of the programs had begun to offer classes in less than one year from the date when planning for the program began (Eastman, 1972, pp. 106-107). Gordon Misner, president of an association of police educators, the Academy of Criminal Justice Sciences, has described this process in harsh language: "The infusion of LEEP money has brought into being the greatest number of harlots the world has probably ever seen. . . . An awful lot of hustlers, and some college presidents serving as pimps, [are] all looking for this LEAA dollar. In fact, I think what is going on now in criminal justice higher education is perhaps the most scandalous thing in the history of our education" (Misner, 1977, p. 14).

Both private and public colleges have created police education programs in recent years, though perhaps for slightly different reasons. Given the financial pressure to maintain or increase enrollments (Fiske, 1978a), many private colleges have recently altered their traditional missions in a number of ways (R. E. Anderson, 1978; Coughlin, 1978), including the creation of police education programs. The LEEP funds led some small liberal arts colleges into part-time, evening, adult education for the first time in their institutional histories. Such drastic changes in mission can cause intensive conflict among administrators and traditional faculty (Fry and Miller, 1976). The changes can also turn students and faculty in police education programs into second-class citizens, denied the same level of institutional resources that other areas of study receive. At one small college, for example, the sudden creation of a LEEP-funded program raised the question of "whether cops really belonged on campus, at least in such large numbers" (Fry and Miller, 1976, p. 265). And even though LEEP funds apparently helped save the college from going bankrupt, the college still failed to make any long-term commitment of resources to police education. This private college is not an exceptional case: one third of the private colleges receiving LEEP funds in 1975-76 failed to provide even one full-time faculty member to their police education program (Table 7).

It is public institutions, however, that provide most of the college programs for police. For many public institutions, educating the police represents little change in mission. Public institutions also derive relatively less financial benefit from LEEP funds than do the private colleges charging higher tuition. Yet many public institutions offering police education programs have also failed to provide institutional support commensurate with what they provide to comparable programs. Like their private counterparts, many public institutions are under pressure to maintain enrollments, so much so that in Maryland, for example, several public community colleges were caught falsely inflating their enrollment figures (Goll, 1977). Police education provides a new source of students at a time of steady decline in the number of people in the traditional college-going age groups. Those programs staffed with inexpensive part-time faculty can provide a revenue surplus that can be used to support other programs in which enrollments are declining.

The practice of supporting some areas of teaching at the expense of others, of course, is necessary for maintaining a well-balanced institutional program of course offerings. Departments of philosophy, for example, are essential components of any college, yet they are rarely self-sustaining in terms of their enrollments. But it is one thing to draw surpluses to support the less popular programs from such well-established and often high-quality programs as law schools, and quite another to draw them from new programs requiring extensive development. Failure to reinvest at least part of the surpluses in the faculty and support services of those programs suggests a lack of long-term institutional commitment to them.

Inadequate Faculty Resources. The strongest evidence that some colleges have not made long-term commitments to their police education programs is the widespread use of part-time faculty to do most of the teaching. This problem, to be sure, is not unique to police education. The use of part-time faculty is rapidly increasing in many areas of higher education. The national ratio of part-time to full-time instructors dropped from 1:4 in 1972-73 to 1:3 in 1976-77. At four-year colleges and universities, the number of full-time instructors increased by only 9 percent from 1972 to 1976, but the number of part-time instructors increased by 38 percent. At two-year colleges, the 1972-1976 change is even more dramatic: full-time instructors increased by only 11 percent while part-time instructors increased by 80 percent. Part-time instructors now outnumber full-time instructors at the two-year level (Magarrell, 1978).

The general increase in the use of part-time faculty can be attributed to two primary causes: cost and flexibility. One study (Tuckman and Vogler; reported in Magarrell, 1978) found that part-time faculty members are paid less per course than full-time faculty, receive fewer fringe benefits, and are given little or no office space. Almost three quarters of them have contracts only for the term in which they are teaching. Untenured part-time faculty cost less in the terms they are used and also do not have to be paid when there is no student demand for their courses. They permit an institution to preserve its student/faculty ratio during times of fluctuating enrollment and to offer new courses and programs without making long-term commitments to continue them (Magarrell, 1978). Police education programs are a prime example of the general trend.

As Table 7 shows, over one quarter of the criminal justice programs participating in LEEP did not have a single full-time faculty member, even though some of them enroll over 1,000 students. Without a special waiver from LEEP officials, the absence of full-time faculty violates LEEP guidelines (U.S. Law

Table 7. LEEP-Supported Institutions with Criminal Justice Programs
That Had No Full-Time Faculty Members in 1975-76,
by Type of Institution

Type of Institution	Number with Criminal Justice Programs	Number with No Full-Time Faculty Member	Percent with No Full-Time Faculty Member
All institutions	871	234	26.9%
Public	695	173	24.9
Private	176	61	34.7
All 2-year colleges	454	130	28.6
Public	439	121	27.6
Private	15	9	60.0
All 4-year colleges	162	50	30.9
Public	60	9	15.0
Private	102	41	40.2
All universities	255	54	21.2
Public	196	43	21.9
Private	59	11	18.6

Source: Computed from National Planning Association, 1976, p. V-159.

Enforcement Assistance Administration, 1975, p. 6). Even where full-time faculty members are used, they are generally outnumbered by the part-time faculty. In all the criminal justice programs combined, less than half of the faculty members are full time (Table 8). At two-year colleges, almost three quarters of the faculty members are part time. When these 1975-76 data are compared with 1971-72 data for all faculty members nationwide, the contrast is striking. The percentage of part-time criminal justice faculty is more than twice as high as the percentage of all part-time faculty nationally. (Given the increased use of part-time faculty in other areas of higher education, however, a comparison with 1975-76 data on all faculty would show less of a difference.)

Another indication of the lack of institutional commitment to providing adequate faculty resources for police education is the high student/faculty ratios in college programs for the police. Both the federal LEEP requirements (U.S. Law Enforcement Assistance Administration, 1975, p. 6) and the accreditation standards of the Academy of Criminal Justice Sciences (1976, p. 5) define a full-time-equivalent student/faculty

Table 8. Part-Time Faculty as a Percentage of All Faculty Members
in LEEP-Supported Criminal Justice Programs in 1975-76,
and of All Faculty Nationally in 1971-72, by Type of Institution

Type of Institution	Status of Faculty Members in LEEP-Supported Programs in 1975-76			Percent of All Faculty Nationally Part Time in 1971-72
	Full Time	Part Time	Percent Part Time	
All institutions	2,897	4,032	58.2%	24.4%
Public	2,188	2,963	57.5	22.6
Private	709	1,069	60.1	28.2
All 2-year colleges	838	2,134	71.8	39.5
Public	816	2,086	71.9	39.8
Private	22	48	68.6	35.7
All 4-year colleges	500	587	54.0	21.5
Public	237	131	35.6	15.7
Private	263	456	63.5	28.3
All universities	1,559	1,311	45.7	18.2
Public	1,135	746	39.7	14.6
Private	424	565	57.1	27.2

Source: Computed from National Planning Association, 1976, pp. V-160, V-162.

ratio of greater than 60:1 as unacceptably high. Yet, according to the best estimate of the National Planning Association (1976, p. V-163), over 60 percent of the LEEP-supported criminal justice programs exceeded that standard in 1975-76.

Finally, the teaching loads of the full-time faculty are often quite high, as are the number of different courses they are required to prepare for. Brandstatter (1967; quoted in Mathias, 1976, p. 381) observed over a decade ago that many faculty members in police education programs must teach eighteen hours a week and that twenty-five hours is not unheard of. Course preparations have run as high as twenty different courses in two years.

Inadequate Support Resources. Critics often charge that colleges provide inadequate resources to their police education programs. Misner (1975, p. 16), for example, has observed that "Too many programs in the criminal justice field are in it primarily for the money and have made no significant investment in library resources." Other criminal justice educators have commented on the failure of college libraries to obtain books related to policing and criminal justice (Brandstatter, 1967; quoted in Mathias, 1976, p. 382; Riddle, 1978). The fact that the accreditation guidelines of the Academy of Criminal Justice Sciences include standards for library resources, as well as for such support services as adequate classrooms, office space, and clerical assistance, demonstrates their concern for the problem as well.

The charges of inadequate support resources, unfortunately, cannot be evaluated with recent data. Even the congressionally mandated, multimillion-dollar "Nationwide Survey of Law Enforcement Criminal Justice Personnel and Resources Needs" failed to investigate this vital aspect of police education in its field studies. The heads of 204 police education programs responding to a 1970 survey, however, did assess the adequacy of the library materials available to their programs at that time; one third of the two-year and one half of the four-year program heads reported that their library materials were inadequate (Eastman, 1972, p. 168).

Quality Versus Access?

In the name of providing greater access to higher education, a number of colleges have employed questionable practices in administering their police education programs. Greater student access to a particular college, of course, means higher enrollments at that college. In order to increase enrollments in police education programs, some colleges have reportedly lowered their academic standards for admission and for granting credit for noncollegiate experience and instruction. They have also engaged in extensive off-campus instruction without providing adequate student services. These practices may well have attracted students who would otherwise not have pursued a college education, but they have also lowered the quality of the education the students received. We believe that police education can be made accessible without the use of these questionable practices.

Admissions Standards. The sensitive issue of admissions standards clearly reflects the tension between traditional conceptions of academic quality and broader access to higher education. A planning group at the City University of New York's John Jay College of Criminal Justice, for example, attacked the use of admissions standards as a measure of quality (Pearson and others, 1978, p. 16): "Quality among the traditional universities is usually associated with the competitive admission of students, using criteria that are heavily academic in nature such as test scores and high school grades. The students so selected possess strong academic skills and are usually able to proceed through a rigorous academic program. . . . Whether students selected in this way are best equipped to pursue criminal justice careers is an open question. Much depends upon their motivation for this career. It is at least as arguable that academic criteria for admissions should be modified to take account of evidence of the student's interest and practical experience in the field."

Much the same, of course, could be argued about admissions standards in professional education in engineering, law, and medicine. But the educators in other professional fields at least use the rhetoric of seeking and educating the "best and the brightest" for their professions. These criminal justice educators speak of "the education of average Americans" (Pearson and others, 1978, p. 17), a far cry indeed from Vollmer's "truly exceptional men." (Vollmer should be forgiven for reflecting the sexism of his times.) A stronger argument in favor of less selective admissions to education for a field that clearly requires above average intelligence is that many highly capable people are otherwise excluded by cultural biases in admissions tests and poor secondary education. That is no justification, however, for providing a less rigorous college education, including any necessary remedial instruction in academic skills.

It is important to distinguish admissions standards in higher education generally from admissions standards in specific institutions. Police education programs are most often found at the less selective colleges, as defined by *Barron's Profiles of American Colleges* (1976). The surveys use three criteria to measure selectivity of admissions: (1) median SAT or ACT scores, (2) high school rankings, and (3) the proportion of applicants whom the institution accepted, all for the most recent freshman class. The results are used to divide 1,349 four-year colleges and universities into six categories of selectivity. Of the 521 of these colleges identified by the commission as having police education programs, less than 5 percent are in the top half of the six selectivity categories. Table 9 suggests that, with only a few exceptions, the more competitive a college's admissions standards, the less likely it is to offer a police education program. This pattern is even stronger if the 917 public community colleges, 531 of which have police education programs, are added to the noncompetitive category. This pattern may only reflect the reluctance of more selective institutions to create specialized, occupationally related programs at the undergraduate level. Although it may suggest that admissions standards to police education programs are at the lower end of the spectrum in higher education generally, the pattern does not necessarily suggest that specific institutions have lowered their own standards to attract students to police education programs.

Police education programs, in fact, once had more "selective" standards than other programs in the same institutions. As recently as the 1950s, admission to a police education program was determined by the same procedures as admission to a police department: a physical examination and a background check for a criminal record (National Planning Association, 1976, p. V-104). Today, according to a field survey of twenty-six programs, admission to police education programs is open to almost all applicants. Moreover, almost one quarter of the programs said that their admissions standards were "not the same" as (and presumably lower than) those of other programs in the same institution (National Planning Association, 1976, p. V-105).

There is certainly a strong case to be made for letting every high school graduate who applies enroll in a police education program. The adoption of that standard at an institution where admissions standards for other programs are higher, however, can have unfortunate consequences for the quality of the

Table 9. Percentage of All 4-Year Colleges and Universities
Having Programs for Police, by Selectivity of Admissions

Selectivity	Percent of All Barron's Respondents Having Programs for Police		Percent of All Public Respondents Having Programs for Police		Percent of All Private Respondents Having Programs for Police		Percent of All Colleges Having Programs for Police in Each Category	
	Percent	(Number)	Percent	(Number)	Percent	(Number)	Percent	(Number)
Noncompetitive	41.5%	(27/65)	49.1%	(26/53)	8.3%	(1/12)	5.2%	(27/521)
Less competitive	42.1	(185/439)	68.9	(126/183)	23.0	(59/256)	35.5	(185/521)
Competitive	42.6	(286/671)	68.5	(148/216)	30.3	(138/455)	54.9	(286/521)
Very competitive	18.5	(20/108)	34.6	(9/26)	13.4	(11/82)	3.8	(20/521)
Highly competitive	6.3	(3/48)	0	(0/5)	7.0	(3/43)	.6	(3/521)
Most competitive	0	(0/18)	0	(0/0)	0	(0/18)	0	(0/521)

Sources: Barron's Profiles of American Colleges, 1976; Harris, 1975; Kobetz, 1975; Bruns, 1975; lists of LEEP-participating institutions, fiscal years 1975-1977, U.S. Law Enforcement Assistance Administration.

police education program. With less academic respectability, a police education program in those circumstances may generally be treated by other students and faculty, as well as by college administrators, as marginal to the institution, a "weak sister" or "second-class citizen." Both the level of resources allocated to the program and the quality of the educational experience of students in the program may suffer accordingly.

There is no reason why low selectivity must mean less rigor in the nature of the academic program, either within institutions or from one institution to the next. Yet that is often the reality of higher education. Of the 261 police education programs responding to the commission's survey of books used in their courses on police, those programs in less selective institutions were much more likely to use the training-type books. They were also much less likely to have program faculty with graduate degrees (but more likely to have faculty with extensive criminal justice experience) and somewhat more likely to use predominantly part-time faculty (Sherman and McLeod, 1978). Judging by these "traditional" measures, there does appear to be an inverse relationship between quality and access in police education. Exceptions to this pattern are plentiful, to be sure, but the pattern is nonetheless evident. While the students at the less selective colleges deserve no less quality in their curriculum and their faculty, less is often what they get.

Credit for Extrainstitutional Learning. Another questionable practice justified on the grounds of increased access to higher education is the granting of academic credit for both police academy training and life experiences of questionable intellectual value. With proper concern for academic standards, life experience credits can be a meaningful way of recognizing intellectual achievements. Yet there is great potential for the abuse of this practice. According to one *New York Times* review of this issue in higher education generally, many institutions seem to be "making nontraditional education synonymous with entrepreneurial quackery" (Goldman, 1977). A few police education programs award credits the way supermarkets sell "loss leaders," using them to attract students to enroll in the program. Once again, these practices suggest a far greater concern for high enrollments than for high quality.

Consider the practice of awarding credit for police academy courses. Very few of the courses offered in any police academy in the country have sufficient conceptual content to justify college credit. On these grounds, several national organizations have agreed that academic credit should not be awarded for training courses conducted by law enforcement agencies. The President's Commission on Law Enforcement and Administration of Justice (1967b, p. 128) took this position in its *Task Force Report on the Police*; the International Association of Chiefs of Police has recommended that "no credit should be allowed for police training or experience" (Crockett, 1968, pp. 1, 12); and the Academy of Criminal Justice Sciences accreditation guidelines (1976, p. 3) require that "credit should be given only when the institution [sic] is under the direction and control of a degree-granting institution."

These recommendations seem to have had little impact on the colleges educating the police. A survey of 171 police education programs in 1970 (Eastman, 1972, p. 163) found that over half of them granted academic credit for the completion of various police training courses. An earlier survey found that almost half of the 132 colleges responding granted from one to twenty-one semester hours of credit for basic municipal or state police academy training, FBI training, military service, or on-the-job experience (Tenney, 1971, p. 53). More recently, field visits to twenty-six criminal justice programs found that 75 percent of the community colleges and 30 percent of the universities awarded credit for routine agency training (National Planning Association, 1976, p. V-94).

Ironically, the granting of credit for police training contradicts the philosophy underlying the equally widespread practice of granting credit for life experience: that colleges should be certifying competence rather than the mere receipt of formal instruction (Harris and Grede, 1977, p. 309). Although some colleges award credit for training only on the basis of a competence test, most—judging from the way the findings of the surveys of these practices are stated—seem to accept automatically the certification of the training agencies. This practice puts a college in the position of credentialing other credentials. Competency-based credit for life experience, such as a College-Level

Examination Program (CLEP) examination (for which there is none in police science or criminal justice), would seem to be more meaningful than automatic granting of credit for training.

Yet the current practices in granting life experience credit in police education are probably even more questionable than the practice of giving credits for training. One police education program chairman proudly told the commission director that he had arranged for the top police officials in his city to receive three years of life experience credit—so that they could quickly earn their degrees and would then encourage their subordinates to enroll in the program. His story illustrates Misner's claim (1975, p. 16) that decisions about academic credit "are often more political than they are academic." For while the police officials may well have been able to meet rigorous standards for the evaluation of their life experience, the program awarding them credit seemed more interested in enrollments than in maintaining standards.

The American Council on Education (1977) recently addressed this issue in a policy statement on awarding credit for extrainstitutional learning. The statement, which has been endorsed by the Council on Postsecondary Accreditation, observes that "experience . . . is in itself an inadequate basis for awarding credit" and proposes several guidelines for the evaluation of experience. The most important guideline from the standpoint of police education programs is that credit should be awarded only in areas where the institution's faculty members have expertise or where nationally validated examinations or other recognized procedures are available. Since no nationally validated examinations for police education exist, colleges must rely on their faculty. And if their police education program faculty are part-time instructors employed by local criminal justice agencies, there may be a conflict of interest in their academic evaluation of the work experience of their colleagues who enroll as students. At the very least, there seems to be a need to restrict the evaluation of life experience to full-time faculty members whose own expertise has been acquired in ways other than (or in addition to) life experience.

Off-Campus Classroom Instruction. A third practice that

some police education programs justify on the basis of increased student access is extensive off-campus instruction. "Extensive" means that students may spend most of their college career without ever setting foot on a college campus. Instead, they attend classes in convenient off-campus locations arranged by the college, a practice that one police educator describes as "ambulance chasing" (Schembri, 1977). Police precinct stations are a common off-campus setting for college classes, even though LEEP guidelines specifically require that "courses shall be convened in academic or neutral environments. A police department squad room, for example, would not be considered a neutral setting" (U.S. Law Enforcement Assistance Administration, 1975, p. 9). Some colleges have even used profit-making subcontractors to provide their outreach courses hundreds of miles away from their campuses (Johnson, 1977).

Although it should be possible to provide a high-quality educational experience in off-campus locations, the practice seems to entail major problems. A report to the New York State Education Department on off-campus collegiate instruction in Westchester County, for example, recently criticized the "inadequate supervision, faculties, curricular offerings, counseling, and other services" found in the extension programs (Michalak, 1978). Commenting on the report, the director of the Division of Academic Review of the Education Department pointed to the financial reasons for the problems of quality: "Now colleges smell money whether it's 13 miles away or 1,300 miles away, and they go after it."

The relationship between access and revenues is illustrated by the experience of the New York Institute of Technology's College Accelerated Program for Police (CAPP). CAPP makes extensive use of off-campus locations, although it does require students to attend special lectures on campus several times a year. Most of the teaching is done by part-time instructors. As of 1978 the institutional cost per student in CAPP was $294 per semester, compared to about $1,050 at nearby John Jay College (which does most of its teaching on campus, or more precisely, in its two large buildings in midtown Manhattan). In the spring semester of 1976, CAPP enrolled 11,706 students, at a cost of $2,514,528, while earning $2,784,284 for a net surplus of $269,756 (D. C. Anderson, 1978, p. 37). But the economics of access are not always so favorable: by the spring of 1978, CAPP enrollments were down to 1,994, and the program was estimated to be losing $92,000 for the semester.

Regardless of financial considerations, there are distinct educational disadvantages to off-campus instruction in police education programs. Access to libraries and extracurricular activities is clearly reduced, but the quality of the classroom experience itself also suffers because the classes are often composed of in-service police officers, sometimes from the same organization. The provost of New York Institute of Technology acknowledged this problem in his defense of off-campus instruction: "Admittedly, this makes it difficult to avoid excessive homogeneity in the student body, a price we must be willing to pay at the present time if we wish to make access a reality." But access to higher education means more than just access to an instructor's lectures. It also means (at the very least) access to classroom discussions involving other students, discussions which are usually more stimulating if the students represent a wide variety of economic, cultural, and perhaps racial backgrounds, as well as different ideological perspectives. If on-campus instruction offers a greater mix of students, then off-campus instruction is probably of poorer quality.

David Anderson's comparison of CAPP to John Jay captures some of the difference in educational experience (1978, p. 38): "Anyone who strolls the halls of John Jay's main building, a converted shoe factory on West 59th Street in Manhattan, senses the palpable difference between accelerated off-campus education and more deliberate traditional education. John Jay students, a stable mix of men and women, blacks, Hispanics, and whites from all parts of the city, walk the halls together, pass the time in a cavernous cafeteria, a rathskeller, and numerous lounges, or wait to visit with professors whose offices are only a few steps from the classrooms."

The assumption that heterogeneity constitutes better educational quality is admittedly difficult to prove. But given the traditional inbreeding of American police departments, a more heterogeneous student body seems to be necessary if police education is to break through the traditional assumptions and values of the police occupational subculture. Heterogeneous classes would seem to be particularly important for in-service students, who constitute most of the enrollment in the off-campus classrooms.

Role of Community Colleges

A great deal of police education is provided by the most accessible institutions of all: the public community colleges. Public two-year colleges now enroll more students than any other type of institution, accounting for 46 percent of all higher education enrollments (Golladay, 1977, p. 56). They have filled an earlier generation's dream of "breaking the access barriers" (Medsker and Tillery, 1971), placing higher education within commuting distance of virtually all Americans. They have also provided almost half of the college programs for police (Table 10) and quite probably a major portion of the students (al-

Table 10. Distribution of College Programs for Police Officers, by Type of Institution

Type of Institution	Number of Institutions in U.S.[a]	Number of College Programs for Police	Percent with College Programs for Police	Percent of All Colleges with Programs for Police
All institutions	2,509	1,070	42.6%	100.0%
Public	1,422	837	58.9	78.2
Private	1,087	233	21.4	21.8
All 2-year colleges	1,067	531	49.8	49.6
Public	917	513	55.9	47.9
Private	150	18	12.0	1.7
All 4-year colleges and universities	1,442	539	37.4	50.4
Public	505	324	64.2	30.3
Private	937	215	22.9	20.1

[a]Includes both accredited and candidate institutions.
Sources: Bruns, 1975; Harris, 1975; Kobetz, 1975; lists of LEEP-participating institutions, fiscal years 1975-1977, U.S. Law Enforcement Assistance Administration.

though enrollment data are unavailable). The quality of police education thus depends heavily on how well the community colleges are educating the police. Our findings are not encouraging.

In the commission's study of books used in college courses on policing (Sherman and McLeod, 1978), the most powerful determinant of the conceptual level of the books was whether the program was located at the two-year or four-year level. Eighty-two percent of the two-year programs responding to the survey reported using highly prescriptive "training-type" books, compared to only 36 percent of the four-year programs. Further evidence of the effect of the community colleges on the police education curriculum is reported by Tenney (1971, p. 49), who found that 10 of the 13 two-year programs (compared to 2 of the 8 four-year programs) he studied had a paraprofessional training curriculum, and by the National Planning Association's study (1976, p. V-154) of course titles in LEEP-supported programs, which found a higher proportion of training-type courses (24.7 percent) in two-year public colleges than in any other type of college.

The effects of being in a community college are not confined to a police education program's curriculum. Police education program faculty in community colleges have substantially less education than four-year police education program faculty —but substantially more experience (Sherman and McLeod, 1978). Fully one third of the program faculty in two-year public colleges supported by LEEP do not have any graduate degrees (National Planning Association, 1976, p. V-155), a violation of both LEEP requirements and the accreditation guidelines of the Academy of Criminal Justice Sciences. Community college programs also make the most extensive use of part-time faculty relative to the number of full-time faculty (see Table 8).

These findings could be defended as wholly consistent with the career education mission of the community college: the curriculum *should* be job related, the faculty *should* be experienced, part-time faculty *should* be hired from local agencies to create closer linkages between work and learning, and the faculty's education *should not* be as important a qualification as their professional experience (Harris and Grede, 1977, especially pp. 291-316). This position assumes, however, that the career education which community colleges provide is for "middle-manpower" paraprofessional occupations. If that conception of police work is rejected, then the present state of police education in the community colleges requires strong measures for improvement.

Just as the community colleges may have served the social function of "cooling out" (Goffman, 1952) the aspirations of individual students to attend universities (Clark, 1960a, 1960b), they are also serving to cool out the institutional aspirations of the police to become a profession. Police education began with the police seeking out the university, but current higher education policy is to educate most police in institutions that lack the teaching resources and research capacities of universities. By making higher education in community colleges locally accessible to large numbers of police officers and students aspiring to be police officers, higher education policy has kept much pressure to accept these students off of the four-year state colleges and universities. Instead of sharing university campuses with legal education and medical education, police education has typically shared community college campuses with education for manual and clerical trades and crafts. Higher education policy has employed the community colleges as a way of keeping education for lower status occupations out of the research-oriented institutions (Bennis, 1978), while still providing those occupations with some access to higher education.

It is one thing to defend the community colleges on the grounds of access, and quite another to ask what happens to people or institutions once they get there (Karabel, 1972). The consequences of locating police education in the community colleges rather than in multiversities may be to impede the long-term development of the police institution. Most of the symbolic meanings Bittner (1970) attributes to higher education in the process of professionalization are lacking in the community college. What seems to be educational upgrading may in fact be educational downgrading, since the growth of two-year degrees among police officers may define police work as merely para-professional and thereby repel potential applicants who possess four-year degrees. These consequences can occur no matter how good the quality of instruction may be.

There are also important consequences for individual students pursuing police education in two-year colleges. Students enrolled in two-year colleges are surrounded by other students who are more authoritarian and less open to change than students in other kinds of colleges (Medsker and Trent, 1965; cited in Feldman and Newcomb, 1969). And, compared to students at other kinds of colleges, two-year-college students are less likely to get to know the faculty in their major fields, to be verbally aggressive in the classroom, or to be involved in student government or athletics (Astin, 1977). Data specifically about students enrolled in police education programs, however, are unavailable.

Perhaps the strongest argument against providing police education in community colleges is that they adversely affect student aspirations for further learning. Students drop out of college at all levels, of course, but they seem more likely to do so if they spend their first two years in a community college. The "cooling-out" hypothesis about the effects of community colleges on individual students in general has considerable support. Although two thirds of all entering community college students enroll in "transfer" programs—liberal arts courses that will be accepted for credit upon transfer to four-year colleges and universities—only one third of the students who complete a two-year program actually do transfer (Medsker and Tillery, 1971, p. 58). Only 14-17 percent of B.A. aspirants enrolling in community colleges ever earn a B.A., whereas 50 percent of the students beginning their studies in four-year colleges complete the B.A. An enormous number of community college students "drop out, get cooled out [via pessimistic, "realistic" counseling], pushed out, [or] disappear" (Zwerling, 1976, pp. 234-235). Data from the American Council on Education's massive decade-long Cooperative Institutional Research Program on 300 institutions and 200,000 students show that "Even after controlling for the student's social background, ability, and motivation at college entrance, the chances of persisting to the baccalaureate degree are substantially reduced" when students begin their college education in a two-year college (Astin, 1977, p. 234).

Data on students in police education programs are not available. Even if they were, they would not be comparable, because police education programs are often considered "terminal" rather than "transfer" programs. But the fact that police education programs are considered "terminal" strongly suggests an attempt to thwart further learning.

The terminal nature of police education programs in community college discourages further learning in several ways. First, it lends a note of finality to the curriculum, as if to say that this is all a police officer needs to know. The two-year degree requirement many police departments impose on recruits simply reinforces this image of finality. Second, it provides students with their heaviest specialization in their first two years of higher education. Where distribution requirements must be met, transfer students may face the prospect of spending much of their junior and senior years in introductory freshman courses. The most serious obstacle to further learning, however, is the fact that many courses from two-year police education programs are not accepted for credit toward a B.A. degree by four-year colleges (Swank, 1975).

The National Planning Association's (1976, pp. V-101-103) 1975 field study of thirteen community college criminal justice programs concluded: "The transfer issue may not be as controversial as it may have been in the past." Ten of the thirteen programs claimed that their curriculum was designed to be fully transferable, and about the same number reported that their students had had no difficulty in transferring credits during the previous two years. Nonetheless, almost three fifths of the universities surveyed in the same study reported that they had refused to grant transfer credit for two-year-college courses, primarily those in the vocational skill training category. The paraprofessional career training model, it would seem, not only duplicates the police academy but also slows down the progress of a student aspiring to a baccalaureate degree. When he discovers that up to a semester of courses cannot be transferred (as might happen if the curricular recommendations presented in Stinchcomb, 1975, are followed by the community college), a student might well be discouraged from pursuing the B.A.

Despite the evident cooling-out effects of community college programs, those programs have also served to draw in large numbers of police officers who would not otherwise have obtained a college education. Many of those officers have probably even gone on to complete a four-year degree. To the extent that the community colleges serve to draw police officers into what becomes a broad four-year program of study, they play a valuable role in police education. With the policy changes we recommend, it should be possible for community colleges to do more drawing in and less cooling out.

Recommendations

Any consideration of the colleges educating the police must be tempered by the empirical evidence showing relatively modest differences among different types of colleges in their impact on students. Different kinds of colleges enroll different kinds of students, and the initial differences in student characteristics are only slightly magnified by their different college experiences (Feldman and Newcomb, 1969). When the impact of college is defined as the changes in the intelligence and attitudes of students during the college years, the differences in impact among different colleges are relatively small. Nonetheless, there are significant correlations between the "quality" of a college and lifetime earnings, even when student background characteristics are controlled for. And, although the overall differences among institutions may be less than what is commonly supposed, "institutions clearly do differ in the degree and kind of change they effect among some, if not all, of their students. The very fact that institutions differ implies that some could do better in outcome achievement. Indeed, it is largely through efforts at the institutional level that the system can improve" (Bowen, 1977, pp. 257-260).

Regardless of their differences in impact, different types of institutions provide different levels of quality in their police education programs. Some institutions are starving their police education programs of resources, while others are labeling their students as paraprofessionals and perhaps cooling them out of university-level aspirations. The praiseworthy fact that many of these same colleges provide students with readier access to higher education does not excuse the lower quality that is often found in the more accessible programs.

A variety of strategies are available for compelling some of the colleges educating the police to provide a higher-quality education, from accreditation to federal funding requirements. These strategies are considered in later chapters. The present recommendations specify the changes that should be aimed for in the colleges educating the police. The most important of these is institutional commitment:

> 4-1 *Colleges should offer a police education program only as a long-term commitment demonstrated by institutional support commensurate with that provided to comparable programs.*

The police and their educational needs will be around for some time to come, regardless of the future of federal funding. The boom in police education may well decline, but some students will continue to be interested in programs of this nature. The mere availability of federal funds is no reason to create a police education program, especially if doing so represents a drastic change in a college's institutional mission. Once a long-term commitment is made to a police education program, there is no reason for failing to allocate adequate resources to it.

The most important kind of resource is full-time faculty. The Academy of Criminal Justice Sciences (1976, p. 5) recognizes this point in its accreditation guidelines, which require that the percentage of "annual credit-hour production of criminal justice courses" taught by part-time faculty not exceed 50 percent in associate degree programs, 30 percent in baccalaureate programs, and 25 percent in graduate programs. These standards, however, are insufficient to guarantee a high level of faculty involvement in the program. The part-time faculty should merely supplement, and not take the place of, the full-time faculty:

> *4-2 Colleges should rely on a core of full-time faculty to staff their police education programs and should rely much less on part-time faculty. In no case should part-time faculty be employed for more than 25 percent of a program's annual credit hour production.*

Support resources are also vital elements of program quality, particularly the library collection. Acquiring good habits of library research is a key to lifelong learning. A college without adequate library holdings in a student's field of interest cannot provide the environment necessary for learning how to learn through independent reading. Building a good collection of research materials in policing and criminal justice will require buying the classics as well as newer books and journals:

> *4-3 College libraries should engage in retroactive acquisition programs, as needed, in order to bring library resources for police education up to the present level for other programs in the college.*

Resources alone, however, cannot guarantee a high-quality program. Programs must also maintain high levels of academic standards. Although there may be apparent conflicts between accessibility and high standards, we believe that these two objectives are highly compatible. For example, it should be possible to attract students to a high-quality program without treating college credits for police training and life experience as free giveaways or marketing devices. Life experience should be evaluated carefully for evidence of intellectual accomplishment. Credit for police training courses, if it is awarded at all, should be evaluated as life experience rather than granted automatically:

4-4 *Colleges should grant no academic credit for attendance at police agency training programs.*

4-5 *Life experience credit for police service should be awarded only after careful review consistent with the guidelines recommended by the American Council on Education and endorsed by the Council on Postsecondary Accreditation.*

Geographical access to police education programs should not be achieved at the price of educational quality. Off-campus classroom instruction deprives students of the many hidden benefits of simply being on a college campus, especially the informal contact with other students. Precinct houses and other off-campus classroom settings usually offer an excessively homogeneous environment, impeding a broad learning experience:

4-6 *Classroom instruction in police education programs should take place on college campuses in order to encourage greater student interaction with diverse kinds of people.*

Student access to community colleges has played an important role in increasing the national educational level of the police. But community college police education programs have also helped to define police work as paraprofessional in nature. Some programs—particularly the terminal two-year degree programs, in which many credits are not transferable to a four-year degree program—have acted as a brake on the educational achievement of police officers and other students. The terminal degree programs are also the major source of the paraprofessional caste of two-year police education. Supported by federal vocational education funds requiring "training" courses, they are often housed in the same academic units as programs in cosmetology and auto mechanics. We believe that community colleges offering police education programs should place them in the academic mainstream of the colleges, defining them as the first two years of a four-year program:

> *4-7 Community colleges should phase out their terminal two-year degree programs in police education. Meanwhile, special efforts should be made to increase opportunities for community college students by ensuring articulation between two- and four-year programs.*

The colleges educating the police can almost guarantee that police education will be of low quality. Starving a program of resources, lowering academic standards, and encouraging termination at the two-year level make low quality almost certain. Yet even by avoiding these practices, the colleges cannot guarantee that police education will be of high quality. The most they can do is to help make high-quality learning experiences possible. The rest is up to the faculty and the students.

5

⊂━○━⊂━○━⊂━○━⊂━○━⊂━○━⊂━○━⊂━○━⊂

Faculty

*I do not believe we can any longer regard
experience as either a sufficient or as an
essential characteristic of a faculty member in
criminal justice or police education programs.
All of education rests on the notion that
accumulated human experience can be
absorbed vicariously through the process of
teaching and learning. If we cannot accept this
proposition, our participation in the
intellectual academic enterprise is spurious.*
                              Riddle, 1978, p. 28

No question in police education is more sensitive than who
should educate the police. For the proponents of a traditional
liberal arts curriculum for police education, the question of faculty background does not arise: the police should take courses
from the same faculty as anyone else going to college. But for
those who adopt any of the curricular models directly related to
police work, there is widespread disagreement over the kinds of
qualifications that are necessary and appropriate for teaching in
a police education program.

   The commission believes that many of the present faculty
in police education programs are poorly qualified for their important task and that immediate steps must be taken to improve
their quality. This chapter examines the historical origins of the
present faculty in police education programs, the intense debate

over police experience versus graduate education as qualifications for teaching, and the important consequences of different faculty backgrounds for teaching and research. It describes
the meager current efforts at faculty development and offers
some recommendations for upgrading the faculty of police education programs.

History

August Vollmer's ([1936] 1971) plan for the faculty
educating the police was to use established scholars in the traditional disciplines who could apply their expertise to the
problems of policing. His plan was adopted in most of the early
police education programs he helped to create. As police education began to spread at the two-year colleges, however, the faculty members were increasingly drawn from police departments.
These ex-practitioners lacked the scholarly training of the arts
and sciences faculty, but their experience was assumed to compensate for their lower level of education. This trend was rein-
forced by the passage of the George-Dean Act in 1936 (supple-
menting the Smith-Hughes Act of 1917), which provided
federal funds to support industrial and technical education in
the community colleges. Since expertise in most of the occupational fields covered by the act could be acquired only through
experience, police education was subjected to the same conception of using practitioners as faculty. In California, apparently
the first state to apply the George-Dean funds to police education programs, several years of police experience became a minimum requirement for all faculty in those programs (Myren,
1970).

Over the same period, and quite apart from the specialized programs in police education, scholarly research on crime
and criminal justice slowly developed in sociology, psychology,
law, and political science. Hardly any of the scholars in these
fields had served as police officers, but they provided the base
of knowledge on which the field of criminal justice was con-
structed in the late 1960s and early 1970s. Some of the scholars
and teachers trained in this tradition joined the faculties of

police education programs after 1968, in the period of their mushrooming growth. The demand for them soon outpaced the supply, however, and the colleges rushing to create police education programs were forced to turn to current and retired police officers to cover the burgeoning classes (Riddle, 1978). And where those classes consisted largely of in-service police officers, they may also have responded to the insular police distrust and suspicion of academics by hiring "real cops" as instructors.

In addition to the practitioners and the scholars from traditional fields, a third group of faculty members can now be found in police education programs: scholars trained in an interdisciplinary doctoral program in criminology or criminal justice. These doctoral programs were first created in the late 1950s and early 1960s (notably at the University of California at Berkeley, Florida State University, the University of Maryland, and the State University of New York at Albany), before the boom in criminal justice. The demand for undergraduate faculty in criminal justice programs fueled the expansion of the Ph.D. programs in the early 1970s. Although the program at Berkeley has since been closed (Phelps, 1977), there are now nine others in existence. Yet the rate at which they are graduating their Ph.D. students is very low. Even though most four-year programs in criminal justice now seem to prefer to hire Ph.D.s in criminal justice (although some programs require that even these Ph.D.s have police experience), it is unlikely that this group of faculty —with or without police experience—will constitute more than 3 to 4 percent of the faculty in police education programs in the near future.

The compromises with traditional faculty standards forced by the rapid growth of police education programs and fostered by police insularity are now often defended as the most appropriate standards for such a "nontraditional" field. Yet there is nothing "nontraditional" about the practice of educating people for specific careers. The history of faculty qualifications in other areas of undergraduate education for the "useful arts" shows a similar reliance on nonscholarly practitioners in the early stages of their development, quickly followed by a concerted effort to make scholarship more important than experience as a faculty qualification (Cheit, 1975). Whether police education will follow that pattern remains to be seen.

The Education or Experience Debate

The debate over faculty qualifications affects thousands of instructors hired for their experience rather than their education. The educational qualifications of the faculty educating the police are usually much lower than those of the faculty in other academic fields. As Table 11 shows, almost one quarter of all

Table 11. Percentage of Faculty Members with No Graduate Degrees in LEEP-Participating Criminal Justice Programs in 1975-76, and of All Faculty Nationally in 1972-73, by Type of Institution

| Type of Institution | Percent with No Graduate Degrees | | | |
	Full-Time Criminal Justice Faculty, 1975-76	Part-Time Criminal Justice Faculty, 1975-76	All Criminal Justice Faculty, 1975-76	All Faculty Nationally, 1972-73
All institutions	11.6%	31.7%	23.3%	7.4%
Public	14.3	37.1	27.4	NA
Private	3.1	16.6	11.2	NA
All 2-year colleges	31.6	43.7	40.3	12.3
Public	32.3	43.9	40.7	NA
Private	4.5	33.3	24.3	NA
All 4-year colleges	4.8	15.3	10.5	4.7
Public	5.9	12.2	8.2	NA
Private	3.8	16.2	24.3	NA
All universities	2.9	19.4	10.3	7.7
Public	3.1	22.4	10.7	NA
Private	2.6	15.6	10.0	NA

Source: National Planning Association, 1976, pp. V-155-158.

criminal justice faculty in the LEEP-supported programs have not completed any graduate level degrees, three times the percentage of college faculty generally. The difference is even greater at the two-year level, where the percent lacking graduate degrees is almost four times higher in criminal justice programs.

Comparable data for the percentages holding doctorates or other terminal graduate degrees are unavailable, but it is reasonable to suspect that the contrasts at that level would be even sharper.

There is also a clear tendency of the colleges hiring the faculty to trade off degrees for practical experience in their criteria for selection. As Table 12 shows, the less education crimi-

Table 12. Mean Years of Criminal Justice Agency Experience of
Faculty Teaching in LEEP-Supported Criminal Justice Programs,
by Faculty Degree Level and Type of Institution, 1972-73

| Faculty Degree Level | Type of Institution (N = 761) | | |
	University (N = 20)	Other 4-Year (N = 150)	2-Year (N = 410)
Certificate	17.0	31.0	11.9
Associate	7.0	18.0	13.0
Baccalaureate	14.1	12.1	10.1
Master's	8.0	7.0	10.6
Doctorate	5.6	5.8	11.5

Source: Foster, 1974, p. 110.

nal justice faculty members have, the more years experience in criminal justice agencies they are likely to have, at least in the programs supported by LEEP. The commission's survey of police education programs also found a significant inverse correlation between the average educational level and average number of years of agency experience among both full-time and part-time faculty (Sherman and McLeod, 1978).

Unlike the widespread use of part-time faculty, the extensive use of experienced faculty lacking graduate education does not violate the LEEP guidelines. In fact, federal policy clearly encourages the current state of affairs (U.S. Law Enforcement Assistance Administration, 1975, p. 5): "Qualifications for faculty of crime-related studies should include academic preparation in appropriate fields AND practical criminal justice experience. It is preferable [though not required] that faculty members possess at least a master's degree; some members should possess doctoral degrees" (italics in original). The national guidelines for LEEP are translated into even greater emphasis on experience in some states by the state planning agencies administering the LEEP funds. Harry Mansfield, director of the Tennessee Law Enforcement Planning Agency, for example, wrote the commission that "Any professors that are hired with grant funds must have at least one year of working experience in the criminal justice area." He posed the argument most often made in support of requiring faculty to have practical experience: "Since most of the students taking criminal justice courses are already employed in criminal justice agencies (in-service students), it is quite difficult for a professor to get up and instruct policemen on police-related subjects when they have never experienced what they may be talking about. Policemen find it hard to relate to someone who only has the book knowledge."

Robert Flowers, the head of the equivalent agency in Texas, emphasized the distinction between preservice and in-service students while making the same point to the commission: "Professors without prior experience can usually 'get by' with preservice students, but not with veteran officers who are in academic programs." President Wayne Shepherd of the Chiefs of Police Association of Utah justified an experience requirement for faculty members in terms of their impact on the subsequent performance of their students as police officers; judging from the performance of his largely college-educated police force at the University of Utah, he observed: "It is easy to tell those who have been trained by professors and staff with no police background. We found that they require a closer supervision and an attitude change back to reality."

This position is consistent with the modern conception of "career education" for "middle-manpower" occupations. The career education movement's objective of developing job skills dictates that "Teachers . . . must, first of all, be competent practitioners in their own fields" (Harris and Grede, 1977, p. 223) and that advanced degrees should not be required. There is even a certain contempt for scholarship implied by some of the arguments for practical experience, as if graduate education were a hindrance to teaching rather than an asset (see, for example, Kirkham, 1974). While that may be true for teaching technical skills, it is hardly true for teaching concepts, ideas, and methods of reasoning.

Not all state planning agencies take the position that experience is more important than education. For example, the head of Delaware's state planning agency, Christine Harker, wrote the commission that "Instructors' backgrounds for all but a few courses ought to be identical to those instructing in any course. . . . However, I feel that it is much more important to have an instructor *in any course* that has sufficient content knowledge, the ability to teach and communicate, and the ability to motivate. That he have a police background for a police course is not essential." Similarly, the head of Wisconsin's state planning agency, Charles M. Hill, Sr., wrote: "While a police background and personal experience are desirable, they are not necessary. . . . More important is an academic background in the complexities of the police function in a democratic society." Nonetheless, over half of the state planning agency executives responding to the commission's survey (eleven out of twenty-one) thought that at least some faculty members in every police education program should have had police experience.

Sworn police experience among police education faculty has come to serve as a badge of honor, an almost mystical symbol of membership in the police tribe (see Joseph and Alex, 1972). Anyone who has not been a police officer is a "civilian" and, in a certain sense, an enemy (Westley, 1970) of the police. Police experience serves to separate the insiders from the outsiders in police education (Hoffman, Snell, and Webb, 1976).

These distinctions are not necessarily invidious. The symbolic meanings of police professors' being insiders could lend support to the process of professionalizing the police, and help to foster police scholarship. Bittner (1970, p. 81) has developed this argument at some length: "It is clearly not for lawyers, sociologists, or psychologists to develop an intellectually credible version of what police work should be like. This must be left to scholarly policemen, just as the analogous task is left to scholarly physicians, social workers, or engineers. . . . For the main reason for having professional schools of police work is to make a home for police work-study. It must be their own home, or the enterprise will be dispirited and doomed to failure. The development of a fully reasoned meaning of the police role in society, that might give rise to a range of rationally methodical work procedures, must be worked out from within the occupation; it cannot be imparted to it by outsiders. Outsiders can help in this task, but they cannot take it over. The main reason for this is not that outsiders are not adequately informed but that supplying knowledge from external sources would leave police work intellectually inert."

The existence of a scholarly role within the police career structures might well serve to raise the intellectual sophistication of police work. Unfortunately, the present practice of hiring retired or active police officers to teach heavy undergraduate course loads allows little time for scholarly endeavor (although low teaching loads, of course, would not necessarily result in more scholarship). Nor do the colleges offering police education programs seem to mind the absence of scholarly research. As a field study of fourteen of the better criminal justice programs found, research usually has a very low priority in police education (Pearson and others, 1978, p. 7): "Virtually all of the institutions indicated that they were looking for teachers over researchers, even though most made the ritual statement that it would be nice if individuals did in fact do research. . . . One prominent institution made the interesting observation that they did not want to hire 'stars.' " Undergraduate police education programs generally fail to provide either the resources or the incentives for their faculty members to undertake research (Saunders, 1970; Goldstein, 1977). As a 1970 survey of 197 police education programs found, 95 percent of the two-year and 57 percent of the four-year programs do not consider research to be a "basic factor in faculty promotion or determination of annual salary increments" (Eastman, 1972, p. 81). Despite the apparent trend away from a "publish or perish" to a "teach or perish" incentive system in higher education generally (Fiske, 1977), the police institution cannot afford the almost complete lack of scholarship in undergraduate police education.

The graduate programs in criminal justice are a more likely place to find faculty scholarship. They are also the closest
existing approximations of Bittner's conception of graduate
schools of police work. A number of ex-police officers are on
the faculties of the 9 Ph.D. and the 121 master's programs. But,
with very few exceptions, they have failed to advance the scholarship of police work. The recent explosion of research on policing has occurred largely in the traditional arts and science disciplines. As Donald Riddle (1978), President Emeritus of the
John Jay College of Criminal Justice, has observed, almost none
of the books about the police worth reading have been written
by professors of police science. Most of those who do write
books prefer to write textbooks based on their personal experience in police work rather than undertaking systematic research
designed to generate new knowledge.

The heavy reliance of faculty members with police experience on their knowledge gained from practice (rather than
from research) carries over into their teaching. William P. Brown
(1965, p. 9) described this pattern over a decade ago as "using
the colleges to transmit the rather meager supply of information
which has been gathered by the police over the years." Judging
by their persistence in using the same prescriptive textbooks in
1977 that were used in 1968 (see recommendation 3-7), the
pattern has changed little. The reliance on conventional wisdom
in teaching content serves to reduce the chances that education
will serve as a force for change in policing. As commission member Lee P. Brown (1974, p. 120) has argued, when they are
"taught by the retired or ex-law enforcement official, too many
of the existing criminal justice programs are a perpetuation of
what has already been recognized as a failing system." The
American Bar Association (1973, p. 218) describes such efforts
as serving "only to reinforce the most parochial concepts prevalent in the police field."

The lack of scholarship in both research and teaching
associated with the police-experienced faculty members should
not be blamed on those professors as individuals. Many work
quite hard at preparing for their classes and may take a deeper
interest in their teaching than the more scholarly faculty. But
the structure of their career experience and the lack of scholarly

training at the graduate level almost guarantee that the content of their teaching will be prescriptive rather than conceptual in nature. "Second-career faculty members," according to a criminal justice educator who has evaluated many police education programs, "tend to be second class" (Newman, 1978). "I know of no high-quality criminal justice program—or for that matter, no high-quality law, social work, or other professional school—built and staffed by second-career faculty. There are *individual* exceptions—practitioners who make the transition from agency to university criteria of excellence—but collectively, *en masse*, this is almost always academically fatal."

The most common criticism of the police-experienced faculty members is that their teaching relies heavily on "war stories": anecdotal accounts of the more exciting incidents of their police careers. Not all experienced faculty teach this way, of course, nor is the practice confined to experienced faculty. No matter who uses it, this teaching technique in police education, from all accounts, is largely devoid of conceptual content. Yet it could be a valuable method of exploring the complexities of the police role in a democratic society. If the war stories were systematically organized around major conceptual and policy issues, they would be quite similar to the case studies used at the Graduate School of Business and the John F. Kennedy School of Government's public policy program at Harvard University. Rather than planning how to save a company from bankruptcy or an urban renewal project from failure, case studies in police education could be used, for example, to systematically explore methods of coping with family fights under different family circumstances. The knowledge gained by police experience is of great potential value to a police educator. The problem is that extensive police experience seems to inhibit more conceptual thinking, fostering an epistemology that is far more concerned with the particular details of each incident than with the general problems they may illuminate.

Quality of Part-Time Teaching

The education or experience debate is closely tied to the heavy use of part-time faculty in police education programs. As

Table 11 shows, part-time faculty are much less likely to have
earned a postgraduate degree, no matter what type of college
they teach in. And as Table 13 shows, part-time faculty some-

Table 13. Mean Years of Criminal Justice Agency Experience
of Part-Time and Full-Time Faculty Teaching in Police Education
Programs, by Type of Institution

		Mean Years of Experience	
Type of Institution	Number of Institutions	Full-Time Faculty	Part-Time Faculty
All institutions	281	10.61	10.88
Public	241	11.33	10.96
Private	40	5.73	10.41
All 2-year colleges	147	13.74	11.93
Public	142	13.67	11.91
Private	5	16.39	12.52
All 4-year colleges and universities	134	6.94	9.34
Public	99	7.76	9.10
Private	35	4.45	9.97

Source: Commission Survey of Police Education Programs (Sherman and
McLeod, 1978).

times have more experience working in criminal justice agencies
than full-time faculty members (although this pattern varies by
type of institution). The heavy use of part-time faculty therefore raises important questions about the quality of their teaching, quite apart from the issues of institutional commitment discussed in the previous chapter.

Those who favor practical experience as a qualification
for the faculty educating the police generally argue that the
quality of part-time teaching is quite high. Part-time faculty
members not only have more experience; they also have closer
contact with the problems they teach about. Far from being
sheltered in an "ivory tower," many part-time faculty are also
full-time employees of criminal justice agencies. Some hold key
positions in their local criminal justice system—as district attorneys, chief juvenile court judges, and chiefs of police. Their
positions are said to make their teaching a unique contribution
to a police education program, one that cannot be matched by

full-time faculty members. If quality teaching depends on an intimate knowledge of the day-to-day operations of policing and criminal justice, then the more part-time faculty who are full-time practitioners the better.

For those who value scholarly breadth and depth in the faculty educating the police, however, the quality of part-time teaching is necessarily inadequate. Whatever their educational backgrounds may be, part-time faculty members, and particularly those who hold another full-time job, have less time to keep up with the current scholarly literature in their fields. They are also less likely to engage in research and publication, at least according to a national study of part-time faculty in all fields (Tuckman and Vogler; cited in Magarrell, 1978). For all the lack of scholarship among the full-time faculty, the part-time faculty in police education may be even less scholarly.

Regardless of the relative merits of scholarship and experience, part-time faculty members of whatever background simply have less time to devote to a police education program. Like part-time faculty generally, they offer few of the non-teaching services, such as advising students and serving on faculty committees, that directly affect the overall quality of police education. Over half of all part-time faculty do not even have an office on campus where students can meet with them (Magarrell, 1978). It is not surprising, then, that, in a field study of twenty-six police education programs, the program heads rated full-time faculty members higher than part-time faculty members—not only in teaching ability but also in counseling ability, knowledge of the program, and even in efforts at job placement—notwithstanding the presumably greater ability of part-time faculty to hire students in their agencies (National Planning Association, 1976). Part-time faculty members may cost less, but a police education program clearly gets less from them in return.

Other fields of professional education have incorporated part-time faculty as clinical instructors who supplement the core academic faculty. The clinical instructors are explicitly recognized for their expertise as practitioners, with little expectation that they be scholarly. Instead, they keep the curriculum up to date with current developments in their field of practice. A similar arrangement in police education might make the best use of a select group of part-time faculty.

Faculty and Curriculum

Many of the arguments about the faculty educating the police are based on impressionistic or speculative evidence. In order to examine the arguments empirically, the commission requested information about faculty backgrounds in its survey of books used in police education programs. The study was designed to test several hypotheses about the impact of faculty characteristics on the content of the curriculum.

Using the scale of conceptual abstraction described in Chapter 3 (see Table 6 and the accompanying discussion), the hypotheses predicted that, on the average, the more education and the less criminal justice experience a program's faculty had, the higher the conceptual level of the books used in the program's courses would be. As Table 14 shows, both of these hypotheses were correct. At the higher levels of conceptual abstraction, the average educational levels of the faculty were higher and the average numbers of years of criminal justice experience were lower. A third hypothesis received somewhat less support: The more full-time faculty members there are relative to the number of part-time faculty members, the higher the conceptual level of the books used. The findings failed to show any connection between the average length of teaching experience of the faculty and the books they used.

The study also found that the selectivity of the college, the level of the program (two year or four year), and the proportion of the students in the program who are (according to the program's director) oriented to police careers (preservice plus in-service) are all highly correlated with the conceptual level of the books used. Some of these characteristics are more strongly correlated with the book level than are the educational level and criminal justice experience of the faculty. But even when all the other factors are held constant, there is still a generally strong correlation between faculty characteristics and the

Table 14. Mean Abstraction Level of Books Assigned in Police-Related Courses in College Programs for Police Officers, by Faculty Characteristics

| | Mean Abstraction Level | | | | | |
Mean Faculty Characteristics	Task-Prescriptive Text	Policy-Prescriptive Text	Descriptive Text	Descriptive Research Report	Explanatory Text	Explanatory Research Report
Educational level[a]						
Full-time faculty	4.23	5.41	6.44	7.07	7.03	6.50
Part-time faculty	4.65	5.11	6.24	6.14	6.79	6.33
Years of agency experience						
Full-time faculty	18.01	12.22	8.04	5.97	4.67	1.00
Part-time faculty	16.27	11.43	10.14	7.09	8.56	8.33
Percent of programs in which part-time faculty outnumber full-time faculty	77.8	65.1	65.0	23.1	50.0	100.0

[a]Number of years post-high school: B.A. = 4, M.A. = 5, professional degree (J.D., M.D., and so on) = 7, research doctorate (Ph.D., Ed.D., D.Crim., and so on) = 8.

Source: Commission Survey of Police Education Programs (Sherman and McLeod, 1978).

conceptual level of the books used—and hence the type of curriculum offered—in police education courses (Sherman and
McLeod, 1978). The debate over education and experience,
then, is not an empty one. To a large extent, the content and
quality of the curriculum depend on who the faculty members
are: "Once the faculty is in place, the catalog has largely been
written" (Carnegie Foundation, 1977, pp. 8-9).

Upgrading the Faculty

Commission member Charles B. Saunders, Jr. (1970), predicted a decade ago that the federal law enforcement program
would diminish the general quality of teaching in police education by expanding the number of students at a much faster rate
than the number of qualified faculty. It has and it did. Despite a
few attempts to increase the supply of scholarly faculty for
police education programs, the U.S. Law Enforcement Assistance Administration has been unable to keep up with the rapid
growth of criminal justice education. The National Planning
Association (1976, p. V-181) has described the situation as "a
classic example of the consequences of a government program
structured to have a major impact on the demand for a particular service without adequate consideration being given to the
ability of the system to deliver the required supply." Part of the
blame for this situation rests with the Congress, which paid
scant attention to faculty development needs in preparing the
Omnibus Crime Control and Safe Streets Act of 1968. But
much of the blame also rests with LEAA.

Under Section 406(e) of the 1968 Safe Streets Act, Congress provided LEAA with several million dollars for discretionary support of several aspects of law enforcement education,
including faculty development. These funds were probably insufficient to cope with the problems created by the rapid
growth. Yet providing more money may have made little difference, given the way LEAA spent it. Most of these funds were
spent on a generally unsuccessful attempt to create Ph.D. programs in criminal justice at seven universities that were selected
on political rather than academic grounds (Twentieth Century

Fund, 1976). Some funds were also provided for Ph.D. dissertation fellowships, but for several years doctoral students at the seven specially selected universities were the only students eligible for the fellowships. No funds were made available for the much more expedient solution of "retooling" Ph.D.s from traditional academic disciplines into criminal justice faculty through postdoctoral fellowships or summer institutes. Many Ph.D.s in history, for example, could have applied their historical knowledge to the history of criminal justice, becoming sufficiently acquainted with it for teaching purposes during an eight- to ten-week summer institute, and could have gone on to make valuable contributions to police education as they learned even more about policing. They would certainly have been more readily adaptable to teaching in police education programs than the practitioners who lacked graduate education.

In recent years an organizational restructuring of LEAA has permitted a more coordinated approach to federal support of criminal justice education and training. Since 1976 both LEEP and the 406(e) funds have been administered by the Office of Criminal Justice Education and Training—OCJET (*Manpower Planning . . .*, 1976). OCJET has abandoned the largely abortive attempt to produce more Ph.D.s and concentrated on faster ways of developing a more scholarly faculty. For example, OCJET is now planning a one to two month summer faculty development program for criminal justice faculty. Judging by the results of a similar program sponsored by the National Institute of Corrections in 1973 (O'Leary, 1976), the project could result in a substantial increase in the conceptual level of the curriculum adopted by the faculty participating in the project.

In addition to the 406(e) funds, Law Enforcement Education Program funds have also been used to support faculty development in police education. Teachers in programs supported by LEEP funds have been fairly high on the list of priorities of students eligible to receive LEEP funds (U.S. Law Enforcement Assistance Administration, 1975). Of the students receiving LEEP support in 1972-73 at the University of Southern California (of whom 96 percent were graduate students), 30 percent were full- or part-time faculty members in other colleges, 9 percent at four-year colleges and 21 percent at two-year colleges (Carter and Nelson, 1973, p. 493). Yet much more federal support for various faculty development programs is required if the investment in LEEP is to become worthwhile.

However meager the current federal effort may be, it is almost the only source of initiative in faculty development. The Academy of Criminal Justice Sciences has organized a number of faculty development workshops around the country, but the relatively large registration fees may have limited faculty access to these workshops. Few colleges are willing to pay high costs for intensive development of their police education faculty—or, for that matter, any of their faculty (Eble, 1972). A 1970 survey of 193 police education programs found that 25 percent of the two-year and 36 percent of the four-year programs had no institutional provision for sabbatical leave; 32 percent of the four-year programs had no provision for travel and expense funds to attend professional conferences (Eastman, 1972, pp. 125-126). Both deans and, where they exist, program chairmen have failed to exercise the leadership they could and should be exercising, cost considerations notwithstanding. Faculty development could be accomplished on any campus at no cost if, for example, good teachers in all fields were used, at teaching clinics or centers for the improvement of instruction, to assist the new police faculty in learning the art of pedagogy (Bennis, 1978). Teaching techniques must build on substantive knowledge, however, and there can be no better faculty development program in police education than fellowships for faculty to continue their own learning.

Rather than developing their police education faculty, some institutions have moved instead toward supervising and controlling them. The New York Institute of Technology, for example, which uses many part-time faculty for the extensive off-campus instruction in its College Accelerated Program for Police, guards against poor teaching by "continuous supervision" and "observation of instruction" (Salten, 1977). Other colleges require their instructors to submit detailed outlines of each class session at the beginning of each term. Some colleges even dictate the textbooks to be used in each course.

It is hard to see how supervision and tight control can

improve the teaching quality of a faculty member who lacks the proper scholarly background for the subjects he or she is teaching. At best, this approach to upgrading the faculty may curb the excessive use of war stories and ensure that the lectures follow the text. At worst, it may turn professors into bureaucrats following orders instead of scholars devoted to seeking and conveying knowledge.

Recommendations

The present faculty in police education programs are well qualified for teaching a paraprofessional training curriculum. They may well accomplish the objective of making police officers more efficient at their present tasks. But they are woefully underqualified for teaching either a liberal arts or a professional curriculum of police-related studies. Given their often uncritical acceptance of current police practices, they are most unlikely to accomplish the objective of educating the police institution for change.

From the standpoint of the commission's goals for police education, the most glaring defect of the present faculty is their lack of scholarly training at the graduate level. Without a full understanding of the meaning of scholarship and the resources of higher learning, the present faculty are not able to connect theoretical knowledge to practical problems. Graduate degrees represent more than mere credentials. The commission's research strongly suggests that the level of education of the faculty is directly related to the conceptual level of the curriculum. The police institution has much greater need of infusions of new conceptual knowledge than recirculation of its conventional methods and assumptions. The best way to ensure that police education faculty will contribute new perspectives to policing is to require that they be well educated themselves:

> 5-1 *Faculty members in police education programs at any level should be required to have completed at least two full years of postgraduate education.*

Even the two-year minimum is lower than it has to be. Ample numbers of Ph.D.s in fields other than criminal justice have had difficulty obtaining academic employment since the early 1970s. Many of them, particularly in history and English, are fine scholars who would be an asset to any police education program. But despite the claims of criminal justice educators that their field is multidisciplinary, very few fields other than sociology, psychology, public administration, and law are represented on criminal justice faculties at any level. The general failure of federal agencies to sponsor "retooling" programs to prepare scholars trained in other disciplines for teaching criminal justice reflects the apparent lack of true multidisciplinary interest in police education programs. The substitution of Ph.D.s in the social sciences and humanities for many or most of the present faculty might greatly increase the conceptual level of the curriculum and make a more valuable contribution to policing:

> 5-2 *Police education programs should actively seek out Ph.D.s in arts and science disciplines to serve as faculty members. The Law Enforcement Assistance Administration (or any successor organization) should fund programs for "retooling" these Ph.D.s into criminal justice scholars and teachers.*

The major obstacle to the implementation of this recommendation is the widespread assumption that police educators must be (or have been) police officers in order to be effective teachers. We reject that assumption. Although there is great merit in Bittner's (1970) conception of the scholarly police professional, that conception will not be realized until scholarship becomes more highly valued in police education programs. As long as the antiintellectual biases of the present ex-police faculty dominate police education, the valuation of research and scholarship will remain at its currently low level. The scholarly role in a police profession can grow only in an atmosphere created by scholars from the traditional disciplines. While those with police experience should not be excluded on these grounds, the primary concern should be their academic preparation for teaching:

> 5-3 *Educational background, teaching ability, research, and commitment—rather than prior employment in a criminal justice agency— should be the most important criteria of faculty selection in police education programs. Prior criminal justice employment should be neither a requirement nor a handicap for faculty selection.*

The commission does not consider field experience in police work to be irrelevant to educating the police. But that experience can be gained in other ways besides service as a sworn police officer. Internships or research in police departments can serve the same purposes equally well. To the extent that experiences other than employment avoid the development of a police occupational world view (Skolnick, 1966; Muir, 1977), they may even be preferable to police employment. The proposition that one must personally experience a role in order to understand it (Kirkham, 1974) denies the principle of vicarious learning, on which all higher education is based (Riddle, 1978).

If the first three recommendations are followed, police education programs will be forced to reduce their use of part-time faculty hired on the basis of practical experience rather than academic qualifications. Yet some of these faculty members may make unique contributions to the program. Where part-time faculty members can offer high-quality instruction in the more practical aspects of police work, they should be recognized for that contribution with a distinctive role. Where neither their experience nor their teaching ability is particularly unusual, there should be no departure from the standards recommended above:

> 5-4 *Part-time faculty appointments in police education programs should be limited to people with unique practical expertise. Such appoint-*

*ments should be distinguished by the title of
clinical professor.*

Given the present faculty of nonscholarly ex-practitioners, the prospects for fusing teaching with research in police education are not sanguine. Nonetheless, every effort should be made to develop the research potential of the present police education faculty. As James Osterburg wrote to the commission: "We will not be getting criminal justice material written that is suitable for a liberal arts curriculum until and unless we provide the criminal justice equivalent of a Guggenheim." The same could be said for developing a professional curriculum comparable to professional education in engineering or architecture. Although it is unrealistic to expect most of the faculty in two- or four-year programs to continually undertake major research efforts, research fellowships for all police education faculty might help them grow as scholars and improve their teaching:

> 5-5 *Both the Law Enforcement Assistance Administration (or any successor organization) and private foundations should consider developing a program of one- or two-year fellowships for full-time faculty in police education programs to pursue their graduate education or to engage in research or the development of new courses.*

Colleges offering police education programs should not wait for outside funding of faculty development. Every college has excellent teachers who can be called on to assist new instructors in learning how to teach. No matter what field they come from, these teachers can be of great assistance to the police education faculty that now rely on anecdotal teaching. Through instructional clinics or other arrangements, the "war stories" might be refined into a case method for teaching (or discovering) general principles of police work:

> 5-6 *Expanded opportunities should be provided on the campus for the continuing improve-*

*ment and development of the teaching skills of
faculty members in police education programs.*

In the long run, the quality of teaching in police education and criminal justice programs may depend on the quality of the people who are attracted to the field. To attract more first-rate people, criminal justice will have to achieve greater academic respectability than it has at present. Business education was assisted in achieving greater academic respectability in the 1950s by the creation of endowed chairs of business administration at leading universities by private foundations, and the same approach may well assist criminal justice. The recent creation of the Daniel and Florence Guggenheim chair in criminal justice policy and management at the John F. Kennedy School of Government at Harvard could have an important impact on the development of the field. Equally important, perhaps, would be the endowment of chairs at institutions educating large numbers of present and potential police officers, so that teaching as well as research can be enhanced by the chairs. The effect of such endowments would be not only the attraction of senior scholars from other fields into police education but also the creation of a long-term incentive for scholars considering a career in police-related research and teaching:

> 5-7 *Private foundations should consider the possible creation of named chairs in criminal justice or police administration at colleges or universities with a long-term commitment to police education.*

6

Student Experiences

For professional higher education to have its fullest impact on the criminal justice system, the educational experience must be a sustained and uninterrupted one in which habits of thought, ethical standards, and patterns of behavior become well established in the individual prior to the commencement of a career in which all of these become highly subject to revision and compromise.
Tenney, 1971, p. 28

The sum total of the quality of higher education is reflected in the nature of student educational experiences. The content of the curriculum, the resources provided by the colleges, and the performance of the faculty are important elements of educational quality only because of their impact on students. Yet the students' learning experiences do not depend on these influences alone. The full impact of higher education on students as whole persons also depends on how education fits into the totality of their lives. The timing of their education in relation to their careers and life cycles, their motivation for pursuing their education, and their degree of immersion in student life on campus may be as important for the quality of the educational experience as what goes on in the classroom.

    The prevailing quality of the educational experience among police students—although increasingly typical of the

139

experience of college students generally—is not as good as it could be. Many, if not most, educated police have attended college as part-time commuter students while working full time as police officers. A substantial body of educational research suggests that that kind of educational experience results in much less cognitive learning and personal growth than full-time residential education prior to beginning a career. A decade ago widespread in-service education of police students was required by the short-term goal of raising the educational level of police personnel very quickly, but that goal has largely been accomplished. The time has come for both federal policy and police department practice to replace the short-term goal of educating the recruited with the long-term goal of recruiting the educated. It is only then that higher education may begin to be an agent for change.

This chapter describes both the in-service and the pre-service college students who are studying for police careers. It examines their motivations, their educational experiences, and the likely consequences of those experiences. Finally, it offers some recommendations about how to improve their educational experiences.

A Statistical Profile

According to a 1974 U.S. Census Bureau survey of sworn law enforcement officers, 46 percent of the police in this country have completed at least one year of college, and 9 percent have completed four years of college (see Table 3). Almost half of these college-educated officers began their college education after entering police work, and many others have continued the education they began before joining a police department. As Table 15 shows, only 28 percent of the police officers surveyed in 1974 had completed at least one year of college before entering police work, and only 5 percent had completed four years of "preservice" education. "In-service" education accounted for a 64 percent increase over educational levels at entry in the number of educated officers, producing 40 percent of all officers with any college education in 1974. In-service education

Table 15. Educational Attainment of Incumbent Sworn Law Enforcement
Personnel in 1974 and at Their Time of Entry

Educational Level	Education at Entry		1974 Educational Level		Increase (+) or Decrease (−)	Percent- age Change
	Number	Percent	Number	Percent		
All incumbents	492,819[a]	100.0%	491,009[a]	100.0%	—	—
Less than 8 years	15,572	3.2	13,602	2.8	− 1,970	−12.7%
9-11 years	49,928	10.1	38,164	7.8	−11,764	−23.6
12 years-	288,208	58.5	211,297	43.0	−76,911	−26.7
13-15 years	113,859	23.1	184,807	37.6	+70,948	+62.3
16 or more years	25,252	5.1	43,139	8.8	+17,887	+70.8
Subtotal: some college	139,111	28.2	227,946	46.4	+88,835	+63.5

[a]The difference between these two numbers reflects the difference in the response rate to the two questions.

Source: National Planning Association, 1976, p. II-150.

probably accounts for well over half of the total credit hours earned by police. Given the continuing LEEP support for about 65,000 police officers each year since 1974 (according to LEAA figures), it is quite likely that more than half of the police officers who are college graduates received at least some of their education as part-time, in-service commuter students.

Yet preservice education also seems to be increasing. The same census survey (Table 16) showed that almost two out of

Table 16. Percentage Distribution of Educational Attainment
at Time of Entry of Law Enforcement Personnel Serving in 1974,
by Year of Entry

Educational Level at Entry	Year of Entry		
	1960-1964	1965-1969	1970-1974
All entrants	100.0%	100.0%	100.0%
8 years or less	3.5	2.9	2.5
9 to 11 years	10.7	8.1	6.6
12 years	62.9	67.0	52.4
13 to 15 years	20.2	19.9	29.8
16 or more years	2.7	2.1	8.7
Subtotal: some college	22.9	22.0	38.5

Source: National Planning Association, 1976, p. II-148.

every five officers hired since 1970 (and still serving in 1974) had completed at least one year of college before entering police work, compared to only one in five of those hired in 1960-1964. The percentage of police recruits holding a college degree may have increased by over four times from 1965-1969 to 1970-1974, from 2 percent to 9 percent. These figures probably exaggerate the real trend in preservice education, however, since college-educated officers are much more likely to quit police work after five or six years of service (Levy, 1967; Cohen and Chaiken, 1972). Those who joined in the 1960s and quit before 1974 were omitted from the survey, so the true level of preservice educational attainment of all police recruits in the 1960s may be greatly underestimated. Whatever the rate of increase, though, the level of preservice education of those hired even in recent years is still quite low.

In order to compensate for the low level of preservice education of the people traditionally hired by police departments, the U.S. Law Enforcement Assistance Administration (1975) has consistently given higher priority to LEEP funding for in-service students. According to figures supplied by LEAA's Office of Criminal Justice Education and Training, about 80 percent of the students whom LEEP supported in its first five years were in-service students; after an administrative policy change in 1973, the in-service students increased to about 90 percent of the total. The proportion of in-service students who were police officers in any given year has varied from just over 80 percent to the 1978 level of about 75 percent, or about 65,000 in-service police officers now supported by LEEP. About one fourth of all police officers surveyed by the Census Bureau in 1974 had received LEEP support, with minority officers slightly more likely and female officers much less likely to have received support (National Planning Association, 1976, p. V-176). Although LEEP gives higher priority to full-time students than to those enrolled part time, most police officers receiving LEEP funds attend college part time. As of 1978 an estimated 72 percent of all LEEP recipients had been enrolled as part-time students, so it is reasonable to assume that most police students had been enrolled part time as well.

The LEEP data offer the only available statistical profile of students studying for criminal justice careers. Although this profile is not representative of the preservice students, it probably does reflect the characteristics of the in-service students, since these students are far more likely to participate in LEEP. The LEEP students are overwhelmingly male (90 percent), white (84 percent), and married (72 percent). Over half of them are veterans (54 percent), making many of them eligible for educational benefits from both LEAA and the Veterans Administration. LEEP students are very much a part of the "new majority" of college students, who are older than the traditional college-going age. Ninety-six percent are 25 years old or older, and over one quarter (26 percent) are 40 years old or older. Almost half (46 percent) list their degree objective as less than a B.A., but over a thousand of them are aiming for a doctorate.

No one knows what the relative proportions of preservice and in-service students are in police education, partly because preservice students are hard to define. Many "preservice" students, including almost half of the lucky few who have received LEEP support (U.S. Comptroller General, 1975), fail to enter police or criminal justice agencies (many of whom, however, did not even seek police employment). Their preservice status merely reflects a statement of interest in a criminal justice career, and students' vocational interests have certainly been known to change. The perceptions of those interests by the heads of the police education programs responding to the commission's survey are reported in Table 17, but the basis of their distinction between students hoping to enter police work and all others is far from clear. The reported numbers of in-service police officers enrolled in the programs are probably more reliable. These data, of course, are only a sample of the students enrolled in the three "directly related" police educational curricula. They omit both in-service and preservice students enrolled in a general liberal arts or another professional education curriculum. But they do suggest that the charges of excessive homogeneity of the students in police education programs (American Bar Association, 1973; Twentieth Century Fund, 1976) are well founded. Over one quarter of the programs responding to the survey reported

Table 17. Percent Distribution of In-Service and Preservice Students[a] in Police-Related Education Programs in 1977

Type of Student	Percent in Program										Total
	0-10%	11-20%	21-30%	31-40%	41-50%	51-60%	61-70%	71-80%	81-90%	91-100%	
In-service students											
Number of programs	48	63	36	26	34	8	5	9	3	1	233[b]
Percent of programs	20.6	27.0	15.5	11.2	14.6	3.4	2.1	3.9	1.3	0.4	100.0
Preservice students											
Number of programs	23	30	45	30	42	30	16	10	3	0	229[b]
Percent of programs	10.0	13.1	19.7	13.1	18.3	13.1	7.0	4.4	1.3	0.0	100.0
All other students											
Number of programs	29	45	43	34	26	13	15	12	10	6	233[b]
Percent of programs	12.4	19.3	18.5	14.6	11.2	5.6	6.4	5.2	4.3	2.6	100.1
Total in-service and preservice students											
Number of programs	7	8	13	15	17	25	30	45	44	25	229[b]
Percent of programs	3.1	3.5	5.7	6.6	7.4	10.9	13.1	19.7	19.2	10.9	100.1

[a]Counting students as individuals, not as full-time-equivalent enrollments.
[b]The difference in these numbers is due to differences in the rates of response to the survey questions.
Source: Commission survey.

that more than 40 percent of their students were in-service police officers, and almost three quarters of the programs said that
more than half of their students were either in-service police
officers or hoping to become police officers.

As of this writing, there appears to be a sharp decline in
the percentage of students who are in-service officers. A number
of sources have reported to the commission that in-service enrollments have greatly decreased since the expiration of the GI
benefits for veterans who served during the war in Vietnam.
There are also reports that the market for in-service education
has dried up: those officers who wanted a college education
have obtained it, and the other officers have no interest in going
to college. At the same time, total enrollments in many police
education programs are reportedly quite stable. Preservice or
other students seem to be replacing the in-service students
(Pearson and others, 1978). The lack of any hard data on
these trends, however, makes any analysis of them highly
speculative.

Whatever the current trends in in-service enrollments may
be, it is clear that many programs are organized to meet the
needs of the in-service students. Consequently, both preservice
and in-service students attend many classes in the evening, even
at liberal arts colleges traditionally oriented to daytime residential education (Fry and Miller, 1976). A 1970 survey of one
hundred programs found that 92 percent of them had evening
classes and that 13 percent of them were offered *only* in the
evening (Tenney, 1971, p. 52). Seventy-five percent of the programs reported that they repeated day courses in the evening, a
procedure designed to accommodate the frequent changes in
work schedules of in-service students. While this situation may
have changed since 1970, much impressionistic evidence suggests that it has not. Notwithstanding a decline in the numbers
of in-service students, police education students in general may
continue to be offered an educational experience that is based
on the assumption that all of them are in-service students. The
results of that assumption have important consequences for the
quality of police education.

In-Service Education

The commission believes that, however necessary it may be, in-service education has not been as valuable for the police institution as preservice education. In-service educational opportunities, to be sure, have been used to great advantage by a few highly motivated officers. For most officers, however, part-time in-service education has probably been much less worthwhile than a traditional full-time educational experience would have been. The reasons for the lesser value of an in-service education include both the students' motivation to learn and the nature of the commuter students' experience. The few examples of full-time residential education of in-service students on leave from their police departments suggest that such experiences are far more valuable.

Motivation to Learn. What students get out of a college education depends on what they put into it, as professors are fond of pointing out. The effort that students put into their college education may depend on their motivation for enrolling in college. No matter how good the faculty or how strong the curriculum, a student's motivation may make the difference between learning and merely "serving time" in the classroom.

Why do police officers working at full-time jobs and laden with family responsibilities decide to go to college? What is their motivation for undertaking such an arduous schedule? Ideally, one might hope that their motivation would be learning for its own sake, or learning to help them understand and perform their jobs better. But the true motivations appear to be quite different. While there are no representative surveys of the motivations of in-service students, the commission has found some scattered evidence that consistently suggests three kinds of motivation: promotion, second careers, and money. These objectives may be little different from those of other working adult students, but that makes them no less consequential for the quality of the educational experience.

Virtually all the in-service students (as well as the preservice students) testifying at the commission's regional public forums said that they were going to college in order to improve their chances of rising to a supervisory rank. Not one of them mentioned improving their performance as a police officer or learning for its own sake. All of them implied that managing or supervising police work is more important and more difficult than doing police work. The tasks of a patrol officer, they suggested, are so simple that one does not need a college education to perform those tasks well. Many expressed frustration at having earned a college degree and then not having been promoted. A 1973 survey of LEEP-supported students at the University of Southern California adds extra evidence on the extent of this outlook in in-service police education: of 176 in-service students, 57 percent indicated a desire to become a chief police administrator, and 24 percent said they aspired to the rank of captain (Carter and Nelson, 1973, p. 492).

Going to college at night in order to "get ahead" has a long and fine tradition in the American history of upward mobility. What is good for the advancement of individuals, however, may not be good for the advancement of occupations. Pursuing education as a means of getting out of the work of the line police officer has the effect of denigrating the importance of police work itself. While police supervision may have both greater prestige (Treiman, 1977) and greater monetary rewards than line police work, and while the quality of police supervision clearly affects the quality of line police work, no one is more important in police work than the patrol officer, just as no one in education is more important than the teacher and no one in medicine is more important than the doctor. By defining management positions as more important, in-service students only make police departments more bureaucratic and less professional, more like factories than like hospitals (see Guyot, 1977).

A second motivation of in-service students has more serious implications for the status of police work. A number of officers testifying before the commission said that their ultimate goal in pursuing a college education was to leave police work, advancing themselves by getting a "better" job. One officer said he wanted to become a secondary school principal; others said they merely wanted to have something to fall back on after they retired in their early or middle 40s, as the provisions of many police pension plans allow them to do. A 1971 survey of over 238 graduates of police education programs suggests that many in-service students do leave police work after completing their college education. Of the 108 respondents who had been employed in law enforcement at the time of their graduation from college (1962-1970), 40 of them (37 percent) had left law enforcement work by the time of the survey (Tenney, 1971, p. 61).

Whatever their impact on policing, in-service students who are motivated by a desire for personal advancement seem more likely to take their education seriously than those in-service students who attend college for immediate financial motives. Two sources of financial incentives have encouraged many officers to go to college: federal veterans' benefits and police department salary differentials.

Under the GI Bill, many police officers who served during the Vietnamese War have received several hundred dollars a month in cash benefits for being enrolled in college. One study estimated that over 100 million dollars a year in veterans' benefits supported police education in the early 1970s (National Planning Association, 1976, p. V-34), compared to the only 40 million dollars a year spent by the Law Enforcement Education Program. Indeed, many officers have "double-dipped" into federal benefits, receiving support from both LEEP and the Veterans Administration. The motivation of these students for going to college may not be purely financial, but many observers believe it is. One police officer, for example, surveyed his college-going colleagues in several northern New Jersey police departments and concluded, "One of the strongest motivations in the departments I surveyed is the money aspect. Officers go [to college] because of ... veterans' benefits, and to most of them it is a part-time job" (Hall, 1977).

Students whose financial motives come from an increase in salary awarded for attaining various levels of college education must at least wait until they pass the courses to realize the financial gain of their education. Yet they may still be more interested in credentials than in learning. The definition of each course credit as equally valuable in terms of salary increments may encourage a crassly utilitarian view of the purpose of higher education.

Another motivation for in-service college students has recently been reported, one that may be true of adult education in general. In his interviews at John Jay College in New York, David Anderson (1978) found that many officers go to college for relaxation and therapy, as an escape from jobs that they hate. They find the classroom far more rewarding than police work, and the classes help to distract them from the frustration of their jobs. These students can be said to pursue learning for its own sake. But none of them are enrolled in courses or majors directly related to policing. Courses in drama or psychology—anything *but* police courses—draw them to college. The motivations for those enrolled in police education programs, then, may be quite different from the motivations of in-service students who major in other fields.

The motivations of in-service students enrolled in police education programs seem to contradict the policy objectives of higher education for police officers. Those students most interested in learning have no interest in serving out their careers as educated police officers. Those who are not as eager for advancement may also be less interested in learning. For those who do work hard at their studies and remain police officers, their frustration at not becoming a supervisor may cause their performance to deteriorate, rather than improve, after they have earned a college degree. Some of these contradictions might be resolved by a restructuring of police departments to allow for more advancement in pay and prestige while doing police work rather than supervising it. But given the present structures of police departments and police careers, these contradictions are an almost inevitable consequence of in-service education. And, because of these contradictions, much of the potential impact of higher education on the police institution is lost.

The Commuter Student Experience. No matter what their motivations may be, in-service students are almost always part-time commuter students. Some police officers do attend college full time while working full time as well, but that may only make their educational experience even less worthwhile. For there is good reason to believe that the hurried and brief contacts of the commuter student with campus life produce less cognitive learning and personal growth than the full immersion of the full-time residential student in campus life.

More than half of all American college students now live at home with their families and commute to college (Harrington, 1972). Given the increasing trend toward more adult education (Harrington, 1977), the future of American higher education may well be found in the large, urban, commuter campus (Freedman, 1969). Such campuses provide a very different educational experience from the traditional residential campus community. As Riesman and Jencks (1962) point out, commuter campuses have many similarities with the social organization of a factory; students come each day, accomplish their tasks, and leave. A study of Wayne State University in Detroit (Ward and Kurz, 1969; cited in Harrington, 1972), for example, found that commuters arranged their class schedules to minimize their time on campus. This form of social organization has important consequences for student attitudes toward their colleges: "Whereas students at a residential college often talk about their 'college' with the same kind of romanticism most Americans reserve for their families, [a commuter school's] students more often displayed the kind of cynicism typically saved for employers" (Riesman and Jencks, 1962, p. 173).

Commuter students do not make the complete break with their past that is typical of residential students. When they go home at night to their families, they must often suppress the political and social views they have heard during the day—or suffer stressful arguments with their parents. They also find fewer friends on campus, identifying more with people they had known during high school (Klotsche, 1966). Caught between their old lives and their campus lives, they suffer poorer mental health than residential students (Graff and Cooley, 1970).

Even when they attend college full time, commuter students behave differently from residential students (Chickering, 1974). Commuter students have less frequent and intensive con-

tact with faculty members. They less often participate in extracurricular activities or assume positions of leadership. They attend fewer cultural events and have fewer discussions of political, religious, and social issues. Commuter students who live
with their parents less often do extra reading, check out books
from the library, argue with instructors in class, or discuss their
school work with friends. At Wayne State University (see Harrington, 1972), commuter students holding jobs complained
that they suffered from a loss of energy and mental acuity during their late afternoon and evening classes; many had to with-
draw from classes because of unexpected changes in working
hours.

These differences in behavior may partly reflect the general differences in social background between commuter and
residential students. Commuter students are generally lower in
socioeconomic status (George, 1971; Chickering, 1974), and
disadvantages in background clearly affect college performance
(Feldman and Newcomb, 1969). But as a major study of several
nationally representative samples of students has shown, students who live with their parents fall short of the general learning and personal development levels of all students of similar
background, while those who live in college dormitories exceed
the average achievements of students with the same backgrounds (Chickering, 1974, p. 84):

> Whatever the institution, whatever the
> group, whatever the data, whatever the methods of
> [analysis] the findings are the same. Students who
> live at home with their parents fall short of the
> kinds of learning and personal development typi-
> cally desired by the institutions they attend and
> which might reasonably be expected when their
> special backgrounds are taken into account. Stu-
> dents who live in college dormitories exceed the
> learning and personal development that are pre-
> dicted when their advantages in ability, in prior
> educational and extracurricular activities, and in
> community and family backgrounds are taken into
> account. During the freshman year and during all

four years for several different large samples, examined through simple retest comparisons and
through complex multivariate analyses, the findings remain consistent.

This study, admittedly, combined two very different aspects of a college experience: commuting to college and living
with parents. Another study has found that campus residential
living is not necessarily preferable to off-campus living away
from parents in apartments or rooms (Bradshaw, 1974; cited in
Bowen, 1977). The crucial variable is probably the degree of immersion in the student subculture, or the extent of contact with
other students who are also discovering new ideas and new ways
of seeing the world (Feldman and Newcomb, 1969). Off-
campus housing among other students can clearly provide as
much immersion in the student subculture as dormitory living.
In-service police officers, however, seem to have little time (or
inclination) to immerse themselves in a student subculture.
Their primary social bonds are to their families and their fellow
police officers. Their family obligations probably limit the
amount of time they can devote to life in the student subculture. Their police department peer groups probably limit
their interest in the student subculture. The commuter-student
experience of the in-service police officer, then, may be quite
similar to that of younger commuter students who live with
their parents. Both lack the severing of previous social ties that
facilitates learning and personal growth.

Midcareer Residential Education. Not all in-service police
education has been delivered on a part-time commuter basis.
Under the Law Enforcement Assistance Act of 1965, the Office
of Law Enforcement Assistance—LEAA's predecessor—awarded
graduate fellowships for full-time residential study to fifty-four
police officers in 1967-1969. A similar program was conducted
by LEAA in 1970-71, but it has not been repeated since because of a legal "Catch-22": the program cannot be supported
by other than LEEP funds because it has the same purpose as
LEEP, but LEEP funds cannot be awarded to individuals in
amounts large enough to support residential education (Foster,

1978). Nonetheless, the LEAA evaluation of the 1967-1969 OLEA program suggests that midcareer residential education is very effective for the reasons suggested above: it temporarily severs most of the student's previous social ties and thus facilitates learning and personal growth (Tenney, 1971).

The fifty-four OLEA fellows all left their police departments on a one-year leave of absence and moved with their families (including an average of three children) to one of three colleges: John Jay College in New York, Michigan State University, and the University of California at Berkeley. All were college graduates, and thirteen of the fifty-one respondents to the evaluation survey had previously undertaken some graduate work. But almost none of them had ever experienced full-time education in "an atmosphere removed from their working environment" (Tenney, 1971, p. 69). The sudden removal from their usual surroundings caused some problems of personal adjustment, but it also enhanced their educational experiences. Several of the fellows elaborated on this point in their responses (Tenney, 1971, p. 69):

> "I couldn't understand, when I applied, why students were being asked to remove themselves from their home settings for the year. Subsequently, I came to realize that there were many insights available only through that sense of detachment."
>
> "[The] opportunity . . . without pressures of working in a law enforcement capacity made it possible to become totally involved in the educational process."
>
> "An experience that could not be duplicated under any local part-time or full-time graduate program."
>
> "Students should have to move away."

There is no evidence that these students learned any more in their residential experience than they would have in a local program of the same quality, but some of the students themselves clearly seem to think that their residential education was indeed superior. Even more of them felt that the distance from their jobs allowed them to evaluate more objectively the organizations they served.

These experiences are quite similar to those reported by the Sloan fellows at the Massachusetts Institute of Technology School of Management. The Sloan fellows were selected from middle-management positions in industry to attend MIT for a one-year master's program. The most meaningful aspect of their education was the opportunity to break loose from their organizations for a year. The change of environment consistently enabled them to gain a sense of perspective, not just on their organizations but on their lives as well (Bennis, 1976). Similar benefits are reported by graduates of the three-month program of the Federal Executive Institute.

The problem with midcareer residential education is that it is probably too expensive to make available to more than a very few police officers. By the time they have assumed the obligations of raising a family, in-service students would probably want to remain on full salary during an educational leave, something that most police departments could not afford for more than a few students. Some of the OLEA graduate fellows received only a modest stipend, and they reported serious financial problems. Even those who remained on full salary suffered financially from the year away.

Another limitation to the general use of residential in-service education is that it is often thought to be more suited to graduate education for potential police executives than to undergraduate education for line police officers. The OLEA fellows, for example, were chosen for their leadership potential, and the subsequent LEAA fellowships were called the "Executive Development Fellowship Program." The one-year time period—which probably seems more affordable to both the officers and the sponsors—is just right for earning a master's degree, but it does not allow enough time to complete a baccalaureate. (It should be noted, though, that the English police send officers to a university for three full years to earn baccalaureates; Stead, 1978.)

Nonetheless, both of these apparent limitations can be

overcome. The financial hardships on family life can be largely avoided if residential education fellowships are offered earlier in police officers' careers, perhaps within the first five years, when they are less likely to have children and are therefore more mobile. To ensure that fellowship recipients do not switch career plans in college, the fellowships might be administered as loans forgivable if they complete five years of police service after their year of residential education. The year-away concept is equally valuable for undergraduate education, even if a degree cannot be completed. As Harrington (1972) concluded in his study of commuter education, one year of residential education early in a college career, followed by commuter education, could greatly improve the total college experience. Chickering's (1974) data support this contention by showing that the biggest effect of residence on learning is in the first years of college (p. 132): "It is quite clear that the impact and value of those residence hall experiences taper off rapidly after the first or second year." Apparently, one year or so of immersion in a student subculture is sufficient to develop new ways of thinking and greater receptivity to learning.

Undergraduate resident fellowships for line police officers would not only improve the quality of their education but would also change the prevailing conception of education as a tool for advancement out of police work into management. Undergraduate resident fellows might even be required to stay on the street for five years after their year of educational leave, although they would have to be allowed to advance in rank and salary (while still doing line work, not supervision) in order to prevent the requirement from appearing to be punitive. The explicit purpose of such a program could be to improve the quality of police *work*, and not of police *management*. Alternatively, it could be defined as a benefit that some officers elect to use, as educational leaves are commonly used in Europe (von Moltke and Schneevoigt, 1977).

A program of undergraduate resident fellowships would also affect the educational roles played by various colleges in police education. The one year away might be used to pursue a basic core curriculum in the liberal arts, which could serve as a foundation for more specifically work-related education later on. As Harrington (1972) suggests, this approach would reverse the present role of the community college. Instead of taking students at the beginning of their education, who may later go on to residential study, community colleges or other commuter campuses could serve as continuing education and learning centers, where officers could complete the undergraduate education they began at a residential campus.

Finally, a program of resident undergraduate fellowships for line police officers should not preclude a program of graduate fellowships for police managers. Poor management is one of the most pressing problems of the American police, and residential study might help improve the performance of police managers. It might even help develop a profession of police managers comparable to the profession of city managers, fostering much greater mobility of chief police executives from one city to the next. But graduate education for police managers should be broader than the police administration and criminology programs attended by the OLEA fellows. Schools of management can provide a much more rigorous learning experience in their M.B.A. programs; the new emphasis on *public* management at the UCLA and Yale schools of management may inspire other schools as well to balance their current emphasis on profit-making organizations (which is less relevant to police administration). Given the size and complexity of many urban police departments, there is every reason for police managers to be educated at the finest schools of management in the country. Many smaller and far less important organizations are run by Harvard M.B.A.s; so why not major police departments?

Many different approaches to in-service residential education are possible. Yet, with a few scattered exceptions, neither police departments nor federal policies support such educational experiences. The commission believes that a more selective investment of the 40-million-dollar LEEP funds in residential education for in-service students could have a far greater impact on policing than the current use of those funds to support part-time commuter education. Given the low tuition at many public community colleges, LEEP funds for commuter students provide relatively marginal financial assistance. Once in-service students are "hooked" into education by a residential experience, they might be more likely to pay for their own continuing commuter education toward a degree and, after the degree, for lifelong learning. This approach might even be able to include the same number of in-service officers whose education is currently supported. The cost of one year of residential education at a public institution, for example, may be little more than the LEEP payments presently made for four years or more of commuter education.

No matter how it is structured, however, residential in-service police education will always be more difficult and more costly than preservice education. In the long run, the most effective way of achieving the commission's objectives for educating the police is for police departments to hire more preservice college graduates. Yet even their educational experiences warrant close scrutiny, for the wrong kind of preservice education may be of little value to policing.

Preservice Education

Ample numbers of college students feel called to police work, even though few are chosen. In a survey of almost 200,000 freshmen entering 374 representative colleges and universities in the fall of 1977, 1.7 percent of the respondents named their probable career occupation as "law enforcement officer" (Astin, 1978; cited in *Chronicle of Higher Education*, January 23, 1978, p. 12). Of the forty-two occupations listed in the survey, law enforcement ranked nineteenth in frequency of student interest. Given the projection of almost one million baccalaureates per year to be awarded in the late 1970s (Golladay, 1977, p. 64), and assuming that students interested in law enforcement have the same dropout rates as other students, there will be 17,000 more college graduates each year seeking careers in police work. Since police departments will be hiring around 50,000 new recruits a year from now to the mid 1980s (National Planning Association, 1976, p. II-94), it may be possible for them to quadruple the percentage of new recruits who are college graduates (see Table 16). And with the pent-up demand for law enforcement jobs among present college alumni now working in other fields, it may even be possible to fill all new recruit classes with college graduates, at least in urban areas.

Like the in-service college educational experience, however, there may be major limitations on the quality of learning that occurs in preservice college education. Both student motivation and the commuter experience may reduce the benefit of a preservice college education for both students and the police departments they may serve.

Motivation to Learn. The present generation of adolescent college students appear to be highly vocational in their motivation to learn (Bird, 1975). By 1976, 95 percent of American undergraduates listed "training and skills for an occupation" as either "essential" or "fairly important" goals of their college education (Carnegie Foundation, 1977, p. 223). It is little wonder, then, that many colleges are responding to student demand by developing police-related curriculums that provide more training than education.

Many observers are suspicious of the "new vocationalism," particularly in criminal justice students. To Goldstein (1977, p. 295), for example, "the student demand itself is suspect, reflecting a search for relevancy that may be an escape from more rigorous and demanding courses of study." Other critics have suggested that college students are majoring in police-oriented programs not because of the new vocationalism but because the programs are the new safe or easy courses in higher education—an important comment on the conceptual level of the curriculum and the quality of teaching. (In a now-dated study of student ability, however, police science students in a community college were found to have academic backgrounds and high school achievement similar to those of business administration students; see Lankes, 1971.)

A serious motivation to learn vocational skills at the undergraduate level might inhibit a more general learning experience. Students whose only interest is in the romanticized "nuts and bolts" of police work may have nothing but anti-intellectual contempt for more abstract conceptual knowledge.

A student whose main interests are fingerprinting and firearms may put little effort into studying history and literature. The result may be that preservice college graduates of the vocational training model of police education programs will wind up with roughly the same outlook on police work and society as the traditional graduates of police training academies.

Some preservice students are probably more interested in doing police work than in managing it. In this respect, their motivations fit the police goals of police education better than the typical motivation of their in-service counterparts. But it is by no means clear what proportion of preservice students share that interest. Almost all of the small group of preservice students the commission met with at the University of Cincinnati, for example, expressed the desire to become police administrators. The motivation for preservice police education may generally be no more appropriate for creating an educated police rank and file than the motivation of in-service students.

Among those college students who do not major in a criminal justice or police education program, however, there is less reason to suspect that their motivation limits their learning experiences. While they may be just as concerned with finding a job as police education majors are, they may have a better sense of how the liberal arts constitute the best vocational education for difficult and complex careers. That is not necessarily true for the preservice students majoring in other professional education programs, but it may be true for the police recruits who have majored in arts and science disciplines. Their motivation for entering police work, at least in the short run, may be a desire to do police work rather than to manage it. It is not surprising, then, that some police chiefs prefer to hire preservice graduates who have majored in fields *other than* specialized police education programs.

The Commuter Experience. Because most police education programs have been created at colleges accessible to in-service students, and because the programs have been organized to meet the needs of the in-service students, preservice students in police education programs have much the same educational experience as the in-service students. Judging by the near majority of police education programs that are in community colleges, both preservice and in-service students are typically commuters, and both suffer similar disadvantages of commuter education. The preservice student's commuter experience, however, is different from the in-service student's experience in two key respects. First, the preservice students are more likely to live with their parents, which may limit their growth and learning in comparison to the in-service commuter students who live away from their parents. But a more important difference, which may enhance their learning experience in comparison to in-service students, is that preservice students do not have the reference group of the police subculture counteracting the impact of the student subculture.

Once again, however, there may be a major difference between police education majors and all other preservice graduates. Since commuter colleges are more likely to emphasize vocational training programs than residential colleges are (Harris and Grede, 1977), it seems likely that liberal arts graduates more often attend residential colleges. Perhaps because of this difference in educational experiences, liberal arts graduates learn more and grow more in college (Feldman and Newcomb, 1969). But since residential education is primarily the preserve of the privileged or more advantaged students, a policy of recruiting police officers solely from residential campuses would discriminate against lower socioeconomic groups. Although some reformers have made no secret of their desire to raise the social class backgrounds of police recruits, there is great opposition to closing off police work to the newest urban immigrants (Fogelson, 1977).

Preservice Residential Education. If one year of residential education is feasible for in-service students, it is an even more realistic proposal for preservice students. Preservice LEEP fellowships for residential education of one to four year's duration could be awarded to college students who are willing to commit themselves to working in a police agency. The problem with such commitments is that many preservice graduates have difficulty finding police employment (U.S. Comptroller General, 1975). But there are other ways of providing preservice residential experiences in police education programs. Commuter colleges can easily organize short, intensive residential programs, as Chickering (1974, pp. 132-133) has suggested: "Suppose groups of twenty or thirty students . . . came together in residence situations where they could eat, drink, talk, sleep, write, read, exchange reports and experiences uninterrupted for two or three days, a week, or longer? . . . Such residential periods need not be continuous, frequent, nor scheduled on a regular basis. In the typical course, one or two a semester [might] make a great difference." The cost of brief residential sessions would be relatively small and could be paid for by LEEP funds or the students.

Preservice Work Experience. The growing emphasis on vocational goals for higher education has spurred renewed interest in making work experience a part of higher education. Cooperative education programs at Antioch College, Northeastern University, and other institutions have exposed many students to police work, and a number of them have followed up that brief contact with a career in police work. Campus police forces at several of the larger universities have also given college students in a number of fields the opportunity to sample what police work is like. And since August Vollmer's tenure as police chief of Berkeley, some college students have also worked as sworn police officers in their college towns.

All these preservice work experiences enrich a college education for any student, regardless of whether the experiences lead to police careers. They also help to maintain a more open atmosphere within police departments, since the presence of college students may reduce the we-versus-they "siege" mentality often found in urban police departments. For students who become police officers, internships allow them to make an intelligent choice of careers, informed more by a knowledge of the daily humdrum of police work than by the glamorous images of television shows. Officers who begin police work as cadets or interns may experience less reality shock (Becker and others, 1961) at discovering the true nature of police work.

The Safe Streets Act of 1968 recognized the benefits of preservice work experience by authorizing a program of criminal justice internships. Unfortunately, the Law Enforcement Assistance Administration has defined the eligibility requirements for the internships in the same narrow way that it has defined the eligibility for LEEP support. Only students enrolled in police education programs are eligible to receive a stipend for an internship in a police department. For those students enrolled in a program offering a narrow training curriculum, the internship probably does little to enrich their education. Quite the opposite: it reinforces their parochial concern with techniques and procedures. What could be a broadening experience for a liberal arts student never exposed to the police has instead become a narrowing experience for students who have already spent too much of their education on police topics.

Recommendations

Throughout this discussion of the nature of student experiences, the powerful influence of LEEP funds is clearly evident. The present structure of LEEP has been described as a choice of "quantity over quality" (Stanley, 1978), giving large numbers of students small amounts of money for part-time study rather than fewer students enough money for full-time residential study. The strong grass-roots support that LEEP has generated in almost every congressional district has preserved it from a number of presidentially proposed budget reductions. Despite its political support, LEEP has been the target of almost every critic of the quality of police education, and some have seriously proposed its abolition. We believe that the goal of educating the police for change should be worth at least the present LEEP funding of $40 million per year, the equivalent of the cost of only two strategic air force bombers (FB-111s). Rather than abolishing LEEP, we would like to see its influence redirected toward the support of higher-quality student experiences:

>   6-1 *Congress should continue to fund the Law En-*
>   *forcement Education Program (LEEP) at its*
>   *present level, provided the program is restruc-*
>   *tured in the ways suggested here.*

The basic need for restructuring LEEP is to raise the limits on the amount that can be paid to each individual in a year to a high enough level to support full-time residential education. Moreover, the amounts should be high enough to cover the moving costs and family support expenses involved in the recommendations offered below (concerning one-year residential fellowships). The current limits are $400 per semester (or $250 per quarter) for grants to each in-service student or $2,200 per academic year for forgivable loans to each preservice student to cover only the costs of tuition and other educational costs, such as books and fees; living costs are not allowable. Amounts up to $10,000 per year (in forgivable loans or grants), covering both educational and living costs, would mean that fewer students would be supported, but those who were supported would get a much better education:

> 6-2 *Congress should amend the statutory authori-*
> *zation of LEEP to allow more intensive educa-*
> *tional experiences through more extensive sup-*
> *port of individual students than the present*
> *authorization for grants and loans allows. The*
> *limits on the support of each student should*
> *be high enough to cover all costs of full-time*
> *residential education.*

There is no reason why LEEP should be the only source of support for residential education for the police. State and local governments now provide various educational incentives for in-service commuter education. Given the evidence of the greater educational effectiveness of residential education, they would be well advised to redirect some of that support to one-year educational fellowships. The New York City Police Department and several others now offer one-year leaves at full pay to officers selected on a competitive basis regardless of rank. This policy could be used to develop potential managers as well as people who will continue to do police work. The field of policing will profit from these fellows' learning a variety of subjects, from computer science to history:

6-3 *Federal, state, and local governments should devote greater resources to supporting one-year residential educational fellowships for both police officers and potential police managers. These fellowships should be offered in a diverse range of disciplines.*

In general, we have been opposed to the emphasis of any one discipline or field of study in police education, but one exception to this pattern seems advisable. The complexity of modern police management demands the most sophisticated managers and managerial methods available. The knowledge to be gained in the graduate schools of management (or business) in the leading universities could be an excellent preparation for service as a police executive. The Law Enforcement Assistance Administration (LEAA) once sponsored a brief training institute for police chiefs at the Harvard Business School, and a full two-year M.B.A. program seems equally justified. Programs combining public and private management might provide even better preparation. Since the cost might be prohibitve for local agencies, we suggest that LEEP funds be set aside specifically for this purpose:

6-4 *The administrators of LEAA's educational assistance programs should develop a program for sending potential police executives to the highest-quality schools of management to earn graduate degrees.*

The least expensive approach to increasing the proportion of full-time residential student experiences among educated police officers is to hire more preservice college graduates. The original intent of a key congressional sponsor of LEEP, in fact, had been to foster more preservice education, but the bill was modified in response to police concerns that existing personnel be given an opportunity to upgrade themselves (National Planning Association, 1976). Now that almost half of all officers have completed at least one year of college, it is appropriate to give greater emphasis to preservice students. At the same time,

LEEP funds should remain available to in-service police officers to encourage lifelong learning:

> 6-5 *The Congress and the administrators of LEEP should give equal priority to supporting the education of both in-service police officers and other students planning to pursue police careers. Government policies at all levels should give highest priority to encouraging college education of officers before they begin their careers.*

The quality of preservice education, however, may not be substantially better than the quality of in-service education if the prevailing curriculum is the vocational training model. Since the present statutory authorization of LEEP requires that preservice students enroll in programs "directly related" to law enforcement and criminal justice, many of them do (or would, if preservice funds became more available) enroll in the narrow training programs. Preservice funding of liberal arts students has been avoided on the grounds that they may not be as committed to a police career as students majoring in police education programs. The failure of many police education majors to find police work (U.S. Comptroller General, 1975) and the success of many liberal arts majors in doing so (Hoover, 1975), however, weakens that argument considerably. The argument is even more strained in the denial of law enforcement internships to liberal arts students, who may derive much greater benefit by concrete experience with policing than students who are already well versed in police issues. Finally, until there is a core of systematic knowledge that every police officer needs to learn—beyond what is taught (or should be taught) at training academies—restrictions of LEEP support to specialized police education programs make little sense:

> 6-6 *The Congress and the administrators of LEEP, in order to support the pursuit of a wide range of academic majors and courses by students*

participating in both LEEP and the Law En-
forcement Internship Program, should remove
any requirements that course work be "direct-
ly related" to law enforcement and criminal
justice. In-service students, presumably already
familiar with the basic issues of policing,
should be encouraged to study relevant sub-
jects other than police science and criminal
justice.

Whether in-service or preservice, students in most police
education programs are not offered sufficient opportunities to
immerse themselves in learning environments. In this respect, of
course, police education is no different from any other program
on the same campuses. But all commuter college programs
could profit by adopting the recommendation we offer for police education:

6-7 Every nonresidential police education program
should provide and require brief, intensive resi-
dential periods of study at least once each
semester or quarter.

A great deal can be done to improve these and other aspects of the quality of police education. The curriculum, the
resources, the faculty, and the student experiences in police
education can all be redirected to better achieve the objective of
educating the police institution for change. But no matter how
high the quality of police education, it will have relatively little
impact on policing unless police departments are restructured to
make better use of educated personnel.

7

≡⊃○⊂⊃○⊂⊃○⊂⊃○⊂⊃○⊂⊃○⊂⊃≡

Changing the Police

*The police establishment [should] face up to
the fact that a college education can only
benefit policing if the police establishment is
prepared to accept change.*

Ladinsky, 1977, p. 2

In the first part of this report, we argued that a primary objective of police education should be changing the police. In the second part, we argued that the poor quality of much police education limits its potential for changing the police. In this final part of the report, we now consider the steps that must be taken to achieve the objective of educating the police institution for change. In this chapter we shift our focus from the colleges to the police departments, arguing that police department policies have failed to take advantage of higher education as a resource for change. In the next and final chapter, we examine both the colleges and the police departments, as well as the other major institutions that control police education, in order to show how police education can be changed.

Police departments vary widely in their posture toward higher education, just as they vary in most other important respects. Some have ignored education entirely, while others have sought to use education as the foundation for a program of planned change in the role of the police in the community. Most urban police departments, however, seem to have adopted

167

the rhetoric of police education as a public relations device, supporting police education as a way of improving their department's public image. At the same time, they have successfully avoided the potentially disruptive effects of having educated personnel. Using a variety of policies to ensure that educated officers remain loyal to the values and norms of the police subculture, these departments have prevented education from becoming an agent of change. Like the colleges exploiting police education for profits, these departments have exploited police education for credentials.

This chapter suggests some directions for changes in policing that higher education might help achieve. It shows how education can be a resource for change as well as a source of beneficial disruption and dissatisfaction. It examines the present formal (and informal) policies of police departments toward education and some of the major controversies over what those policies should be. Finally, it offers some recommendations for the policies that are needed for changing the police through higher education.

Directions for Change

The problems of policing discussed in Chapter One will never be solved completely. Conflicting objectives for police work, inadequate methods for achieving those objectives, police violations of the law, and poor relations between the police and (at least some) citizens may all be inevitable problems in policing a free society. Yet they are all problems of degree. The fact that a few departments have substantially reduced these problems demonstrates that changes can be accomplished. Drawing from the experience of those departments, as well as from the ideas of some major philosophers of policing, we can summarize briefly three directions for change in the substance of policing, the behavior of police officers at work: doing new tasks, doing the same tasks better, and not doing illegal or unethical "tasks."

Doing Different Tasks. Given the enormous amount of time police now devote to "preventive" patrol, and given the questionable value of merely driving around the streets (Kelling and others, 1974), there seem to be ample resources available for the police to perform some new and different tasks. Some of that time, for example, could be devoted to crime prevention activities, such as visiting people's homes to make recommendations about how they might make their homes harder to burglarize. Some of that time could be devoted to seeking out and identifying community problems before they become more serious—unsafe housing conditions, for example. Some of that time could be devoted to having the police officer play the role of a neighborhood ombudsman, taking complaints and requests for any and all municipal services needed in the neighborhood and making the necessary inquiries with other city departments or appropriate private agencies. In these and other ways, police officers might become advocates of the communities they serve, rather than mere shift employees.

New police tasks probably will not be developed unless several conditions are met. One is that police departments develop new organizational structures that will allow police officers greater flexibility in using their time and greater stability of assignment to the same geographical area. The radio dispatching of calls for police service, in particular, must be redesigned in order to maintain an available supply of police officers for emergency situations without wasting the time of all officers in merely waiting for something to happen. Some experiments with new tasks, in fact, have failed because a higher priority was given to availability for radio dispatches than to performing the new tasks (Sherman, Milton, and Kelley, 1973).

Perhaps the most important condition for doing new and different tasks is the development of creativity, analytical intelligence, imagination, and initiative among police officers. The San Diego Police Department's Community Profile program, for example, in which patrol officers conducted systematic research on the social conditions of their areas, required a good deal of creativity in determining where to find relevant information. The program required much intelligence for analyzing the information, and a good deal of imagination and initiative for putting the information to use in their work (see Boydstun and Sherry, 1975). Given the research findings discussed in Chapter

Two (Feldman and Newcomb, 1969; Astin, 1977; Bowen, 1977), there is some reason to believe that more and better higher education for police officers may help produce the personal qualities necessary for creating this kind of new police role.

Doing the Same Tasks Better. There is also great room for improvement in the way police perform their present tasks. New ways must be found to identify and apprehend criminals, as well as to keep the peace and manage conflict among neighbors, friends, and lovers. The present state of police knowledge about the relative effectiveness of different ways of performing these vital tasks is at best unsystematic. The kind of practical, applied knowledge that is needed to do these tasks more effectively can be developed only through continuing and careful experimentation, in which the police departments conducting the experiments have a sophisticated appreciation of the requirements of scientific research procedures. Just as some major hospitals are devoted to teaching and research as well as to patient care, perhaps some police departments can define themselves as research oriented, providing knowledge services to the police profession as well as police services to their community. The Kansas City, Missouri, and San Diego, California, Police Departments, for example, have played that role in recent years, but many more "research departments" are needed.

At least two conditions seem to be necessary for any improvement to occur in crime detection or peace keeping. One is the development of more effective management in police departments. The inadequacies of police management first identified over fifty years ago (Fosdick, [1920] 1969) still exist today. Police administrators are still chosen primarily by examination from the ranks of the police, with almost no possibility for lateral entry from other occupations into middle or top police management. More important is the generally inadequate training and education of police managers at all levels, especially the chief police executive's (International Association of Chiefs of Police, 1976). As John Stead's (1978) report to the commission on the extensive training and education of police managers in Europe shows, the American practices lag far behind. If police managers in this country were recruited and trained differently, they might pay more attention to finding ways to improve police performance and might be much more open to experimentation and careful research.

Another necessary condition for doing present tasks better is that police officers participate in the design of new approaches and cooperate in their rigorously scientific testing. The officers who perform the basic police tasks have some of the best ideas about how those tasks might be done better, but they are often unable or unwilling to articulate those ideas. Moreover, when new ideas are tested, it is not uncommon for some police officers to attempt to sabotage the experiments, in contempt for both the idea being studied and the research process itself. More and better higher education for police officers may not solve these problems, but it may at least improve the climate for research in police departments.

Not Doing Unethical "Tasks." Despite the apparent decline in the public and media attention given to police misconduct in recent years, the problems persist. Police officers often use fatal force unnecessarily (if legally), despite the increasing restrictions on police use of weapons (Milton and others, 1977). They still misuse their discretion to arrest people who show insufficient respect, rather than those who should be arrested on the grounds of law or department policy (Sykes and Clark, 1975). And some still participate in corrupt and criminal activities for personal gain (Beigel and Beigel, 1977).

Despite the widely shared hypothesis that better-educated police are less prone to performing these undesirable "tasks," the available evidence is not encouraging. One study, for example, suggests that college-educated officers in one department use fatal force more often (Milton and others, 1977), although the finding could be explained by the fact that the college-educated officers in the study were generally younger. Many officers convicted on corruption charges in recent years have been college educated. Although these scant data say nothing about the relative probabilities of educated and noneducated officers committing acts of misconduct when all other factors are equal, they do suggest that education alone does not immunize officers from improper behavior. What may be more important is to change the organizational character of police departments: the prevailing norms and assumptions of the police subculture that presently support police malpractice (Muir, 1977). Whether more and better higher education for police officers can produce that kind of change may well depend on the nature of police department policies toward higher education.

A Resource for Change

Ideally, police department policies should treat higher education as a resource for change, providing a series of opportunities for experiments with new tasks, programs, and organizational arrangements. As Thomas Reppetto's (1978) report to the commission points out, the organizational design of the educated police department can be very different from the present quasi-military designs developed at a time when many police officers were functionally illiterate. With changes in organizational design, managerial practices, and other factors in the control of most police executives, education might have a much greater impact on police behavior than it does when education is the only variable that changes. To expect education to be the sole, or even the primary, agent of change is probably unrealistic, as we have already noted.

Some proposals have assumed that police departments should be reorganized into a new hierarchy, in which the complexity of the tasks performed by officers in each rank matches their level of education. The President's Commission on Law Enforcement and Administration of Justice (1967b), for example, suggested that police departments move toward a three-level structure for line officers providing police services. The lowest level under this plan is the community service officer; this officer would need to have only a high school diploma at the time of appointment and would perform such routine police tasks as directing traffic. The next level is the police officer, who would perform tasks similar to those of present patrol officers; the applicants for this rank would usually have to hold a degree from a two-year or four-year college. At the top of the hierarchy is the police agent, who would perform the most complicated, sensitive, and demanding police tasks, from patrolling a high-crime neighborhood to specializing in homicide investigations; the applicants for this rank would have to hold at least a baccalaureate degree. The President's Commission argued that this structure would allow more recruitment of both minority-group members (as community service officers, whose college education could be supported by the department, so that they could be promoted to the higher ranks) and preservice college graduates. It also argued that the plan would provide a much better fit between the different levels of difficulty of police tasks and the different levels of ability among police officers.

Another proposal for using education as a resource for change is to organize police departments more collegially, abolishing the hierarchical command structure in favor of peer-controlled work groups (Angell, 1971). If all police officers were well educated, and considered themselves professionals committed to a code of ethics, the traditional bureaucratic structures of central control could be replaced with neighborhood-based teams of officers who would be of equal status within the team. A central coordinating staff, under this model, would provide only training and support services, as well as investigating possible violations of ethics. The theory of this proposal is that a collegial organization would produce better police-community relations and better police morale. Whether educated officers would adapt better to this kind of organizational design is an open question, but it is true that other collegial organizations (law firms, hospitals, universities) usually have well-educated personnel.

Many other organizational designs making use of higher levels of education among police are possible, of course, and none of them can be evaluated properly without careful research on experimental attempts to adopt the designs. All of them, however, pose a threat to the established power relations in police departments. Most police supervisors and managers, as well as many police officers now lacking higher education, have nothing apparent to gain and perhaps everything to lose by the adoption of these organizational designs. Higher education may be a resource for change, but change is hardly a universal goal among police departments. Where organizational designs are not modified to take account of increased levels of education, education can be a source of disruption and dissatisfaction (Berkeley, 1971). Fearing the disruption, perhaps, more than welcoming the resource for change, most police departments have failed to take full advantage of the growth of police education. Instead, through a number of formal and informal policies, they have succeeded in defusing education as a potential source of change.

Police Policies and Education

A large number of police department policies presently limit the impact of police education. Formal policies on recruitment, selection, promotions, salary structures, and educational benefits often limit the quantity and the quality of education among their officers. Equally important are the informal policies, which often seem to punish officers for being more educated than their peers or supervisors. Reasonable arguments can be made both for and against most of these policies; unless they are changed, however, higher education will have little impact on the quality of police performance.

Recruitment and Selection. A prime example of the widespread resistance to using education as a resource for change is the failure of most police departments to recruit and select more college-educated police officers. As Table 18 shows, only 5.5 percent of the 2,639 police agencies responding to a 1975 survey require that their recruits have some level of college education, and more than one in ten have no educational requirements at all. These figures are admittedly an improvement over the findings of a 1961 survey of 300 police departments; less than 1 percent of those departments required any level of college education, and 24 percent had no educational requirements at all (O'Connor, 1962; cited in President's Commission on Law Enforcement and Administration of Justice, 1967b, p. 126). The 1975 figures also show a very slight increase over the find-

Table 18. Minimum Education Required at Entry for Sworn Law Enforcement Personnel, 1975

Minimum Education Required	Police Agencies				Sheriff's Agencies			
	All Police Agencies (N = 2,639)	Fewer Than 150 Employees (N = 2,392)	150-399 Employees (N = 150)	400 or More Employees (N = 97)	All Sheriff's Agencies (N = 550)	Fewer Than 150 Employees (N = 487)	150-399 Employees (N = 41)	400 or More Employees (N = 22)
All responses	100.0%	100.0%	100.0%	100.0%	100.0%	100.0%	100.0%	100.0%
No minimum	11.2	12.2	1.3	1.0	13.1	14.4	2.4	4.5
Less than high school diploma	2.1	2.0	3.9	2.1	2.7	2.5	4.9	4.5
High school diploma	81.3	80.9	82.0	88.7	81.8	81.5	82.9	86.4
One year of college	1.9	1.9	2.0	1.0	1.1	0.6	4.0	4.5
Two or three years of college	3.3	2.9	10.0	7.2	0.9	1.0	0	0
Bachelor's degree	0.3	0.2	0.7	0	0.4	0	4.9	0

Note: Detail may not add to totals due to rounding.
Source: National Planning Association, 1976, p. II-170.

ings of a 1972 survey of 493 police departments having more than fifty officers (Eisenberg, Kent, and Wall, 1973). When the 1975 survey data are adjusted by excluding all departments under fifty officers, they show that 6.5 percent of that much larger sample requires its recruits to have some level of college (National Planning Association, 1976, p. II-192), compared to the 6 percent responding to the 1972 survey. But this trend (if it is measured correctly) toward higher educational requirements is far from rapid, especially in comparison with the dramatic recent increases in the actual educational levels of new recruits (see Table 16).

There is an important distinction, of course, between seeking out more college-educated police recruits and requiring that all recruits be college educated. Another 1975 survey, for example, found that while less than 1 percent of the 344 responding police chiefs supported the idea that all recruits should hold a baccalaureate degree, almost 20 percent claimed that they actively recruited on college campuses (Beckman, 1976, pp. 317-318). The latter figure must be treated skeptically, since the survey questionnaire could have been interpreted as asking whether the department recruited people who had been to college. Nonetheless, many police executives and union leaders who at least pay lip service to the value of higher educational *levels* for police personnel are opposed to *requiring* a college education (for example, J. Wilson, 1975). The reasons for their opposition to college requirements reflect a growing concern in many fields with the issues of credentialism and educational discrimination.

The major argument against requiring police recruits to be college educated is that there is not enough proof that a college education is necessary for performing police tasks. This argument has three logical flaws. One is the assumption that a college education can be proved to be necessary for performing the tasks involved in any occupation, but that is simply not the case (Bird, 1975). The college requirement for G.S.-7 positions in the federal government, for instance, have never been "validated" for the full range of tasks performed by people at that level, and certainly not for the federal law enforcement agencies which recruit beginning agents at that level. Nor has a law school education been demonstrated to produce more component or even minimally competent lawyers; yet the lack of such evidence has not slowed the steady abolition of clerkship without law school as a means of admission to the bar. The few studies that have examined the relationship between educational background and police performance are admittedly inconclusive (National Planning Association, 1976; Smith, 1978), although they all suffer from severe methodological problems; but similar studies on any other occupation would probably be equally inconclusive, given the extreme difficulty of measuring good job performance.

A second flaw in the argument of insufficient proof is the assumption that a degree must be *necessary* in order to be fairly required. There are many paths to learning any set of skills, no matter how complex, and formal education is only one of them. Some people will always be able to acquire certain kinds of knowledge, skills, and personality traits without formal education, but they are the exceptions in contemporary society. While it may not be necessary to be college educated to acquire the qualities we think important for police work, the *probability* that college-educated people have those qualities is greater. The same assumption underlies degree requirements in other occupations.

A final flaw in the logic of the insufficient proof argument is that competence to perform a job as it is presently structured is something different from competence at changing the nature of the job itself. The distinction between upgrading the qualifications required of the people who perform a job and upgrading the nature of the job itself is central to the use of education as a strategy for changing the police. Unfortunately, the distinction has been ignored in the current wave of reaction against credentialism: "the imposition by employers of educational requirements that are not clearly indicated by the requirements of particular jobs" (Gordon, 1974; quoted in Bird, 1975, p. 127). The issue of credentialism has also been complicated by the issue of race. After the Civil Rights Act of 1964 outlawed employment discrimination on the basis of race, some observers began predicting that employment discrimination on the basis of education would also be outlawed (Drucker, 1969). The Supreme Court came very close to doing just that in a 1971 case interpreting the Civil Rights Act (*Griggs* v. *Duke Power Company,* 401 U.S. 424 [1971]). The Court held that the company had discriminated against a black employee by denying him a transfer to an office job as a messenger because he lacked a high school diploma, since there was no evidence that a high school education was necessary for performing that job. The year before, Ivar Berg (1970) had published his indictment of the general trend toward higher educational requirements for many jobs in which the skill levels had reportedly remained unchanged since 1940. More recently the higher education community has joined the attack on credentialism. The Carnegie Commission on Higher Education (1973a), for example, called much "educational upgrading" of jobs artificial, recommending against the practice unless there is a clearly demonstrable relationship between education and performance. And the Carnegie Foundation for the Advancement of Teaching (1977) argued that overeducation for many jobs would lead to dissatisfaction and frustration among the college graduates in those jobs.

The higher education groups' recommendations are ironic, given the historic impact of the Ph.D. requirement in the professionalization of the American professoriat and the institutional transformation of colleges into universities (Rudolph, 1962), despite the absence of any evidence that a graduate education produced better teachers or better scholars. The commission's own research has demonstrated a clear relationship between *aggregate* faculty educational levels and the curriculum used in police education programs, but similar research at the individual level of analysis is lacking for any field of higher education. The point that the anticredentialist movement fails to grasp is that a transformation of aggregate educational levels in an occupation can lead to a transformation of the nature of the job, rather than merely rendering people overqualified for an unchanging job. Federal law may demand that educational requirements be validated in terms of individual competence to perform a job as it is presently structured, but the primary pur-

pose of a college requirement for police recruits is not to screen
for such competence. The purpose is to help create a new kind
of job, which college-educated people in the aggregate will be
more likely to create.

Nonetheless, many police executives cite *Griggs* in oppos-
ing college requirements because fewer blacks than whites hold
college degrees, and the requirement might therefore have the
impact of disproportionately excluding blacks. A similar argument, of course, could be made about any occupational degree
requirement, from the federal civil service to law and medicine.
A more recent case (decided on Fourteenth Amendment
grounds rather than, as *Griggs* was, on Title 7 of the Civil Rights
Act) held that *intent* to discriminate on the grounds of race
must be established to prove that an entrance requirement is un-
lawful (*Washington* v. *Davis* 426 U.S. 229 [1976]), but the legal
issues are not the only concern of many progressive police executives. They argue against college requirements because the requirements might pose an obstacle to increasing the proportion
of blacks in their departments as rapidly as possible.

In his report to the commission on this issue, however,
Gwynne Peirson (1978) questions the sincerity of the concern
for minority hiring, arguing that it is merely a convenient excuse for perpetuating low standards for law enforcement personnel. Peirson also questions the logic of using educational
levels of the general population (or of males in the age range of
police recruiting) to assess the impact of educational requirements on different racial groups. Pointing out that blacks and
other minority-group members in several major police departments are much more likely than white officers to be college
educated (see also Watts, 1978), he argues that the relevant
comparisons of educational levels is with those groups who have
traditionally been attracted to law enforcement careers, and not
with the general population. While it might be hard to define
the groups attracted to law enforcement, there is ample prece-
dent in Affirmative Action plans for using hiring "pools" from
which candidates are drawn for a particular job, rather than the
population at large, as the basis for assessing discrimination.
And some definitions of the hiring pools might show educa-

tional requirements to *benefit* blacks, possibly even leading to charges of reverse discrimination. In any case, Peirson (a black former police officer with a doctorate from Berkeley) concludes: "If mandatory college education were imposed as a prerequisite for entry to the police field, and if higher education standards were similarly imposed throughout the departments, highly qualified minorities, particularly blacks, would be attracted to the occupation." Similarly, an econometric analysis of admittedly scanty national labor market data recently concluded that the imposition of college-degree entry requirements by police departments would not necessarily impede minority recruitment efforts (Carver, 1978).

As evidence of the false concern of white officers, Peirson cites the only legal test to date (of which we are aware) of the racial discrimination argument against college requirements for police (*Ice, et al.* v. *Arlington County, et al.,* No. 76-2194 [4th Cir., May 16, 1977], aff'g No. 74-645-A [E.D. Va., Aug. 10, 1976]). The suit, brought by 111 *white* Arlington County, Virginia, police officers, claimed that their police department's educational requirements and salary incentives discriminated against their eight black colleagues, only one of whom joined the suit. The U.S. Equal Employment Opportunity Commission found that the policies were discriminatory (Case No. YDC5-373, Washington District Office, December 27, 1974), but the federal district court dismissed the racial discrimination claim when the one black officer dropped out of the suit. The case was pursued on the grounds that the salary incentives denied the white officer equal pay for equal work, but the district court was unconvinced: "All Arlington policemen do not perform their duties in like manner. Some do it better than others—some relate better with the public—some create and develop new techniques. . . . All of the evidence disclosed that college-trained policemen make better policemen" (pp. 5-6). The appeals court heard additional evidence on the job relatedness of the educational requirements and upheld the lower court's ruling. Other courts may take a different view of the evidence, but as far as the commission could determine, the *Ice* case is the only one on this issue to have reached the federal courts.

Whatever the resolution of the legal issues, many other arguments will still be made against college requirements for police recruits. Some of the arguments will be difficult to resolve with factual evidence, since they reflect value judgments about the future directions of policing (just as we do here). The argument that a college requirement would increase the prestige of police work, for example, has been rebutted by former Washington, D.C., police chief Jerry Wilson (1975, p. 175), who argues that "conscientious, hard work at a craft is just as important as holding a degree and claiming to be a professional. . . . The nation needs to reassess its sense of what kinds of accomplishments deserve prestige." Other arguments involve empirical facts that are difficult to determine. For example, Wilson also disputes the claim that a college education will help an officer use police discretion more wisely, arguing that police do not—or should not—have any discretion over when to enforce the law (but see Goldstein, 1977). Similarly, he disputes the argument that police work is so complex that it requires a high level of intelligence, arguing that much police work is boring and quite simple.

Some of the arguments over college requirements can be resolved with factual evidence. The argument that higher educational standards are needed to keep up with the rising level of education of the general public (Saunders, 1970), for example, is now clearly refuted by the fact that, since the early 1970s, police educational levels have been higher than the levels of the male labor force aged 20-44 (Figure 1). At the same time, the claim that insufficient college graduates would be available to fill police recruit classes if the requirement were imposed is largely refuted by two other facts: the high unemployment rate (8 percent) of young college graduates ("Jobless Rate Increases . . . ," 1978) and the ample numbers of college graduates taking police entrance examinations in many cities.

There are also different arguments to be considered for different levels of college requirements. Many departments have found the B.A. requirements excessively high, adopting instead an A.A. degree, or two years of college, as the minimum level of education. Some police executives, however, have found that

Figure 1. Percentage of Sworn Police Officers with One or More Years
of College, Compared with the Male Labor Force (Ages 20 to 44),
1960, 1970, and 1974

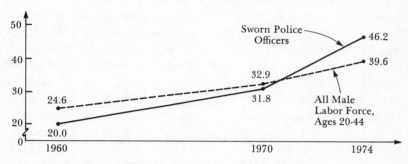

Source: National Planning Association, 1976, p. II-147.

this compromise only makes matters worse, confining the potential pool of applicants to the graduates of the paraprofessional training programs in the community colleges. The Madison, Wisconsin, Police Department, for example, recently abolished its two-year-college requirement in order to seek out a broader range of recruits, including more graduates from four-year colleges (Couper, 1977).

Despite the many arguments against raising the minimum educational requirements for police for police recruits, a sizable minority (41 percent) of the police executives of agencies serving communities of 17,000 or more people in 1975 favored requiring some college. Moreover, 20 percent of the chiefs in those communities anticipated that the minimum educational standard in their agencies would rise within the following two years (National Planning Association, 1976, pp. II-174-175), although it is most doubtful that their predictions were correct. The chiefs' responses might be treated as evidence that many police executives want to use higher education as a resource for change. Nonetheless, the majority remain opposed to any college requirements for recruits.

The matter of educational requirements is only one aspect of the much larger question of how to recruit and select the people most fit for performing and changing police tasks. There is a great need to move toward evaluating individuals rather than credentials, through such methods as assessment centers (Reinke, 1977), and for designing selection procedures that are free from bias and that will make police personnel more representative of the communities they serve. If a college education is of sufficient quality, its impact should be evident in the assessment of individuals by appropriate police selection. Until such procedures are implemented, however, there seems little chance that police departments will seek to hire officers with a critical and sophisticated understanding of police work (compare Gray, 1975). In the short run, the only way to increase the proportion of officers shaped by a four-year, full-time residential education may be to impose the four-year college requirement on all police recruits.

The call for a four-year degree requirement for police recruits may appear to be pointless in the face of the growing national taxpayer revolt against local government (Clymer, 1978), best demonstrated by the recent vote to cut all property taxes in the state of California. Where police officers are being laid off in order to balance constricted budgets, the idea of higher qualifications might be rejected by city and county administrators as a "frill," or at best something that might lead to higher, unaffordable salaries for police officers. But precisely because there may be no new hirings in many jurisdictions for some years, now is the time to introduce higher entry level educational requirements. Given the currently favorable salary levels in many metropolitan area police departments (compared to most other entry level salaries for which college graduates compete), there should be no difficulty in attracting college graduates to apply for police positions without any increase in police salaries.

Salaries and Promotions. It is no accident that some of those who are most opposed to entry-level college requirements are strong supporters of policies encouraging police officers to go to college once they have been hired. Chief Jerry Wilson (1975), for example, couples his strong opposition to college entry requirements with support for the ideas of granting extra pay to educated police officers, giving extra points on promotional examinations for college credits earned, and providing tuition support for officers enrolled in college courses. Wilson's views reflect widespread practices in police departments, in which low minimum entry requirements are coupled with a variety of incentives for officers to attend college. Commission consultant Elinor Ostrom (1978), in her sampling of 150 police departments in medium-sized metropolitan areas, found that only 7 percent of them required education beyond high school for entry but that 20 percent of them required more than a high school education for promotion to supervisory levels. Moreover, well over half of them (61 percent) offered some kind of financial support or salary differential for officers pursuing a college education. In commission consultant Richard Schick's (1978) smaller but more representative sample of police departments, almost 80 percent of the departments offered either promotional preferences or financial incentives.

This pattern is consistent with the principle of educating the recruited rather than recruiting the educated. The consequence of the pattern is to minimize the impact of higher education as both a source of criticism and a resource for change. As we have already argued, the postentry educational experience is generally of poorer quality than most preservice education because postentry studies are mediated by more intense involvement in police work than in student life, limiting the impact of new ideas and perspectives gained from education.

Not all educational salary incentives necessarily have this impact. Salary differentials for officers with B.A. degrees can take effect immediately upon hiring and may therefore serve to attract (but not to help select) preservice college graduates, even though, as we have argued, present salary levels are high enough to attract college graduates in many departments. But salary differentials based on the number of college credits earned are clearly the most blatant kind of credentialism, implying that each additional course taken improves police performance by an equal amount. As we observed in Chapter Six, such a mechanistic assumption fails to recognize the wide variation in educational impact from one course to the next.

Police policies supporting in-service educational experiences, particularly educational leaves of absence, could be an excellent means for developing lifelong learning in the police institution. They cannot, however, serve as a substitute for pre-service education. By tying education mechanically to promotional credits and salary increments, in-service educational incentives can turn college into a cynical game, in which the student's only motivation is financial. As W. L. Penhollow, director of the Riley County, Kansas, Police Department, wrote the commission about his department's educational incentive plans: "I feel the emphasis is usually on the dollar rather than education among those attending classes."

It would be far better to base salaries and promotions on careful assessments of job performance (Landy, 1977), in which the impact of a serious pursuit of a college education should be evident. Automatic granting of educational preferences is merely an extension of the present mindless approach of most police civil service systems. A sophisticated and reliable personnel evaluation system can reward educational attainment in a way that distinguishes those who have learned from those who have merely done their time in the classroom. Rather than rewarding education, though, many police departments seem to punish it, or at least some of the behavior that education encourages.

Punishing Education. Until very recently college-educated officers, especially those who were educated before joining a police department, were quite rare in American police departments. Their education often marked them out for special treatment by both their peers and their supervisors. Some of them tried to hide their education, in order to blend in with the police subculture. Others became iconoclasts, either out of preference or in reaction to the scornful treatment that they and the other "college boys" received. The often negative reaction to their education may be one of the reasons why college-educated police officers, according to at least two studies (Levy, 1967; Cohen and Chaiken, 1972), were more likely to quit police work early in the 1960s. The problem of keeping college graduates once they have been hired has received extensive attention in the police literature (Pomrenke, 1966; Schrotel, 1966; Beckman, 1974), but its causes remain unclear. In the absence of evidence that educated officers leave for other reasons (for example, higher pay in other jobs), it is reasonable to suspect that some of them leave because they are being punished for their education.

However frequent the punishing of education was in the 1960s, it is probably less frequent today. More officers have attended college, so that education is no longer confined to the marginal few. More important may be the increased levels of education among police supervisors (Table 19). The many

Table 19. Educational Levels of All Sworn Law Enforcement Personnel in the U.S., by Rank Level, 1974

Rank	All Educational Levels	Less Than High School Graduate	High School Graduate	College Attainment		
				All Levels	1-3 Years	4 Years or More
Line patrol	100%	8.4%	45.0%	46.8%	39.6%	7.2%
Line investigation	100	4.1	36.1	59.7	44.6	15.1
Supervision	100	5.5	35.3	59.2	49.0	10.2
Management	100	15.7	42.0	42.3	31.0	11.3

Note: Detail may not add to totals due to rounding.
Source: National Planning Association, 1976, p. II-153.

stories about college graduate patrol officers supervised by high school dropout sergeants now appear to be more often myth than fact: supervisors are now more likely than line patrol officers to have attended college and to have graduated. Nonetheless, there is still some evidence that supervisors punish their subordinates for education. One study of the Dallas Police Department, for example, reportedly found that the most highly educated officers received the lowest performance ratings from their supervisors (Gottlieb and Baker, 1974; cited in Goldstein, 1977). And in a recent survey in Saint Louis, educated officers were much more likely to express a negative opinion of their supervisors (Watts, 1978). In a related study, McAllister (1970) found that the more intelligent an officer was, the lower his performance was rated by supervisors.

Another indicator of how police departments treat their educated officers is the rate at which they are promoted. Most police departments take some form of subjective evaluation into account in making promotional decisions (in addition to examination scores), which should reflect their views of educated officers. By this measure, it does not seem that police departments discriminate against educated officers. One study found that educated officers in one city were more likely to be promoted (Weiner, 1974), but a more sophisticated study in New York City found that the apparently positive effect of education on promotions there disappeared when other relevant factors were held constant (Cohen and Chaiken, 1972). A similar study in Saint Louis found almost no difference between educated and uneducated officers in their speed of promotion (Watts, 1978).

Ultimately, perhaps, the treatment of educated police officers may depend on the attitudes of top police managers. Given the fact that managers are the least likely of any rank level to have completed at least one year of college (Table 19), it is not surprising that they are often skeptical of the value of higher education. As one former police manager points out, "Many police administrators who haven't been to college feel threatened by those who do attain the education" (Spreen, 1977, p. 21).

Not all chiefs feel threatened by educated subordinates, however. The attitudes of police executives toward higher education appear to be fairly evenly split. In a 1975 survey of police chiefs serving cities of 17,000 or more people, 40 percent of those responding said that they thought college-educated police were superior officers, while 13 percent held the opposite view; 35 percent said they thought there was no difference between college-educated officers and officers who did not attend college, and 12 percent said they didn't know whether there was a difference (National Planning Association, 1976, p. II-138). Those chiefs who were the least educated were the least likely to rate educated officers as superior: 29 percent of the 279 high school-educated chiefs and 74 percent of the 177 chiefs with graduate degrees rated their college-educated police officers as superior (p. II-139). Older chiefs were also less likely to view educated officers more favorably: only 33 percent of the chiefs in their 60s, compared with 63 percent of the chiefs in their 30s, rated their educated police officers as superior.

As the older chiefs with less education are replaced by

younger chiefs with more education, then, educated officers
may receive better treatment, or at least become less likely to
be punished for their education. An educated management
corps is probably a necessary condition for education to be used
as a resource for change. Time alone should create this condition, if present trends continue. But a number of serious barriers to change will still remain.

Barriers to Change

No matter how many educated officers apply for police
jobs, and no matter how many educated officers become
police chiefs, police education cannot be fully developed as a
resource for change until two major barriers are removed: civil
service law and police union opposition. Civil service law often
prevents departments from making any alteration in police
selection criteria, task assignments, or organizational structures.
Police unions generally stand opposed to any policies that make
distinctions among line officers. Both barriers prevent police
executives from using education to have the police undertake
new tasks and perform old tasks better.

Strict civil service laws are often imposed on local police
departments by state legislatures to prevent political patronage
or corruption in police selection and promotion. In recent years
state commissions on law enforcement training and education
have imposed minimum standards for all officers. The effects of
these legally imposed constraints on police personnel procedures have been two-edged. In some states police departments
have been prevented from imposing college requirements for
recruits; in other states police departments have been forced to
adopt such requirements. The same contrast is found with
salary incentives. When these laws do foster education, they
often specify a limited number of major fields which qualify for
incentives or requirements, or they limit education even further
to police science or criminal justice. No matter what the requirements may be, however, they tend to be extremely rigid
and difficult to change.

The most serious barrier posed by civil service law is the

nearly exclusive reliance it usually places on examinations as the means of selecting police recruits. Most examinations appear to be completely unable to predict police performance, and many have been invalidated by the courts as racially discriminatory (see, for example, *Afro-American Patrolmens League* v. *Duck,* 503 F.2d 294 [6th Cir. 1974]). Doing well on these examinations is often more a matter of luck than of ability. Given the intense competition for the few police openings in recent years, many able college graduates have been kept out of police work by a margin of only a few points on the examination.

Attempts to change civil service laws to allow greater flexibility are often opposed by powerful police labor organizations. Even apart from the laws, the unions pose a strong barrier at the bargaining table to most innovations proposed by police management. Edward Kiernan, the president of the largest police labor organization in the country, the International Conference of Police Associations, has argued that the union position on education is not necessarily negative and that some unions have supported educational incentives even when the police chiefs were opposed to them (Kiernan, 1977). However, Kiernan expressed opposition to almost every one of the proposals of the American Bar Association (1973) for eliminating the barriers to more effective use of college graduates in police work: realignment of duties and responsibilities, lateral movement of officers among police agencies, and changes in the criteria used for rewarding and promoting police personnel.

Police unions are also generally opposed to one of the most promising organizational concepts for making better use of education in police work—the position of master police officer or master neighborhood officer. The master officer rank would be awarded only to those who have demonstrated their superior ability at all phases of police work (Murphy and Plate, 1977) and would be compensated by a salary equal to that of the first-line supervisors. Like the rank of full professor, the master officer rank rewards achievement without removing people from the work they are doing well. Unlike sergeants, master officers would continue to take primary responsibility for providing police services in their area. With sufficient gradations and provisions for merit increases, stratification of line police work on the basis of performance could help reduce the "twenty-year-loser" syndrome common to older officers who are not promoted to supervisory rank.

Like many college faculty unions, however, police unions argue that such "merit" distinctions merely work to the advantage of administrative control, dividing the loyalties of their membership. The police unions have generally opposed the master officer concept on these grounds, arguing that any extra money should be divided equally among all officers, regardless of the administration's assessment of their performance. Given the same attitudes among both police and professors, it seems doubtful that hiring more educated police officers would change the police union's position on this issue.

Recommendations

Although we acknowledge that "the value of college training [for police] is still largely a matter of conjecture" (J. Q. Wilson, 1975, p. 113), we believe that more and better higher education may help change policing in the directions we have suggested. Yet current police department policies and practices have limited the effects of education as either a resource for change or a source of beneficial disruption. The two major elements of the strategy for defusing education as an agent of change are the emphasis on postentry education and the maintenance of traditional organizational designs. The first step in making education more effective should be to end these practices:

> 7-1 Police departments should place less emphasis on educating the recruited and more emphasis on recruiting the educated. The organization, policies, and practices of police departments should be modified to make better use of educated personnel.

Our recommendation implies the chicken-and-egg dilemma of educating the police for change: which comes first, more educated police officers or organizational designs that will make police work more attractive to better-educated people? College graduates who join police departments may be more likely to quit early, possibly out of dislike for the existing police organizational designs and practices. Yet attempts to convert to new organizational designs while the majority of police officers are still not college graduates could fail because the nongraduates might lack the initiative and imagination necessary to make the new designs work. The only way to resolve the dilemma is to undertake both sides of it at the same time. Any movement toward new organizational designs, however, should be attempted only with careful evaluation of their consequences, since very little is known about the kinds of designs that would make fullest use of an educated police service:

> 7-2 *Police departments should conduct properly evaluated experiments with new organizational designs more appropriate for college-educated personnel.*

In order to add both symbolic and practical support to attempts to redesign police departments as educated organizations, a college-degree entrance requirement should be imposed immediately. The requirement will help to define police work as a complex job requiring college-level intelligence. It will also increase the number of educated officers whose education was not filtered by the occupational perspective of full-time police work, people who may be more critical and challenging of accepted practices. Ample numbers of qualified college graduates will be available to fill the openings in most police agencies for the foreseeable future. The fact that large numbers of minorities are now enrolled in college or have recently graduated from college means that a degree requirement would not necessarily obstruct efforts to increase minority representation in police departments. With aggressive programs for identifying qualified minority college graduates and encouraging them to apply to police agencies, the degree requirement can be compatible with Affirmative Action goals. The one step that should be avoided, however, is a compromise requirement that new

officers have completed *two* years of college. A two-year requirement might define police work as paraprofessional, making
it even less attractive to college graduates, perhaps, than a high
school requirement. A two-year requirement would also yield
more graduates of the presently narrow vocational training curriculums in the community colleges, and fewer people with
broader educations:

> 7-3 *All police departments should move now to re-
> quire new recruits to have earned a bacca-
> laureate degree and no police department
> should require two years of college as the
> minimum qualification for police recruits.
> Vigorous recruitment of qualified minority-
> group members should be undertaken in order
> to alleviate any possible exclusionary impact
> of this requirement upon minorities.*

The purpose of requiring a college degree should be to
increase the chances that police recruits will have the personal
qualities needed to help create a new police role. The specific
content of their college education is of lesser importance. Policing can benefit from people educated in a wide range of disciplines, and any attempt to restrict police recruits to graduates
of specialized police education programs would exclude large
numbers of capable college graduates from other fields:

> 7-4 *No major field of study should be specified in
> any college-degree requirements for police
> positions.*

Given the present relatively low turnover rates in most
police departments, the college-degree entrance requirement is
not likely to produce an immediate substantial increase in the
general educational levels of police personnel. In-service education must continue in order to make most police officers college
graduates at any time in the near future. Police department policies should continue to support in-service education, but in a
way that encourages meaningful learning experiences rather

than merely "doing time" in the classroom. One way of making the motivation to attend college somewhat more conducive to learning is to remove the present policies of awarding salary incentives on the basis of credit hours completed. Salary incentives and other rewards should be based on the completion of a well-rounded program of study, and not on the accumulation of credits:

> *7-5 No police salary increments should be awarded*
> *on a credit-by-credit basis.*

Another way of improving the quality of in-service education is to foster complete immersion in education through one-year leaves of absence. While a previous recommendation on this point (6-3) was directed to funding agencies, the idea of one-year fellowships requires the support of police departments as well. While some departments now grant leaves of absence with pay, others are reluctant to let their officers take educational leaves even without pay. There are certain complications involved in granting leaves, particularly in smaller departments, but the long-term benefits probably outweigh any short-term complications:

> *7-6 Police departments should regularly grant and*
> *encourage educational leaves of absence.*

These recommendations may not eliminate the current police strategy of defusing education as an agent of change, but they should at least weaken that strategy. And once police departments become more receptive to education as a resource for change, the quality of police education will become even more important.

8

Changing
Police Education

*Plato's classic scheme of folly, which would
have the philosophers take over the
management of affairs, has been turned on its
head; the men of affairs have taken over the
direction of the pursuit of knowledge.*
                    Veblen, [1918] 1957, pp. 77-78

In order to change the police through higher education, police
education must itself be changed. Changing police education
will depend on the actions of a number of major institutions, as
well as on the collective actions of many individuals. For, as
Veblen has observed, education is no longer the exclusive prov-
ince of the educators. Students, police departments, accreditation authorities, state government, the federal government, faculty members, and college administrators—all exert some degree
of control over the content and quality of higher education for
police careers. This chapter shows how those actors form the
structure of control over police education, making them the
audience for the commission's recommendations about how
police education can be changed.

Not all higher education for the police, of course, needs
to be changed. The education that present and future police
officers now receive in most traditional arts and science pro-

grams is probably quite valuable. Many criminal justice programs taught from either a liberal or a professional perspective are also quite sound. The major concern of this chapter is with changing police education programs that have the following characteristics:

- The implied objective of maintaining the status quo in policing
- A curriculum emphasizing technical police tasks, to the exclusion of moral and conceptual issues
- A faculty lacking adequate postgraduate education
- Student experiences that are primarily part time and nonresidential

None of these characteristics are easily changed. Changing a curriculum, for example, has been described as "harder than moving a graveyard" (Bragdon, 1967; quoted in Rudolph, 1977, p. 3). Most of these same characteristics, however, were present in the early stages of higher education programs for other occupations and were successfully changed through the combined actions of national study groups, funding sources, and formal associations of educators (Cheit, 1975). The goal of this chapter is to design a similar blueprint for change in police education.

Diverse Patterns of Control

Changing police education programs will require different strategies for different kinds of colleges. Like the general structures of control in higher education, the control of police education seems to vary systematically among different types of higher education institutions. These diverse patterns of control are described by Baldridge and his associates (1978, p. 11) in their survey of a nationally representative sample of 300 institutions: "The farther we progress [across eight distinct types of institutions] from community colleges to public colleges to elite liberal arts colleges to multiversities, (1) the more the faculty are influential, (2) the less the administrators dominate, (3) the less the environmental influences affect the institution's autonomy, and (4) the less likely it is that unions will be elected." The same study found that, although students are not directly involved in policymaking (except at elite institutions), campus power is shifting to areas of new strength according to shifting student enrollment.

These findings suggest some patterns in the control of police education. Almost half of all police education programs are located in public community colleges (see Table 10). The rest are scattered among private junior colleges, public colleges, public comprehensive colleges, and private liberal arts colleges, with virtually none in the multiversities or the elite liberal arts colleges. Judging from the study by Baldridge and others, we would expect that the control of police education is generally characterized by weak faculty and strong academic administrators, heavy environmental influences limiting program autonomy, and great sensitivity to changes in enrollment levels. For the most part, our scattered evidence on the control of police education supports these hypotheses, with some very clear differences between programs in public community colleges and in other types of institutions. These patterns of control show the points of leverage at which police education may be changed.

Faculty

The faculty in police education programs often exercise little control over police education, although their influence varies among different kinds of colleges. Those faculty members who have suffered the most criticism in this report are probably the least to blame for the poor quality of police education. Unlike faculty members in elite institutions, many faculty in police education programs have little control over what courses they teach or how they are taught. In the study by Baldridge and others (1978, p. 115), over half (52 percent) of the faculty in public community colleges reported that they have little control over the courses they teach, as did over one third (34 percent) of the faculty in the public and public comprehensive colleges. This pattern is confirmed for police education programs by a number of statements to the commission indicating that detailed outlines of each lecture (much like police academy "lesson plans") must be approved by college administrators before each term begins.

Faculty control in police education programs, in fact, is probably even weaker than faculty control in other programs on the same campuses. The heavy and often exclusive use of part-time faculty in police education means that the faculty are rarely ōn campus when they are not teaching and that they rarely participate in committees and other structures of governance. Their part-time status also means that they are untenured, giving them a very weak bargaining position. If they make any trouble, they can easily be let go at the end of their one-term or one-year contracts.

The detailed case study of faculty power in police education mentioned earlier (Fry and Miller, 1976) illustrates their frequent lack of autonomy. When a small, nearly bankrupt liberal arts college initiated a police education program in 1972 in order to attract students eligible to receive LEEP funds, the college hired several new faculty members with backgrounds in law enforcement, who proceeded to offer a fairly technical curriculum with the approval of the dean. When a new dean was hired in 1973, he attempted to make the police education program more academic and decided that the faculty members were underqualified. As soon as the new dean discovered that he could still obtain LEEP funds for the college while converting the "Administration of Justice" program (with ex-police faculty) into a "Public Administration" program (with traditional, tenured faculty), he fired the part-time police education faculty.

Faculty control clearly varies by type of institution, however, at least in regard to the content of the curriculum. The commission's study of books used in courses on the police revealed a sharp contrast in faculty influence between two-year and four-year colleges. The average educational level of the faculty varied widely in both kinds of colleges and was highly correlated with the conceptual level of the books when two-year and four-year schools were lumped together. Our interpretation of this finding was that the faculty were influencing book selection and that the better-educated faculties selected the more conceptual books. But when the two-year colleges were examined separately, there was no correlation between the faculty educational level and the conceptual level of the books (while at the four-year level the correlation was even stronger under separate examination). It is reasonable to conclude, then, that the faculty in the four-year programs have a great deal more control over the books they assign than their colleagues in the two-year programs.

In order to seek greater control over police education, many faculty members have fought to obtain separate departmental or school status for their programs, instead of being housed in departments of sociology, political science, public administration, or other traditional departments. Obtaining separate departmental and disciplinary status has been described as the most pressing problem facing criminal justice education (Adams, 1976; but see Olson, 1978). There is little question that separate departments would provide greater faculty power in almost any type of institution (McHenry and others, 1977). The danger is that greater faculty autonomy in separate departments may allow some of the more vocationally oriented programs to continue their present curriculums. Even in the four-year programs, faculty influence does not guarantee a more conceptual curriculum; it only allows the strength or the weakness of the faculty to shine through more clearly.

Academic Administrators

The weakness of the faculty in police education programs is generally matched by the strength of the academic administrators. In the community colleges and public four-year colleges, where police education programs are most often found, it is usually the deans who hire, evaluate, promote, or terminate the faculty, as well as deciding what courses the faculty must teach (Baldridge and others, 1978). This pattern contrasts sharply with the collegial model of governance found in the liberal arts colleges and multiversities, where the faculty of each department collectively make the initial decision on most personnel and academic matters, with the deans generally limited to veto power and control over the budget. The principles of professional autonomy and of faculty expertise as the basis for decision making—the result of the "academic revolution" which during the post-World War II years gave greater power to faculty than they had ever enjoyed in the history of American higher education (Jencks and Riesman, 1968)—do not seem to have taken hold in the sector of higher education where police education is generally found.

The fact that the academic administrators make the key decisions does not necessarily mean that they should be held responsible for the quality of police education. Like the faculty they control, the administrators in many of these colleges have relatively little autonomy in choosing the policies that guide their day-to-day decisions. The colleges they administer tend to be extremely subject to external pressures, which largely determine the kinds of decisions they make. This pattern is particularly evident in the community colleges, about which Clark (1960b, p. 175) has observed: "Institutional leadership is minimized, and direction by context [is] maximized. Along a continuum of organizational power in environmental relations, ranging from the organization that dominates its environmental relations to one completely dominated by its environment, the public junior college tends strongly toward the latter extreme." For those who believe that community colleges should be responsive to local demands, however, this statement merely indicates that these colleges are doing their job.

The environmental constraints on academic administrators may not be absolute. We suspect, in fact, that many college deans could be much bolder in their defense of academic quality without losing their jobs. Yet the deans supervising the police education programs in many colleges might not last very long if they ignored two major sources of environmental pressure: the financial pressures for high enrollments and the political pressures for providing the kind of program the local police agencies demand.

Student Enrollments

To a large extent, students in police education programs seem to get the kind of education they want. The phrase "student power to control the curriculum," of course, has taken on new meaning in the current state of academic affairs. Where students once marched in an attempt to influence both academic and nonacademic policies, they now vote with their registration cards to determine quite effectively which academic programs will wither away and which will flourish and grow. The general disappearance of required courses (Carnegie Foundation, 1977) has left many academic departments to the mercy of their "FTEs" (full-time-equivalent students), the academic term for enrollment levels. Police education programs have prospered under this new form of student power, as have most occupational education programs. But the kind of program the students seem to want is quite different from the kind of program we think they need.

The limited evidence we have suggests that many police education students prefer to enroll in programs where the curriculum emphasizes skills training, the faculty have extensive law enforcement experience (and little graduate education), and the amount of time spent on campus is minimal. In the Fry and Miller (1976) study of a small liberal arts college, for example, the part-time, in-service students actively protested the new dean's attempts to change those aspects of the police education program. In statements at the commission's public forums, several students stressed that the more vocationally oriented courses would help them pass the entrance and promotional examinations in police departments. And in the commission's study of books used in police education programs, there was a strong inverse correlation between the proportion of students who were oriented to police careers (in-service plus preservice students divided by total program students) and the conceptual level of the books: the more "careerist" the student body, the less conceptual the books.

The student power of enrollment levels seems to be particularly strong wherever several colleges offer police education programs in the same metropolitan area. In the New York area, for example, many students who had been enrolled at John Jay College transferred to the New York Institute of Technology when it opened its College Accelerated Program for Police. As the president of NYIT puts it, John Jay "was almost wiped out by our successful program" (see D. C. Anderson, 1978, pp. 35-36). The enrollment in the NYIT program at one time was almost 12,000 students (compared to John Jay's high of 9,000), many of whom seemed to be attracted by the convenient locations of the program in off-campus settings close to their workplace or home. While comparative judgments of the quality of the teaching and the content of the curriculum at John Jay and NYIT are difficult to make, there is no question that the NYIT program required the students to spend much less time on campus. Similar patterns of interinstitutional competition for students shaping the nature of police education programs can be found in other metropolitan areas.

Even where there is no direct competition, concern for student enrollment levels may lead college administrators to develop the kind of police education program we recommend against. The administrators may fear that students will drop out of college altogether if they are not offered a program they feel comfortable with. And since, as we have noted, enrollment levels have been important enough financially for some colleges to falsify in order to maintain their level of state aid (Goll, 1977), the student power of enrollments seems to be very strong indeed.

Police Departments

Wherever in-service students constitute a large proportion of the student body in a police education program, the police departments for which they work can also exert considerable influence on the quality of the program. The power of police departments to shape police education goes beyond the indirect effects of the departmental policies discussed in Chapter Seven. Just as some proponents of the career education movement have advocated (Harris and Grede, 1977), many college programs for police have become "handmaidens" to their local police agencies, allowing police officials a great deal of direct operational control over the program. This pattern is far more common in two-year programs than in four-year programs, at least according to the National Planning Association's survey. At the two-year level, the survey found that some programs "become wholly owned subsidiaries of a police agency" (National Planning Association, 1976, p. V-57).

At the University of Cincinnati, for example, an associate degree program in law enforcement technology was created in the 1960s at the request of high-ranking officials in the Cincinnati Police Division (Carte, 1978). The courses offered in the program reflected the police agency's preference for practical subjects, including Traffic Control, Records, and Weapons Resources. The instructors in the college program were all full-time police officers who were hired by the university as part-time faculty. Until quite recently, the chief of police "informed" the dean who the instructors would be and which courses they would teach. While this arrangement neatly fits the proposal for a "marriage" between colleges and employers (Harris and Grede, 1977, p. 296), it does not seem to be a marriage in which both partners are equal. Rather, it fits the proposal to give employers the dominant role in controlling career education (Markland, 1977).

This pattern of co-optation, of course, can be found in many kinds of organizations. Philip Selznick, who discovered the pattern in his classic study of the Tennessee Valley Authority, defines co-optation as "the process of absorbing new elements into the leadership or policy-determining structure of an organization as a means of averting threats to its stability or existence" (Selznick, 1949, p. 13). For locally funded colleges heavily dependent on community political support, or for programs depending heavily on in-service enrollments, the displeasure of an organization as important as the police department could pose a significant threat to the stability of the college. By absorbing the police into the college decision-making process, the college averts the potential threat of police criticism of the college—either for failing to provide a police education program or for providing one that does not meet with the approval of the local police.

Not all colleges offering police education programs, of course, co-opt the local police agencies. As Donald Newman has observed (1974, p. 23), "Criminal justice programs tend to fall somewhere along a continuum from agency pandering to overt hostility." The place of each program on this continuum is probably determined by the degree to which the college depends on local support for maintaining its vital institutional resources, such as students and funding (Baldridge and others, 1978). The positions may therefore change as the colleges' degree of dependency changes. One New York City police official, for example, suggested that John Jay College has been far more active in seeking out suggestions and advice from local police departments ever since the college was almost abolished during New York City's financial crisis. With a high level of federally funded research and other financial support, however, John Jay has been able to maintain much more independence from local criminal justice agencies than many community colleges, which depend almost entirely on local support.

Police agency control of police education programs is often formalized in the programs' advisory committees. Guidebooks for community college advisory committees, in fact, are quite explicit in recommending that these committees be given a powerful role (Rindeau, 1967). One guide suggests that the committee be responsible for "developing curricula based on actual industrial needs, keeping content current, formulating new policies, and providing overall direction and continuing evaluation," as well as recommending qualified instructors (Stinchcomb, 1975, pp. 10-11). In exchange for this formal grant of power, the college should expect the committee to support the police education program by "maintaining contact with the community, soliciting program support, strengthening relationships between police and local resources, encouraging students to enter the program, and generally promoting the program's merits" (Stinchcomb, 1975, p. 10).

One study of the advisory committees found that they were composed almost exclusively of law enforcement professionals (Tenney, 1971), just as the guidebook (Stinchcomb, 1975) recommends. The study's author recommended that representatives of the public at large, as the consumers of law enforcement services, be appointed to the committees as well. But the presence of laymen would probably do little to alter the organizational power of local police departments to influence the program.

Accreditation Agencies

One proposed means of strengthening faculty control over police education and reducing administrative and external control is the use of *specialized* accreditation as a condition of program eligibility for receiving federal funds. This type of accreditation should not be confused with *institutional* accreditation, in which regional or national associations of colleges and universities regularly certify that each of their members has met certain minimum standards as an institution. Rather, specialized accreditation authorities are national groups of educators (or educators and practitioners) who certify that specialized college programs in their occupational field provide an adequate exposure to the major areas of knowledge used in that field as one aspect of preparation for performing the work of the occupation (Selden, 1976). Some examples are the American Assembly of Collegiate Schools of Business, the Society of American Foresters, and the American Library Association. By establishing specific requirements for program objectives, curriculum, faculty qualifications, and student experiences, the specialized accreditation authorities have given their colleagues the extra leverage needed to win campus struggles over resources (Selden, 1960). And in recent years specialized accreditation has been bolstered by the initiative of the U.S. Office of Education in publishing a list of accrediting agencies it recognizes as reliable authority as to the quality of training provided by college programs, as one consideration in determining institutional eligibility to apply for federal funds (Orlans, 1975).

The growing concern over the quality of police education has led several groups of police educators to explore the possibility of establishing a specialized accreditation agency for criminal justice programs. The most active group in this effort is the Academy of Criminal Justice Sciences (ACJS). The 1975 president of the academy noted that the ACJS is seeking recognition as a specialized accreditation authority because of its disillusionment with institutional accreditation: "Naively, I had assumed for some time that institutional accreditation would assure some minimum level of standards in higher education, i.e., a 'floor' or underpinning of standards, to assure public and students alike that they had some guarantee about the overall quality of accredited institutions. We have seen enough in the past five years of LEEP, however, to convince us that institutional accrediting does no such a thing. It guarantees practically nothing in the criminal justice field" (Misner, 1975, p. 14). After obtaining the approval of its membership for a set of accreditation standards (Bassi and Rogers, 1976), the ACJS has moved rapidly to seek the recognition of both the private, voluntary Council on Postsecondary Accreditation (COPA—the federation of both institutional and specialized accrediting authorities) and the U.S. commissioner of education.

The history of specialized accreditation for professional education provides encouraging examples for police education. In the early part of this century, with the support of the Carnegie Foundation for the Advancement of Teaching or the Carnegie Corporation, the fields of architecture, dentistry, law, library science, medicine, music, nursing, social work, and teacher education reformed their professional education through the use of specialized accreditation (Selden, 1960). The early Carnegie reports leading to the establishment of specialized accreditation have been called "the most startling and epoch-making force for the improvement of professional education" (Brubacher and Rudy, 1958; quoted in Selden, 1960, p. 61), with the Flexner (1910) report on medical education the most famous example. It was not long, however, before the proliferating accrediting agencies were attacked by both the president of the American Council on Education and the chairman of the Joint Committee on Accrediting, an organizational forebear of COPA. At a historic 1939 American Council on Education conference on accrediting, both men attacked the "objectionable practices" of the accrediting agencies: destroying institutional freedom, restricting experimentation, employing outmoded standards, encouraging a trade unionist attitude, and assessing excessive costs (Selden, 1960).

   Obstacles to Recognition. At this point in the history of specialized accreditation, there are serious obstacles to the recognition of an accreditation agency for criminal justice programs by either the Council on Postsecondary Accreditation (COPA) or the U.S. Office of Education (OE). College administrators are still strongly opposed to the proliferation of specialized accrediting agencies, most often on the grounds of cost. The accreditation process requires site visits by outside study teams from other colleges, the cost of which must be borne by the college under review. In addition, some agencies require the colleges to pay rather expensive institutional membership fees. More costly, perhaps, is the price of complying with the standards for student/faculty ratios, library and laboratory resources, and so on. And in an era when higher education is becoming increasingly vulnerable to external regulation, college administrators are hardly eager to deal with additional regulators. Since acceptance of the accrediting agency by the colleges offering the programs to be accredited is a major condition of both COPA and OE recognition, the ACJS will probably find it very difficult to obtain recognition.

   Another major obstacle to the recognition of the ACJS as the accreditation agency for criminal justice programs is the competition of other professional associations. Most of the other groups, in fact, have a larger membership than the ACJS. The criminal justice section of the American Society of Public Administration (ASPA), for example, has around 1,000 members, while the ACJS has only around 700; the fact that ASPA allows nonfaculty members to join makes the comparison somewhat inappropriate, but the ACJS has also recently opened its doors to some criminal justice practitioners. Other practitioner groups, such as the Education and Training Section of the International Association of Chiefs of Police, have supported the ACJS efforts to establish specialized accreditation. Unlike the situation in other fields, there is little tension between the academics and the practitioners over who shall control any accreditation agency. Rather, the major conflict is among the diverse groups of academics.

The principal competitor of the ACJS is the 2,400-member American Society of Criminology (ASC), from which the ACJS seceded fifteen years ago (Morris, 1975). Founded in 1941 by August Vollmer as the National Association of College Police Training Officials, the ASC had evolved by the early 1960s into a multidisciplinary group dominated by university professors interested in research on crime. The more vocationally oriented professors, primarily from community colleges, split off from the ASC in 1966 to form the International Association of Police Professors, which later changed its name to the Academy of Criminal Justice Sciences. The ACJS still seems to be composed largely of community college instructors, whose interests lie more in teaching and practice than in research. There is considerable overlapping membership in the two organizations, but it is probably safe to say that the ASC membership is drawn more from the liberal arts and professional criminal justice programs than from the vocational ones, while the ACJS membership is drawn more from the vocational and professional programs than from the liberal arts curriculums.

It is not surprising, then, that the early discussions between the ACJS and the ASC about sharing the authority to accredit criminal justice courses were relatively unproductive. The ASC membership was and is probably split over the question of whether there should be any accreditation agency at all, and the only question the ASC executive committee seemed to consider was whether it should openly oppose the ACJS efforts. Some ASC members were concerned that the ACJS standards would be interpreted by college administrators as maximums or norms rather than bare minimums. ASC members from programs with low student/faculty ratios, for example, feared that the ACJS standard of 60:1 might be used as an argument for reducing the number of faculty members in their programs.

In response to a request by the Office of Criminal Justice Education and Training of LEAA (the current administrators of

LEEP), however, the ASC has agreed to cooperate with the ACJS in forming a Joint Commission on Criminology and Criminal Justice Education and Standards ("Joint Commission . . . Established," 1977-78). With a one-year LEAA grant of $175,000 awarded to the ACJS, the Joint Commission will conduct several research projects and workshops to develop minimum standards for postsecondary education programs in criminal justice and criminology ("ACJS Awarded Standards Development Grant," 1977), but there is no guarantee that the Joint Commission will pursue recognition as an accreditation authority. The ACJS is continuing to pursue its solo effort to gain recognition from COPA. Although there has been some discussion of a possible merger between the ACJS and the ASC, there is still no indication that the much larger ASC membership even favors the idea of accreditation. The Joint Commission also has an advisory committee composed of representatives of related organizations, but not all of these are eager for accreditation either. The Criminology Section of the American Sociological Association, for example, recently voted to instruct its representatives to express "reservations" about the establishment of accreditation procedures for criminal justice and criminology programs (Ward, 1978).

    Consequences of Accreditation. The creation of a specialized accreditation authority for criminal justice education would have at least two major consequences for police education. Perhaps the most important is that it would produce great pressure for a professional education curriculum, since one justification of special accreditation is helping to protect the public from incompetent professional practice (Selden, 1976). Moreover, the "profession" for which the curriculum educates would be criminal justice, not policing. There is considerable question about how much sense it makes to call police officers, judges, prison wardens, and court guards members of the same "profession," and even greater question about the degree to which criminal justice educators can assure the public that the graduates of their programs will be competent in all these fields. In any case, specialized professional accreditation might force many criminal justice programs currently taught as a liberal arts and science major to convert themselves into more practice-oriented professional schools.

A second consequence of the creation of a professional accreditation agency could be that LEEP funds would be restricted to college programs accredited by the agency. Under the current statutory language authorizing LEEP (the Omnibus Crime Control and Safe Streets Act of 1968), if the U.S. commissioner of education published the name of a specialized accrediting agency for programs in law enforcement and criminal justice in his list of national voluntary agencies or associations recognized "to be reliable authority as to the quality of training offered by an educational institution," and if the regulations for LEEP were amended to require programs to be accredited by the agency recognized by the Office of Education, then LEEP funds could be cut off from every college program that has not been accredited by the recognized agency (Seidman, 1975). The accrediting agency does not even have to be recognized by COPA in order for it to be recognized by the commissioner of education. If the ACJS eventually becomes recognized by the commissioner of education, there will be even greater pressure on the liberal arts programs in criminal justice to adopt a more professional emphasis.

At the same time, the recognition of the ACJS by the Office of Education as the accrediting authority for LEEP-funded police education programs may well be the only means of coercing college administrators and the police departments dominating the heavily vocational college programs into accepting more conceptual courses and better-educated faculty. Although accreditation is often described as a *voluntary* system, the term is no longer appropriate once it is used to determine eligibility for federal funds. If the OE determines that an accrediting agency is generally "accepted" by the institutions in its jurisdiction, then all institutions must accept the agency if its accreditation is required for participation in an aid program such as LEEP. Despite the limitations of the proposed ACJS accreditation standards discussed in previous chapters, the implementation of those standards would produce a substantial improvement in the general quality of police education. Given the heavy reliance on LEEP funds of many (though far from all) police education programs, there is no surer guarantee of their meeting the standards than the threat of losing those funds. Police education has much to gain from such a major shift in its structure of control. It may also have much to lose. Accreditation may impose a common denominator on police education programs, making the liberal programs more professional and the vocational programs more liberal.

State Governments

A variety of agencies in most state governments exercise some control over police education programs. The state legislatures, executive budget offices, and state university systems all exercise financial control over police education offered in public institutions. The decisions of these agencies, however, are made in the context of similar decisions about hundreds or thousands of other educational programs. Three other agencies seem to exercise much closer control over police education: state law enforcement training councils, education or higher education departments, and criminal justice planning agencies (Myren, 1978).

State law enforcement training councils vary widely from state to state in both their authority and the use to which it is put. In most states their primary responsibility is to set minimum standards for the selection and training of police officers. In a few states, notably Texas, California, and Florida (Myren, 1978), they have the authority to set educational standards for police officers. This authority includes the power to certify that specific educational institutions offer degree programs that provide sufficient preparation for appointment to police service. This certification procedure may be even more intrusive than accreditation, prescribing specific numbers of hours which students must take in particular courses. The overall thrust of these requirements seems to be toward a paraprofessional police education curriculum. Fortunately, the power of the training councils has been generally limited to two-year programs, and even in those states

there are ways for a liberal arts graduate to be appointed to a
police department.

State education departments or other agencies regulating
higher education also vary widely in their powers from one state
to the next, but in some states they are extremely powerful. In
New York, for example, the State Education Department requires that all new degree programs meet with its approval before they are implemented, and in recent years the department
has ordered a number of Ph.D. programs to close (although not
without a legal battle from the State University of New York).
The department failed, however, to take similar action against
the New York Institute of Technology's police education program when it was criticized by a departmental visitation team
for inadequate library and laboratory facilities, inadequate academic credentials of some faculty members, and insufficient
contact hours between the students and faculty for the number
of credit hours awarded (D. C. Anderson, 1978). Instead, the
department conducted a second evaluation visit and reaffirmed
the registration of the program. But while the New York State
Education Department has failed to use its great power to influence police education, the New Jersey State Higher Education
Department has adopted a set of guidelines and established an
advisory committee for approving new criminal justice programs; other states are moving in the same direction.

State criminal justice planning agencies (SPAs) were mandated by the Omnibus Crime Control and Safe Streets Act of
1968 as the agencies responsible for distributing the annual
block grants awarded to the states under the act. After LEAA
operations were decentralized to regions in 1971, SPAs in some
regions were given almost complete de facto authority to select
colleges for participation in LEEP and to determine how much
money each participating college would receive. The criteria for
these decisions varied widely among the states having this
power, from bureaucratic formulas to political logrolling. Some
SPAs imposed highly vocational curricular requirements on the
colleges, and at least one required that all faculty have law enforcement experience. Others apparently tried to encourage the
program characteristics we recommend in this report. Since the

regional offices of LEAA were abolished in 1977, the SPAs have lost their direct power over the allocation of LEEP funds, and the decisions have been centralized in Washington. But the SPAs have been invited to submit recommendations for the allocation of LEEP funds to the LEAA Office of Criminal Justice Education and Training (OCJET) (Foster, 1978). Given the limited resources at OCJET for monitoring the almost one thousand colleges participating in LEEP, the SPAs will probably continue to play an important, although less powerful, role in shaping the nature of police education programs.

Federal Government

Federal policies have been an important influence on police education programs for almost as long as they have been in existence. Like other areas of federal control, federal power over police education has been the power of the purse: provision of program funds only to those programs complying with federal preferences. Long before LEEP was created in 1968, this same principle was established in the second piece of federal legislation providing funds for vocational education, the George-Dean Act (49 Stat. 1488, 8 June 1936). As we mentioned before, to qualify for funds under this act, colleges in California at one time had to hire police education instructors who had at least several years' experience in police work (Myren, 1970, p. I-8). Even today California community college instructors in police technology programs whose salaries are supported by federal vocational education funds must have at least two years of criminal justice work experience.

The provisions of the vocational education program are often in sharp conflict with the requirements of LEEP, as a president of the Missouri Association of Criminal Justice Educators has pointed out (Baxter, 1977, p. 23): "We are supported to some extent by vocational education funds, and that's training, . . . and we've also got the LEEP program saying 'You're not supposed to be training, you're supposed to be involved in education.' " The problem is probably not extensive: in a survey of 125 community colleges receiving federal vocational education funds, only 30 were found to use those funds to support police education, and only 10 used both LEEP and vocational education funds simultaneously (Myren, Baridon, and Laskowski, 1978). Given the LEEP ban on training programs and the vocational education law's requirement that training be provided, it seems to be impossible for a police education program to be eligible for both federal programs at the same time. Neither of these programs, however, devotes extensive resources to ensuring compliance with its regulations, nor does the Veterans Administration's program of educational benefits, which may provide more federal money for police education than either of the other two programs (National Planning Association, 1976).

A program designed to provide loans to thousands of preservice students and grants to thousands of in-service students, LEEP has never been given sufficient resources for ensuring compliance with its regulations. The LEEP staff has been almost completely occupied with the monumental problems of accounting for the expenditure of up to $40 million a year in amounts of generally less than $1,000 (U.S. Comptroller General, 1975). The program's administration has often been chaotic: in 1971 nine LEEP staff processed 900 applications from colleges in three days (Twentieth Century Fund, 1976). The constant reorganizations of the politically troubled Law Enforcement Assistance Administration have shuffled LEEP from one program unit to the next. When LEAA operations were decentralized to regions in 1971, the regional offices were given the responsibility for monitoring the LEEP-participating colleges in their area—giving one official in each office the responsibility for almost one hundred colleges. The regional officials could scarcely visit each college once a year, let alone ensure that the programs were complying with the LEEP regulations. The recent abolition of the regional offices, however, has centralized monitoring at the LEAA Office of Criminal Justice Education and Training, which has undertaken a complete review of each college participating in LEEP.

However lax their enforcement, the LEEP regulations have had a substantial effect upon police education programs, if not always the effect that LEEP officials intended. In the first year of the program, for example, the regulations proscribed training courses but required most programs to offer fifteen hours of courses "directly related" to criminal justice. As commission consultant David Stanley (1978) points out, the effect of those regulations was to spawn even more training-type programs, probably because that was the only kind of course "directly related" to criminal justice that most colleges could quickly find faculty to teach. There have since been a number of major changes in the LEEP regulations regarding course content and other important academic issues, but many educators seemed to assume that LEEP-participating students had to be offered narrowly vocational courses (see, for example, Fry and Miller, 1976). At the very least, the police education program heads have found the continually changing objectives and regulations of LEEP vague and confusing.

Perhaps LEEP has exerted its most important influence on police education through its priorities for student eligibility. Although these priorities have also changed somewhat from year to year, they have consistently favored in-service police officers over preservice students, with the deleterious educational effects described in Chapter Six. Ironically, a key congressional sponsor of LEEP, Representative William Anderson, was at least as interested in supporting preservice students as he was in supporting in-service students, since his primary concern was with police recruitment efforts (National Planning Association, 1976). For the first five years of LEEP, its administrators instructed the colleges to award 80 percent of their LEEP funds to in-service students and 20 percent to preservice students. In 1973 LEEP officials adopted a new list of priorities, which had the effect of cutting off almost all funding of new preservice students, ostensibly because the number of applicants had grown too large for the available funds. Whatever the reason, it is clear that LEAA staff have made a number of major policy decisions affecting police education throughout the country, with virtually no public debate or congressional oversight.

Whereas most federal programs seem to have a member of Congress taking a special interest in them, LEEP appears to lack that kind of intense and continuing sponsorship. It is little wonder, then, that LEEP has been shunted from one part of LEAA to another. As of this writing, LEEP faces the prospect of still another move. The Office of Management and Budget's reorganization project has decided that LEEP should be moved to the proposed Department of Education as part of an effort to combine all educational loan programs in one agency, largely for reasons of administrative efficiency (Stack, 1978).

The divorce of LEEP from the Justice Department may have some long-term merit. It could foster a system of priorities based on student need rather than on current employment status. It could even lead to the use of other kinds of student loans to support police education, such as the $300-million-a-year National Direct Student Loan Program or the multibillion-dollar Guaranteed Student Loan Program, both of which make the $40 million a year for LEEP pale by comparison. But the change comes at a particularly inopportune time for LEEP. Having settled into its most recent home (OCJET) only in January 1976, LEEP has just begun to address the problems of educational quality described in this report. Moreover, the funds for such projects as the Joint Commission on Criminology and Criminal Justice Education and Standards come from a different statutory provision than LEEP, a program line that is not scheduled to be transferred to the new Department of Education. If the processes for setting priorities for LEEP funding and for spending the discretionary funds for the improvement of criminal justice education are split between two cabinet departments, it seems likely that neither process can be effective. And even if OCJET were transferred to the Department of Education in one piece, its special purpose of improving criminal justice might become subsidiary to administrative concerns in the delivery of federal student aid programs generally. The present concern for the quality of police education might be lost in the shakedown phase of a new cabinet department.

Summary: Control of Police Education

The control of police education is extremely complex, and no simple generalizations can apply to all police education programs. Each aspect of the programs has different determinants and will require different institutional actors to change it.

Objectives. The police education programs guided by the objective of maintaining the status quo in policing are probably heavily influenced by the preferences of local police agencies co-opted by the colleges offering the programs. The major countervailing force to this position could be the federal government, since the objective of LEEP is to *improve* law enforcement, not maintain its status quo. LEEP administrators have not pressed this objective, however, and there could be strong grass-roots pressure on Congress to keep them from doing so.

Curriculum. The police education programs stressing technical police tasks are firmly entrenched in this position by the support of their practice-oriented faculty, their career-oriented students, their enrollment-oriented administrators, and the local police agencies that use the program for what often serves as basic training. State governments often reinforce the pattern by requiring police officers to attend college programs with a technical curriculum. The two countervailing forces both remain to be effectively implemented: accreditation standards and LEEP guidelines banning training courses in programs leading to a college degree.

Faculty. The police education programs in which the faculty lack adequate graduate education are strongly supported in this position by students, who seem to prefer instructors with practical police experience, and by local police departments, whose active and retired personnel are hired as faculty members. The three countervailing forces to this position—the state education departments, accreditation standards, and the LEEP guidelines—have not been actively imposed on these programs.

Student Experiences. The police education programs in which the student experience is primarily part time and nonresidential are supported by the entire structure of American higher education, as well as by LEEP priorities favoring in-service students. There is no countervailing force now evident or even on the horizon, despite the growing evidence against such experiences (Astin, 1978). The only conceivable force for the addition of brief residential interludes to the present commuter experiences is the Congress, which would have to amend the authorizing legislation to allow LEEP funds to be used for that purpose.

The Private Sector: A Missing Influence

The review of the major influences on police education reveals a sharp contrast to most other areas of higher education: a virtually complete absence of private financial support. Neither private foundation grants nor alumni gifts have made more than the barest contribution to the improvement of police education. Medical, legal, business, and engineering education are all as good as they are today largely because of private support. The fact that police officers do not (or should not) accumulate substantial wealth and influence during the course of their careers may explain the absence of major alumni giving, but not the absence of foundation support. The massive amounts of LEEP funds may have discouraged foundation involvement in police education, but there are many things that LEEP cannot do under its present authorizing legislation, such as establishing chairs for distinguished scholars of policing, supporting named fellowships for police students on one-year leaves or longer, endowing libraries, and constructing laboratories and computer facilities. Although there have been a few exceptions, such as the Daniel and Florence Guggenheim Foundation, the Pinkerton Foundation, and the Ford Foundation (which indirectly underwrites the cost of this report), the general absence of the private sector has contributed to the emphasis on quantity at the expense of quality that characterizes police education.

Recommendations

The following recommendations are concerned more with means than with ends. They are intended to complement the substantive recommendations of the earlier chapters by specifying who should do what in order to make those recommendations into realistic possibilities for change. Some of the actors addressed by these recommendations are already doing the things we suggest, but most of them probably are not.

We believe that the essential condition of quality education is that the educational program be controlled by a well-educated faculty, whose judgments on educational matters are guided by their expertise. In our study of books used in police education programs, we found that well-educated faculty generally used highly conceptual books. We have already recommended that faculty education be upgraded. If that recommendation is followed, there should be little danger that faculty members given greater control over their programs will perpetuate the vocational training'curriculums. With a well-educated faculty, the control of police education should be safer in the hands of the educators than elsewhere:

> *8-1 Police education faculty members should seek more control over academic decisions in order to promote the objective of educating the police institution for change.*

College administrators have been reluctant to let police education faculty members make such academic decisions as course design and faculty selection, for a number of reasons. Many of them may have directed the faculty to provide a training curriculum out of responsiveness to requests from local police agencies. But if administrators wish to respond less to what is demanded and more to what is needed, they should take a more active stance in upgrading the academic quality of police education programs, implementing the recommendations offered in this report. Many of our recommendations may be opposed by local agency officials, and it is the college administrators who must deal with that opposition. We encourage deans and others not simply to submit to agency demands but, instead, to exercise leadership in developing police education:

> *8-2 College administrators should strengthen police education as a force for change, especially by protecting police education programs from the pressures of local agencies.*

These recommendations, of course, run against the current tide of higher education administration, in which the autonomy of both colleges and their faculty is being steadily eroded. The general decline in autonomy is the combined result of many different external sources of pressure. In the case of police education, however, there is one primary source of external pressure whose change in posture could reverse the decline in educational autonomy: local police departments. Ironically, while the police have long extolled the virtues of autonomy from outside pressure on their own organizations, they have failed to recognize the value of autonomy for police education programs. Although this lack of recognition may only reflect their definition of college programs as an extension of the police academy, this definition is precisely the problem with police education. Police officials can give much valuable advice to police education programs, but there is no more reason for them to make academic decisions than there is for professors to make operational decisions in a police department:

> 8-3 *Police officials and other members of police
> education program advisory boards should
> avoid direct participation in such academic de-
> cisions as faculty selection or promotion and
> curriculum content.*

Academic autonomy would be greatly strengthened by the creation of a specialized accreditation agency for criminal justice programs, as the ACJS has proposed. Accreditation by the ACJS would also improve the quality of many programs now in violation of the proposed ACJS accreditation standards. At the same time, the recognition of the ACJS as an accreditation authority would have several possible negative consequences: the endorsement of the concept of a nonexistent "profession" of criminal justice, pressure on liberal arts programs in criminal justice to adopt a more professionally oriented curriculum, and the possible use of the minimum standards as normative standards. Moreover, the membership of the ACJS is not broadly based enough to represent the full spectrum of criminal justice education. Any attempt to recognize an accreditation authority for police education programs should be approached cautiously and with the direct participation of a number of national organizations related to the programs:

> *8-4 Accreditation of criminal justice programs should be explored as a possible strategy for changing police education, but neither the U.S. commissioner of education nor the Council on Postsecondary Accreditation should recognize any single organization as the accrediting authority for higher education programs in criminal justice. A more broadly based consortium, such as the Joint Commission on Criminology and Criminal Justice Education and Standards and the organizational members of its advisory group, is required to ensure that diverse curricular approaches are maintained.*

The role of state government in changing police education is potentially very great, although little has been done to realize that potential. Where they have been granted the power to review higher education programs, state education agencies can play a much more active role in improving the quality of police education. If they avoid issues of substance and concentrate on issues of resources, their role can be strong without intruding on the autonomy of faculty decision making in academic matters. They could, for example, force colleges to improve their library resources, reduce their student/faculty ratios, and exercise more rigorous standards for granting academic credit in the police education programs.

Another type of state agency, however, should reduce its role in controlling police education. We believe that police education programs should provide education and not training. It is therefore inappropriate for state law enforcement training councils to act almost like collegiate accrediting agencies. There is a great potential for conflict between the standards established by these councils and the standards established by LEEP and potential academic accrediting agencies. The net effect of the role of these councils may be to prevent police education from becoming more conceptual and less vocational:

> *8-5 State education agencies, and not state law enforcement training councils, should ensure that colleges provide their police education programs with adequate resources and otherwise guarantee their quality.*

Changes are also needed in two federal programs: LEEP and the vocational education program. The distribution of LEEP funds, in particular, should be used more strategically to influence the content and standards of the college programs that LEEP supports. The priorities for student participation in LEEP, addressed in previous chapters, will mean little unless the priorities for program participation are altered as well:

> *8-6 State and federal agencies influencing the distribution of LEEP funds should give lowest priority to narrowly technical police education programs and highest priority to programs with a broader curriculum and better-educated faculty.*

The future status of LEEP is clouded by the proposal to transfer it from the Justice Department to the new Department of Education. Divorcing LEEP from the other programs administered by the Office of Criminal Justice Education and Training (OCJET) would greatly hinder the current efforts to improve the quality of the education now supported by LEEP. Even moving OCJET intact to the new Department of Education would be unsatisfactory, for OCJET's potential concern with educating the police for change could become secondary to the Education Department's concern with the administration of student loan programs generally. One Justice Department budget analyst (see D. C. Anderson, 1978) has argued that police education has not been shown to reduce crime and should therefore be labeled an educational program rather than a crime-fighting program appropriate for the Justice Department; by this same reasoning, however, one could transfer the entire Justice Department to other agencies, since neither the FBI nor the Criminal Division nor the Drug Enforcement Administration, let alone police education, has been shown to reduce crime. But police education will never be able to change the police unless its quality is improved, and that is unlikely to happen as long as LEEP is shuttled from one organizational home to the next on an almost annual basis:

> 8-7 *Congress should keep the current programs of the Law Enforcement Assistance Administration's Office of Criminal Justice Education and Training intact under one administrative unit at the Department of Justice.*

The federal vocational education program, which may have been largely responsible for the vocational character of many early police education programs, should be revised to reflect the current thinking about the complexity of police work. In the 1930s the prevailing view of police work may have placed it in the same category as auto mechanics and cosmetology, but few who understand the realities of policing would still espouse that view. Even though community colleges may be hard pressed to find the funds to replace the vocational education program, it may be better to have fewer police education programs available than to continue to characterize police work as a technical, paraprofessional occupation:

> 8-8 *Congress should amend the statutory authorization of the vocational education program to exclude police and criminal justice programs from eligibility.*

As our national investment in higher education for police officers grows close to a billion dollars, we feel justified in bringing these issues to the attention of a wider audience. Our only fear is that Warren Bennis' (1976, p. 33) prophecy may come true for our work: "Without . . . a thorough understanding of the processes of change, we all might just as well continue to work diligently on blue-ribbon 'task force' committees. Nothing ensures the status quo so much as putting the best minds and best talents on these task forces. For their reports continue to get better as our problems get worse."

1 Appendix

○○○○○○○○○○○○○○○○○○○○○○○○○○○○

Summaries of Consultant Reports

All of the consultant reports are available from the Police Foundation, Suite 400, 1909 K Street, N.W., Washington, D.C. 20006.

Case Studies

Police Education and the University: The Cincinnati Case
by Gene E. Carte

The initiative for creating college programs for police officers came from the Cincinnati Police Division as early as the mid 1950s. Both the University of Cincinnati and Xavier University rejected the requests of Cincinnati police officials to offer police training courses. The police were more successful with Chase Commercial College, which was experiencing financial problems at the time. With the assistance of start-up funds provided by the owner of a local department store, Chase began to offer police-related evening courses taught by police officers in 1958. In 1961, however, Chase decided to phase out all undergraduate programs in order to expand its law school.

Police courses in Cincinnati were then left without a collegiate home until a two-year college was created within the University of Cincinnati to provide practical career courses. A two-year police science program was established in 1962, the course content and instructors of which were almost entirely

225

controlled by the police department. A four-year police science program, later expanded to a criminal justice curriculum, was established when the upper-division College of Community Services was created in 1969. A strong dean of the new college insisted on hiring an academic faculty rather than police officers to teach in the upper-divion program; he also insisted that the curriculum be tied to philosophical issues of justice and American city life. Both the two-year and the four-year programs maintain strong enrollments, despite the now diminished opportunities for police employment in the Cincinnati area. Both programs also continue to experience conflict over certain underlying issues: "agency versus academic control, conflicting ideas about the nature of the subject matter, and a reluctance on both sides to reach a creative understanding about the purpose of their joint venture."

This paper was prepared for the commission's meeting in Cincinnati and presented to the annual meeting of the American Society of Criminology in October 1977. The late Gene E. Carte, the biographer of August Vollmer, was an associate professor of criminal justice in the College of Community Services at the University of Cincinnati.

The Heights and Depths of Criminal Justice Education
by James B. Jacobs and Samuel B. Magdovitz

This report is based on case studies of police education at six different campuses in New York State—John Jay College of Criminal Justice of the City University of New York, St. Francis College, New York Institute of Technology, Elmira College, Corning Community College, and Tompkins Cortland Community College. Intensive interviews with faculty and administrators, as well as institutional records and documents, reveal wide variations in both the mission and the quality of their police education programs.

John Jay College offers a large, full-time, scholarly faculty and a full range of college majors as well as a criminal justice program. Eighty percent of its courses are taught in liberal arts departments, and all faculty members are expected to do research and publish. Some courses are narrowly vocational, but all students must satisfy a number of liberal arts requirements. The two other institutions in the New York area (St. Francis College and the New York Institute of Technology), in contrast to John Jay, rely primarily on part-time faculty to teach—often off campus—in their police education programs. The program at St. Francis, which receives more LEEP funds than most other colleges in the country (but not John Jay), consciously avoids theoretical issues in order to concentrate on "nuts and bolts." The New York Institute of Technology's College Accelerated Program for Police offers a behavioral science curriculum rather than police science or criminal justice, but its off-campus classes are often composed almost entirely of police officers.

The two community college programs, in accordance with their missions, emphasize vocational training. The local law enforcement communities maintain some control over the content of the programs, and the law enforcement courses are taught primarily by criminal justice system employees or by full-time instructors with law enforcement experience. The community college programs maintain high standards and experience high failure rates as a result.

Elmira College's police education program, reportedly undertaken for financial reasons, represents a departure from the college's traditional liberal arts mission. At the time the case study was conducted, the criminal justice courses were taught exclusively by part-time instructors with law enforcement experience. Since police students were largely isolated from the rest of the college, in both their curriculum and their extracurricular activities, their enrollment at a liberal arts college did not seem to provide the traditional liberal arts experience.

The findings of these case studies suggest that police education cannot realistically be an elite education, since only a mass education approach will provide access for most police officers. Nonetheless, it is clear that there are substantial differences among those institutions that are willing to accommodate criminal justice programs.

James B. Jacobs is an associate professor of sociology and law at Cornell University, and Samuel B. Magdovitz is a student at Yale Law School.

Curriculum Issues

Criminal Justice Education for Police
by Donald J. Newman

Police should major in criminal justice programs of high quality, but such programs constitute only 15 to 20 percent of all criminal justice programs currently being offered. Most programs created in recent years have made five serious mistakes: (1) poor conceptualization of program objectives and content, (2) an emphasis on training at the expense of education, (3) a pandering to local political forces, (4) use of inappropriate faculty criteria, and (5) lack of consultation with established high-quality programs. Consequently, many—perhaps most—criminal justice programs at all college levels must now improve their quality or—as the internal and external demands for academic excellence increase—disappear from higher education.

The high-quality programs in criminal justice focus on all aspects of the control of serious crimes in our society. They are truly interdisciplinary, blending legal materials with social science. And they are set in a fully liberal arts context, accounting for no more than one third of the total credit hours required for graduation, so that students are exposed to a broad range of subjects and can learn how to think and write clearly and effectively and to understand moral and ethical problems. High-quality programs also have scholarly faculty members, recruited and promoted according to the criteria of scholarly activity, research, and teaching ability.

Police officers might be able to put together an excellent education from the cafeteria counter of our present general education offerings, but few are likely to do so. Criminal justice, taught as a liberal arts subject, provides an opportunity for a coherent and systematic examination of the central issues of policing in their broadest social context. Police educated in high-quality criminal justice programs should be better able to face the issues and resolve the dilemmas that will continue to confront policing in our society.

Donald J. Newman is dean of the Graduate School of Criminal Justice at the State University of New York at Albany and the author of a leading introductory textbook on criminal justice.

On the Disciplinary and Departmental Character of
Criminal Justice Education for Police Officers
by Bruce T. Olson

This report argues that criminal justice is not a discipline and therefore should not be isolated in a separate department. Moreover, the kind of learning that police work requires is beyond the scope of any single discipline. Therefore, an alternative set of institutional arrangements should be considered, in order to provide a criminal justice education to police officers without creating a discipline or department of criminal justice.

First of all, criminal justice professors should do more counseling than lecturing; that is, they should guide students to the learning resources that will help them develop their intellectual and career interests. The professors should also seek to have the established disciplines divert their intellectual resources to examine criminal justice issues. Students could "major" in criminal justice, taking basic courses in a core curriculum, some of which could be taught by faculty members from fields other than criminal justice. Criminal justice faculty should be administratively autonomous, but not as a department offering (beyond the introductory level) its own courses.

Admittedly, there is ample published material available for creating a full-scale department of criminal justice at all degree levels. But since much of the material comes from research done in other disciplines, it seems more sensible to send criminal justice students to those other disciplines than to offer increasingly specialized criminal justice courses derived from those disciplines.

Bruce T. Olson, a criminal justice consultant based in Davis, California, has been an instructor of criminal justice subjects at the graduate, four-year, and two-year levels. He is currently an adjunct associate professor at the University of Southern California branch in Sacramento.

Liberal Arts and Vocationalism in Higher Education
Curricula for Police Officers
by Donald H. Riddle

The goals of professionalizing the police and of general education are highly compatible. Riddle's answer to the question of "how do you educate a policeman" is not just to "teach them the practices, techniques, needs, and milieu of police work." His answer is to educate them "like anyone else," so that they can acquire intellectual vision and an inquiring mind, the best possible preparation for their work.

The best curriculum for achieving these goals is what is loosely called "liberal arts." All police officers should pursue a general education, but they also need more than that. They should study social science subjects closely allied to the substance of police work, such as race relations, social conflict, and the causes of human behavior. They should also study courses about how police work is done, but these courses should be taught in the broadest possible framework. The gap between vocationalism and liberal arts can best be bridged by teaching vocational subjects with a liberal arts approach.

Since police education still suffers from "vocational courses taught from the narrowest possible perspective," a great deal of effort will be needed to achieve liberal teaching of vocational subjects. Specifically, three strategies for change are recommended: faculty development; curriculum development; and the provision of adequate support to police education programs, particularly library resources. Academic administrators should exercise the leadership needed to implement these strategies and should "abandon the exploitation of students and faculty in police education programs." For while the quality of police education has greatly improved in the past decade, much more needs to be done.

Donald H. Riddle is chancellor of the University of Illinois at Chicago Circle and the president emeritus of John Jay College of Criminal Justice, City University of New York.

Police Policies

Police Department Policies Toward Education
by Elinor Ostrom

In a major study, funded by the National Science Foundation, data on educational policies of 150 police departments in 80 small to medium-sized metropolitan areas were collected in 1974 and 1975. Thirty-four cities of over 100,000 population were included in the sample, and all of the agencies studied had at least 50 full-time sworn police officers.

Only 7 percent of these agencies require their recruits to have some level of college education, and 20 percent require supervisors to have attended college. However, 61 percent of the police agencies studied have some form of educational incentive program. Forty-two percent of the agencies pay a salary differential for those who obtain a baccalaureate degree, 30 percent pay for tuition, 26 percent pay a salary differential according to the number of college credits an officer obtains, and 16 percent purchase books for officers taking college courses.

The presence and type of educational incentive vary by region. Departments in the Northeast and the West are the most likely to have some form of incentive, and departments in the South are the least likely. Departments in the Northeast and the West are most apt to give officers a pay differential per credit hour earned, while departments in the West are the most likely to offer a flat pay differential to officers with a baccalaureate degree.

Personnel policies on education for sworn officers also vary according to certain organizational characteristics. Departments that are unionized and/or under a civil service system are most likely to have personnel policies that give positive incentives to officers who wish to pursue higher education. In contrast, departments with a residence requirement (largely county departments) or with elected chiefs are less likely to have educational incentive systems. Departments serving impoverished communities, and those with sizable numbers of nonwhite residents, are less likely to have educational requirements.

Police department policies toward education vary most strikingly by the size of the departments. Departments that range from 101 to 150 full-time officers are the most likely to have educational incentive programs. Smaller departments (between 50 and 100 officers) and larger departments (more than 150 officers) are less likely to have some form of educational incentives.

Elinor Ostrom is a Professor of Political Science and a member of the Workshop in Political Theory and Policy Analysis at Indiana University, Bloomington.

*Higher Educational Requirements and Minority Recruitment
for the Police: Conflicting Goals?*
by Gwynne Peirson

College requirements for police recruits would help, not
hinder, police departments in their efforts to recruit more minority officers. In the first place, black college enrollments have
increased substantially in recent years. Moreover, black officers
in Los Angeles and Chicago are more likely to be college educated than their white colleagues, and the superiority of black
educational levels is even higher at higher ranks. While the
higher educational levels of black officers may only reflect a discriminatory pattern, in which blacks must be more qualified
than whites in order to succeed, they do show that police work
is not unattractive to college-educated blacks.

Given the long and well-documented institutional racism
of American police departments, Peirson finds it difficult to
accept the sincerity of the concern for minority recruitment
often voiced by white police officials as the reason for their opposition to college requirements. More probably, the opposition
is voiced not "for the sake of minorities but because the police
themselves, a predominantly lower- and lower-middle-class
group, have felt threatened by these proposed standards."

In any event, the educational levels of blacks and whites
in general are not an appropriate basis for assessing the potential
for exclusion of black police applicants if college requirements
are imposed. No one has examined the educational levels of
those blacks and whites who actually apply for police entry
level and promotional positions. Without such evidence, it is
simply not valid to assume that black police applicants are
"educationally deprived" relative to the whites with whom they
compete. And those departments that complain of an inability
to attract black applicants may, in their recruitment techniques,
have been insufficiently sensitive to black concerns. Peirson describes specific examples of how and why police recruitment of
blacks has failed for this reason. He concludes that police hiring
decisions based on college education rather than on current criteria would remove, rather than create, a barrier to the hiring of
minorities.

Gwynne Peirson is a professor of criminology at Howard University and a former detective in the Oakland Police Department.

Organizational Design of the Educated Police Department
by Thomas A. Repetto

The military organizational structures of police departments were designed in the last century for personnel who typically had only a limited education; the military model may be much less appropriate for college graduates than it was for less educated officers. It is not at all clear, however, exactly what kind of structure should replace the current "mechanistic" design of most police departments, in which interaction is more vertical than horizontal, loyalty and obedience are paramount virtues, and greater prestige is attached to internal rather than cosmopolitan knowledge.

The complex nature of police tasks and the threatening nature of the police work environment are unlikely to change, no matter how educated police officers become. The crucial problem is to determine the organizational design that will foster optimum performance of the same police tasks. Several current proposals for restructuring police departments—including the idea of splitting police tasks into social service and crime fighting, each to be performed by different units—seem unsatisfactory, since, in the real world, officers have no way of knowing what kind of situation they will encounter when they are dispatched.

Educated police departments should provide greater recognition of the discretion exercised by the rank and file. They should also move toward greater use of teams, not just for neighborhood team policing but in all areas of police work. By flattening the hierarchical pyramid of the current rank structure and making their police departments more collegial, American communities might receive a much greater return on the already sizable national investment in police education.

Thomas A. Repetto is vice-president of John Jay College of Criminal Justice, City University of New York. Formerly, he was a commander of detectives in the Chicago Police Department.

Structural and Attitudinal Barriers to Higher Education Requirements for Police Officers
by Richard P. Schick

Why have so few police departments required their recruits to be college educated? And why have police departments not provided more incentives for their officers' educational achievement? The answers to these questions are drawn from a 1977 survey of 51 chief executives who constitute a representative sample of police agencies serving all urban jurisdictions of over 50,000 people. A subsequent survey included an additional 11 chief executives from departments identified as having higher education requirements or incentives.

Of the 42 departments responding to the initial survey, only 14 percent required any college education of their recruits, and none required a four-year college degree. At the same time, 79 percent provided some form of incentives for currently employed officers to obtain college credits or degrees, of which pay increases were the most common form.

The 17 respondents from both surveys whose departments had college requirements were asked to identify the institutional actors responsible for the adoption of college requirements. The most common response (16 of 17) was the chief police executive, followed by top management of the jurisdiction (10 of 17). Five respondents mentioned the police personnel department, and four mentioned police union leaders as playing an active role in the adoption of educational requirements. Forty-nine respondents from both surveys said that one or more people were working against college requirements (both successfully and unsuccessfully); most frequently named as the opponents were police supervisors, police rank and file, police union leadership, top city management, and civil service commissions.

Forty-one respondents from both samples said that an institutional actor or actors actively supported educational incentives; chief police executives were named most often, followed by police unions, the elected executives, police personnel units, and police supervisors. Forty-six respondents named actors working against educational incentives; here the police unions, police supervisors, and police rank and file were most frequently named.

The results of this survey indicate that a narrow interest group, primarily from within the police themselves, seems to determine police department policies toward education.

Richard P. Schick is a project director with the Graduate School of Management of Northwestern University.

The Structure of Education and Police Careers in Europe and America
by Philip John Stead

What is the role of higher education in police careers in England and France, and how does police education in these countries compare with that in the United States?

Among the 43 police forces of England and Wales, none have less than 800 officers. All English police must begin their careers as rank-and-file constables, and only secondary education is required for appointment to that rank. Twenty college graduates each year are offered an opportunity to join the force, with a promise of possible accelerated advancement to supervisory positions, but few university graduates seem to apply for the regular constable positions. Consequently, England relies heavily on the National Police College at Bramshill to provide a broad and intensive education for police managers as they are promoted up from the ranks. A very few officers who do well at Bramshill are offered a three-year scholarship (at full pay) to complete a baccalaureate university degree. But most top police officials are not university graduates.

In France, by contrast, police recruitment is stratified by educational attainment. Rank-and-file officers need only pass a secondary school examination, while applicants who hold the *baccalauréat* (equivalent to the Associate in Arts degree in the United States) may enter policing directly as a uniformed lieutenant or a plainsclothes detective. University graduates may enter police work in the middle-management rank of *commissaire*, and graduates of the elite National School of Administration may begin police careers as *préfets*, with top-level police responsibilities. All entry levels have specialized police training programs, lasting from six months to almost two years.

Both England and France, despite their radically different structures of entry level and educational requirements, have lessons to offer the United States in the area of command training and executive development. For as Stead observes, the United States has "no center at which the person likely to be put in charge of a police department with thousands of officers can be *extensively* trained for such heavy responsibilities."

Philip John Stead is a professor of comparative police science at John Jay College of Criminal Justice, City University of New York. He was formerly the dean of academic studies at the National Police College at Bramshill, England.

Influences on Police Education

State Government's Role in Criminal Justice Higher Education by Richard A. Myren

Several state agencies could do much more to improve police education. Others could improve it by doing less. Since most criminal justice programs are in public colleges and universities, the growing trend toward central coordination of public higher education could result in more rational planning of criminal justice programs. Currently, however, the state planning agencies for LEAA funds, which have influenced the decisions regarding the allocation of LEEP monies, play the strongest role in shaping police education. The vocational education units of state education departments have declined in significance as police education has moved on to the four-year level, but they still serve to keep the two-year police education programs very practical in their orientations. A newer agency of state government, the municipal police training councils, also influences police education to remain vocational in orientation at the two-year level.

In contrast to the either generally absent or vocationally oriented influences of state government, a new model for state involvement in the creation and maintenance of criminal justice higher education programs could preserve the values of higher education. The model places initiation of police education in the hands of campus faculty governance bodies, subject to the approval of campus administration and any state system administration or central coordinating council for higher education. This process excludes police practitioner groups and the state police training council from decisions concerning academic content, instructor qualifications, and other educational policy decisions. At the same time, the process allows the states to focus on three important issues in criminal justice programs: (1) the number and geographical spread of programs required to meet both research and manpower needs; (2) articulation of the course content of two-year, four-year, and graduate programs; (3) the quality of instruction at all levels.

Richard A. Myren is director of the Center for Administration of Justice at the American University, Washington, D.C., and a former president of the Academy of Criminal Justice Sciences.

The History and Consequences of Federal Policies
Concerning Higher Education for Police Officers
by David T. Stanley
The Law Enforcement Assistance Administration (LEAA) is the only federal program considered here, since other federal programs affecting police education do not have adequate information systems for assessing either the extent of their support or its impact on police education.

Created without any clear rationale or objectives, LEEP moved from one organizational home to another, "like a tenant behind on his rent payments"—a consequence of the rapid turnover in LEAA administrators. Early in the program's history, LEEP officials gave up on quality in order to ensure quantity of education, since "the linking of institutional award decisions to the quality of criminal justice academic programs would have limited participation to only a few colleges."

Federal programs may have stimulated the growth of criminal justice education, but it is difficult to prove that point. It is also difficult to blame federal policies for the highly vocational character of police education, since LEAA guidelines per- mit much breadth in crime-related degree programs (though they may also encourage narrow vocationalism). And it is espe- cially difficult to assess the consequences of federal policies on the educational levels of police officers (because of the lack of a national data system) and on police performance (because of disagreement over what constitutes good performance, as well as the problems of measuring it).

The report concludes with five recommendations: (1) Fu- ture federal policy on support of higher education for police officers should be determined after government-wide considera- tion of comparable subsidies to comparable groups. (2) If the federal government continues to support police higher educa- tion, it should refrain from influencing the content of such education. (3) More comprehensive and exact data systems on police education are needed. (4) More emphasis should be placed on education for management levels. (5) Continued fed- eral support of research into the results of higher education for police officers is needed.

David T. Stanley is a consultant based in Falls Church, Virginia, and the author of seven Brookings Institution books on govern- mental policy.

The Effects of Education

*Empirical Studies of Higher Education and
Police Performance
by Dennis C. Smith*

If one excludes studies of police attitudes and studies of impressions about police performance, as well as studies in which education is only part of a collection or index of factors tested for their joint influence on police behavior, Smith found that only twelve studies have measured actual police per- formance in relation to higher education: Cross and Hammond (1951), Marsh (1962), McGreevy (1964), Levy (1967), Cohen and Chaiken (1972), Spencer and Nichols (1971), Bozza (1973), Smith and Ostrom (1974), Finckenauer (1975), Van Maanen (1974), Smith (1976), and Ostrom (1976).

Three of the studies found that more educated officers did better on such measures of performance as arrests and civilian complaints. Another found that more educated officers were more likely to resign or be dismissed. A fifth study found that more educated officers received higher departmental performance ratings (Spencer and Nichols, 1971; but see McAllister, 1970, and Gottlieb and Baker, 1974). The remaining studies generally report findings of no relationships between educational level and the measures of performance they used.

All the studies reviewed suffer from one or more serious methodological flaws. All of them crudely measure education as a quantity, ignoring the wide qualitative variations in the nature of the college educations that police officers receive. The measurement of police performance suffers from both a lack of consensus in the field about what good police performance is and a lack of direct observation of police performance. The measures of performance allow education to be confounded with other causal factors, such as motivation, which might be the true cause of any observed effects. Studies comparing police departments (rather than police officers) have suffered from a lack of substantial variation in educational levels across departments. Almost none of them measure changes over time, which is the research design needed to assess properly the causal impact of higher education.

The studies, then, "leave most of the questions of greatest import to relevant policymakers unanswered. The findings across the studies are inconsistent, and each of the studies has been shown to have serious defects as guides to policy formation." But, since the recent increase in educational levels of police officers now makes possible the use of more rigorous research designs, there is good reason to proceed with new research efforts on the effects of education on police performance.

Dennis C. Smith is an assistant professor in the Graduate School of Public Administration at New York University and is currently directing a major study of the effects of police education.

2 Appendix

Participants in the Regional Public Forums

1. West Coast Regional Public Forum

Golden Gate University, San Francisco, March 16, 1977
Otto Butz, president, Golden Gate University
Jack Kuykendall, San Jose State University
Wes Pomeroy, Berkeley Police Department
Randy Hamilton, Golden Gate University
Frank Benaderet, San Rafael Police Department
Joseph McNamara, San Jose Police Department
Michael Hebel, San Francisco Police Department
Stephen Wollack, Wollack, Waibel and Guenther
Ellen Zorychtya, San Jose State University
Tom Anderson, Golden Gate University
Sidney Friedman, De Anza College
Richard Hongisto, San Francisco Sheriff's Office
Ken Geppert, San Jose Police Department
Vernon E. Renner, Criminal Justice Education and Training Resource System
Ken Block, San Jose State University
Al Benner, San Francisco Police Department
Bob Whitaker, Hayward Police Department
Dennis Dalton, Fremont Police Department
Hal Ratliff, San Jose Police Officers' Association

Robert Edwards, Oakland Police Department
Michael Weskey, San Francisco Police Officers' Association

2. East Coast Regional Public Forum

John Jay College of Criminal Justice, CUNY,
New York, June 20, 1977

Gerald W. Lynch, president, John Jay College
Anthony V. Bouza, New York City Transit Police
Michael J. Codd, New York City Police Department
Carl Pforzheimer, New York State Board of Regents
Edward Kiernan, International Conference of Police Associations
John Kerr, Nassau County Police Department
Nicholas Scopetta, New York City Department of Investigation
Anthony M. Schembri, Office of Criminal Justice, St. Francis
    College
David G. Salten, New York Institute of Technology
Frederick T. Martens, New Jersey State Police
Arthur J. Fleming, New York City Police Department
Richard J. Bennett, Youngstown State University
Dorothy Guyot, School of Criminal Justice, Rutgers University
Haig Bohigian, John Jay College
Robert Houlihan, Police Academy, New York City Police De-
    partment
Nesta M. Gallas, John Jay College
Lee Weinberg, University of Pittsburgh
George F. Hall, Palisades Parkway (N.J.) Police
Thomas Carroll, Lehigh (Pa.) Community College
Charles P. McDowell, Guilford College (N.C.)
Theodore A. Gill, John Jay College
Hugh Hinton, University of Toledo
Sydney Cooper, New York Institute of Technology
Richard Ward, John Jay College

3. Midwest Regional Public Forum

University of Illinois at Chicago Circle, Chicago,
December 5, 1977

Donald H. Riddle, chancellor, University of Illinois at Chicago
    Circle

John A. Gardiner, University of Illinois at Chicago Circle
James Osterburg, University of Illinois at Chicago Circle
Steven Schiller, Chicago Crime Commission
Allen Andrews, Peoria (Ill.) Police Department
David Couper, Madison (Wisc.) Police Department
Renault Robinson, Chicago Afro-American Patrolman's League
James B. Zagel, Illinois Law Enforcement Commission
John Jemilo, Chicago Police Training Center
Russell Arend, director of training,. Northwestern University
      Traffic Institute
Jim Jansen, Milwaukee Area Technical College
Jim O'Shea, Oakton Community College (Ill.)
Mel Wallace, McHenry County College (Ill.)
Robert Mendelsohn, Indiana-Purdue University at Indianapolis

References

"ACJS Awarded Standards Development Grant." *ACJS Today,* 1977, *1* (5), 1.

Academy of Criminal Justice Sciences. *Accreditation Guidelines for Post-Secondary Criminal Justice Education Programs.* Normal: Secretariat, Academy of Criminal Justice Sciences, Illinois State University, 1976.

Adams, H. *The Education of Henry Adams: An Autobiography.* Boston: Houghton Mifflin, 1961. (Originally published 1906.)

Adams, R. "Criminal Justice: An Emerging Academic Profession and Discipline." *Journal of Criminal Justice,* 1976, *4,* 303-314.

Adams, T. *Police Patrol: Tactics and Techniques.* Englewood Cliffs, N.J.: Prentice-Hall, 1971.

American Bar Association, Project on Standards for Criminal Justice. *Standards Relating to the Urban Police Function.* New York: Institute of Judicial Administration, 1973.

American Council on Education. *Awarding Credit for Extra-Institutional Learning.* Washington, D.C.: American Council on Education, 1977.

American Justice Institute. *Project STAR: Role Performance and the Criminal Justice System.* Cincinnati: Anderson, 1976.

American Society for Engineering Education. *Report on Evaluation of Engineering Education, 1952-1953.* Washington, D.C.: American Society for Engineering Education, 1955.

Anderson, D. C. "The Off-Duty Degree." *Police Magazine,* 1978, *1* (2), 29-38.

Anderson, R. E. *Strategic Policy Changes at Private Colleges.* New York: Teachers College Press, Columbia University, 1978.

Angell, J. E. "Toward an Alternative to the Classic Police Organizational Arrangements: A Democratic Model." *Criminology,* 1971, *19,* 186-206.

Astin, A. W. *Four Critical Years: Effects of College on Beliefs, Attitudes, and Knowledge.* San Francisco: Jossey-Bass, 1977.

Astin, A. W. *The American Freshman: National Norms for Fall, 1977.* Los Angeles: UCLA and American Council on Education, 1978.

Baehr, M. E., Furcon, J. E., and Froemel, E. C. *Psychological Assessment of Patrolman Qualifications in Relation to Field Performance.* Washington, D.C.: U.S. Government Printing Office, 1968.

Balch, R. W. "The Police Personality: Fact or Fiction?" *Journal of Criminal Law, Criminology, and Police Science,* 1972, *63,* 106-119.

Baldridge, J. V., Curtis, D. V., Ecker, G., and Riley, G. L. *Policy Making and Effective Leadership: A National Study of Academic Management.* San Francisco: Jossey-Bass, 1978.

Banton, M. *The Policeman in the Community.* London: Tavistock, 1964.

Bard, M. *Training Police as Specialists in Family Crisis Intervention.* Washington, D.C.. U.S. Government Printing Office, 1970.

Bard, M. *Family Crisis Intervention: From Concept to Imple-

mentation. Washington, D.C.: U.S. Government Printing Office, 1974.

Barron's Profiles of American Colleges. (10th ed.) Woodbury, N.Y.: Barron's Educational Series, 1976.

Bassi, L., and Rogers, R. H. "The Road to Accreditation." *Journal of Criminal Justice,* 1976, *4,* 243-252.

Baxter, D. "New Horizons for Law Enforcement: Curriculum in Two Year Programs." In M. Neary (Ed.), *Higher Education for Police.* New York: American Academy for Professional Law Enforcement, 1977.

Becker, H. S. "What Do They Really Learn at College?" *Trans-Action,* 1964, *1,* 14-17.

Becker, H. S., and others. *Boys in White: Student Culture in Medical School.* Chicago: University of Chicago Press, 1961.

Beckman, E. "To Attract and Retain." *Michigan Police Officer,* 1974, *2,* 10-11, 59.

Beckman, E. "Police Education and Training: Where Are We? Where Are We Going?" *Journal of Criminal Justice,* 1976, *4,* 315-322.

Beigel, H., and Beigel, A. *Beneath the Badge.* New York: Harper & Row, 1977.

Ben-David, J. *Centers of Learning: Britain, France, Germany, United States.* New York: McGraw-Hill, 1977.

Bennis, W. *The Unconscious Conspiracy: Why Leaders Can't Lead.* New York: Amacom, 1976.

Bennis, W. *Toward a Learning Society: A Basic Challenge to Higher Education.* Washington, D.C.: American Center for the Quality of Work Life, 1978.

Bercal, T. E. "Calls for Police Assistance." *American Behavioral Scientist,* 1970, *13,* 681-692.

Berg, I., with Gorelick, S. *Education and Jobs: The Great Training Robbery.* New York: Praeger, 1970.

Berkeley, G. E. *The Administrative Revolution: Notes on the Passing of Organization Man.* Englewood Cliffs, N.J.: Prentice-Hall, 1971.

Bird, C. *The Case Against College.* New York: Bantam, 1975.

Bisconti, A. S., and Solmon, L. C. *College Education on the*

Job: The Graduates' Viewpoint. Bethlehem, Pa.: CPC Foundation, 1976.

Bittner, E. *The Functions of the Police in Modern Society.* Public Health Service Publication 2059. Bethesda, Md.: National Institute of Public Health, 1970.

Bledstein, B. *The Culture of Professionalism: The Middle Class and the Development of Higher Education in America.* New York: Norton, 1976.

Bopp, W. *Police Personnel Administration.* Boston: Holbrook, 1974.

Bouza, A. Statement presented to the National Advisory Commission on Higher Education for Police Officers, John Jay College of Criminal Justice, New York City, June 20, 1977.

Bowen, H. R. *Investment in Learning: The Individual and Social Value of American Higher Education.* San Francisco: Jossey-Bass, 1977.

Boydstun, J. E., and Sherry, M. E. *San Diego Community Profile: Final Report.* Washington, D.C.: Police Foundation, 1975.

Boyer, E., and Kaplan, M. *Educating for Survival.* New Rochelle, N.Y.: Change Magazine Press, 1977.

Bozza, C. M. "Motivations Guiding Policemen in the Arrest Process." *Journal of Police Science and Administration,* 1973, *1* (4), 468-476.

Bradshaw, T. K. "The Impact of Education on Leisure: Socialization in College." Unpublished doctoral dissertation, University of California, Berkeley, 1974.

Bragdon, H. W. *Woodrow Wilson: The Academic Years.* Cambridge, Mass.: Harvard University Press, 1967.

Brandstatter, A. Address to the Conference on Police Education, University of Maryland, June 8-9, 1967.

Broomfield, T. S. "Conflict Management." In J. L. Steinberg and D. W. McEvoy (Eds.), *The Police and the Behavioral Sciences.* Springfield, Ill.: Thomas, 1974.

Brown, L. P. "The Police and Higher Education: The Challenge of the Times." *Criminology,* 1974, *12,* 114-124.

Brown, W. P. "The Police and the Academic World." *Police Chief,* 1965, *32* (5), 8-12.

Brubacher, J. S., and Rudy, W. *Higher Education in Transition— A History of American Colleges and Universities, 1936-1956.* New York: Harper & Row, 1958.

Bruns, G. *Criminal Justice Undergraduate Programs Catalog.* Tempe: Department of Criminal Justice, Arizona State University, 1975.

Caiden, G. E. *Police Revitalization.* Lexington, Mass.: Heath, 1977.

Carnegie Commission on Higher Education. *College Graduates and Jobs: Adjusting to a New Labor Market Situation.* New York: McGraw-Hill, 1973a.

Carnegie Commission on Higher Education. *The Purposes and the Performance of Higher Education in the United States: Approaching the Year 2000.* New York: McGraw-Hill, 1973b.

Carnegie Foundation for the Advancement of Teaching. *Missions of the College Curriculum: A Contemporary Review with Suggestions.* San Francisco: Jossey-Bass, 1977.

Carroll, T. Statement presented to the National Advisory Commission on Higher Education for Police Officers, John Jay College of Criminal Justice, New York City, June 20, 1977.

Carte, G. E. *Police Education and the University: The Cincinnati Case.* Washington, D.C.: Police Foundation, 1978.

Carte, G. E., and Carte, E. H. *Police Reform in the United States: The Era of August Vollmer.* Berkeley: University of California Press, 1975.

Carter, R. M., and Nelson, E. K. "The Law Enforcement Education Program—One University's Experience." *Journal of Police Science and Administration,* 1973, *1* (4), 491-494.

Carver, R. "The Impact of a Four Year College Requirement on Affirmative Action Hiring in Police Agencies." Unpublished paper prepared for Police Executive Research Forum, May 1978.

Chafee, Z., Pollack, W. H., and Stern, C. S. *The Third Degree.* Washington, D.C.: National Commission on Law Observance and Enforcement, 1931.

Cheit, E. *The New Depression in Higher Education: A Study of Financial Conditions in 41 Colleges and Universities.* New York: McGraw-Hill, 1971.

Cheit, E. *The Useful Arts and the Liberal Tradition.* New York: McGraw-Hill, 1975.

Chevigny, P. *Police Power: Police Abuses in New York City.* New York: Pantheon, 1969.

Chickering, A. W. *Commuting Versus Resident Students: Overcoming Educational Inequities of Living Off Campus.* San Francisco: Jossey-Bass, 1974.

Clark, B. "The 'Cooling Out' Function in Higher Education." *American Journal of Sociology,* 1960a, *65,* 569-576.

Clark, B. *The Open Door College.* New York: McGraw-Hill, 1960b.

Clecak, P. "Views of Social Critics." In H. R. Bowen, *Investment in Learning: The Individual and Social Value of American Higher Education.* San Francisco: Jossey-Bass, 1977.

Clymer, A. "Poll Discloses Property Tax Cuts Are Widely Backed Around Nation." *New York Times,* June 28, 1978, pp. 1, 16.

Cohen, B., and Chaiken, J. M. *Police Background Characteristics and Performance: Summary Report.* Washington, D.C.: U.S. Law Enforcement Assistance Administration, 1972.

Cohn, A. W., and Viano, E. C. (Eds.). *Police Community Relations: Images, Roles, Realities.* Philadelphia: Lippincott, 1976.

Coleman, J. S. "Peer Cultures and Education in Modern Society." In T. M. Newcomb and E. K. Wilson (Eds.), *College Peer Groups: Problems and Prospects for Research.* Chicago: Aldine, 1966.

Collins, R. "Some Comparative Principles of Educational Stratification." *Harvard Educational Review,* 1977, *47,* 1-27.

Colquhoun, P. *A Treatise on the Police of the Metropolis.* Montclair, N.J.: Patterson Smith, 1969. (7th London ed. published 1806.)

Conley, J. "Criminal Justice History as a Field of Research: A Review of the Literature, 1960-75." *Journal of Criminal Justice,* 1977, *5,* 13-28.

Coughlin, E. K. "Colleges Found Paying Price for Improved Finances." *Chronicle of Higher Education,* February 6, 1978, *15* (21), 13.

Couper, D. C. Statement presented to the National Advisory Commission on Higher Education for Police Officers, University of Illinois at Chicago Circle, December 5, 1977.

Cox, C. R. "Police Report Writing: The Most Neglected Part of Training." Unpublished manuscript, 1977.

Critchley, T. A. *A History of Police in England and Wales, 900-1966.* Montclair, N.J.: Patterson Smith, 1972.

Crockett, T. S. *Law Enforcement Education: A Survey of Colleges and Universities Offering Degree Programs in the Field of Law Enforcement.* Washington, D.C.: International Association of Chiefs of Police, 1968.

Crockett, T. S., and Stinchcomb, J. D. *Guidelines for Law Enforcement Education Programs in Community and Junior Colleges.* Washington, D.C.: American Association of Community and Junior Colleges, 1968.

Crosby, R., and Snyder, D. "Distrust of the Police and Crime Reporting." In A. W. Cohn and E. C. Viano (Eds.), *Police Community Relations: Images, Roles, Realities.* Philadelphia: Lippincott, 1976.

Cross, A. C., and Hammond, K. R. "Social Differences Between 'Successful' and 'Unsuccessful' State Highway Patrolmen." *Public Personnel Review,* 1951, *12,* 159-161.

Cumming, E., Cumming, I., and Edell, L. "Policeman as Philosopher, Guide and Friend." *Social Problems,* 1965, *12,* 276-286.

Czajkoski, E. H. "Involving the Humanities in Doctoral Education in Criminology and Criminal Justice." Unpublished manuscript, Florida State University, n.d.

Dewey, J. *Democracy and Education: An Introduction to the Philosophy of Education.* New York: Macmillan, 1916.

Drucker, P. *The Age of Discontinuity: Guidelines to Our Changing Society.* New York: Harper & Row, 1969.

Eastman, E. *Police Education in American Colleges and Universities: A Search for Excellence.* Final Report on Grant No. OEG-0-9-450723-4128(085), U.S. Office of Education. Kent, Ohio: Center for State and Local Government, Kent State University, 1972.

Eastman, G., and Eastman, E. (Eds.). *Municipal Police Adminis-*

tration. Washington, D.C.: International City Managers' Association, 1961, 1969.

Eble, K. E. *Professors as Teachers.* San Francisco: Jossey-Bass, 1972.

Eisenberg, T., Kent, D. A., and Wall, C. *Police Personnel Practices in State and Local Governments.* Washington, D.C.: Police Foundation and International Association of Chiefs of Police, 1973.

Ennis, P. *Criminal Victimization in the United States.* Washington, D.C.: U.S. Government Printing Office, 1967.

Feldman, K. A., and Newcomb, T. M. *The Impact of College on Students.* Vol. I: *An Analysis of Four Decades of Research.* San Francisco: Jossey-Bass, 1969.

Finckenauer, J. O. "Higher Education and Police Discretion." *Journal of Police Science and Administration,* 1975, *3* (4), 450-457.

Fiske, E. B. "A New Balance in Universities: A Shift from Research to Teaching Discerned." *New York Times,* December 7, 1977, p. A24.

Fiske, E. B. "Hard-Hit Schools Turn to Marketers." *New York Times,* January 22, 1978a, Sec. 3, pp. 1, 9.

Fiske, E. B. "Growth of Ethics Courses Shows Major Change on U.S. Campuses." *New York Times,* February 20, 1978b, p. 1.

Fiske, E. B. "Harvard Is Debating Curriculum to Replace 'General Education.' " *New York Times,* February 26, 1978c, p. 1.

Fiske, E. B. "Harvard Tightens Up Curriculum; Ends 'General Education' Program." *New York Times,* May 3, 1978d, p. 1.

Flexner, A. *Medical Education in the United States and Canada.* New York: Arno Press, 1972. (Originally published 1910.)

Flexner, A. *Universities: American, English, German.* London: Oxford University Press, 1930.

Fogelson, R. M. *Big City Police.* Cambridge, Mass.: Harvard University Press, 1977.

Fosdick, R. B. *American Police Systems.* Montclair, N.J.: Patterson Smith, 1969. (Originally published 1920.)

Foster, J. P. "A Descriptive Analysis of Crime-Related Programs in Higher Education." Unpublished doctoral dissertation, Florida State University, 1974.

Foster, J. P. Telephone interview, May 17, 1978.

Freedman, M. B. "San Francisco State: Urban Campus Proto-types." In G. K. Smith (Ed.), *Agony and Promise: Current Issues in Higher Education 1969.* San Francisco: Jossey-Bass, 1969.

Freidson, E. *Doctoring Together: A Study of Professional Social Control.* New York: Elsevier, 1975.

Fry, L. J., and Miller, J. "The Organizational Transformation of a Federal Education Program: Reflections on LEEP." *Social Problems,* 1976, *24,* 259-269.

Gallas, N. Statement presented to the National Advisory Commission on Higher Education for Police Officers, John Jay College of Criminal Justice, New York City, June 20, 1977.

Gammage, A. *Basic Police Report Writing.* Springfield, Ill.: Thomas, 1974.

Gamson, W. A., and McEvoy, J. "Police Violence and Its Public Support." *Annals of the American Academy of Political and Social Science,* 1970, *391,* 97-110.

Gardiner, J. A. *The Politics of Corruption: Organized Crime in an American City.* New York: Russell Sage Foundation, 1970.

George, R. L. "Resident or Commuter: A Study of Personality Differences." *Journal of College Student Personnel,* 1971, *12,* 216-219.

Germann, A. C., Day, F., and Gallati, R. *Introduction to Law Enforcement and Criminal Justice.* Springfield, Ill.: Thomas, 1975.

Goffman, E. "On Cooling the Mark Out: Some Aspects of Adaptation to Failure." *Psychiatry,* 1952, *15* (4), 451-463.

Goldman, A. "Debating 'Life Experience.'" *New York Times,* September 11, 1977, Sec. 12, pp. 1, 16.

Goldsmith, J., and Goldsmith, S. *The Police Community.* Pacific Palisades, Calif.: Palisades Publishers, 1974.

Goldstein, H. *Policing a Free Society.* Cambridge, Mass.: Ballinger, 1977.

Goldstein, T. "Measuring Competence: Debating an Indefinable." *New York Times,* February 7, 1978a, p. E7.

Goldstein, T. "Carter's Attack on Lawyers." *New York Times,* May 6, 1978b, p. 11.

Goll, E. W. "Community Colleges: The Maryland Syndrome." *Change Magazine,* 1977, *9* (10), 40-41.

Golladay, M. A. *The Condition of Education.* Vol. 3, Pt. 1. Washington, D.C.: National Center for Education Statistics, 1977.

Gordon, M. S. (Ed.). *Higher Education and the Labor Market.* New York: McGraw-Hill, 1974.

Gordon, R. A., and Howell, J. E. *Higher Education for Business.* New York: Columbia University Press, 1959.

Gottlieb, M. C., and Baker, C. F. "Predicting Police Officer Effectiveness." *Journal of Forensic Psychology,* December 1974, pp. 35-46.

Graff, R. W., and Cooley, G. R. "Adjustment of Commuter and Resident Students." *Journal of College Student Personnel,* 1970, *11,* 54-57.

Graves, H. S., and Guise, C. H. *Forest Education.* New Haven, Conn.: Yale University Press, 1932.

Gray, T. C. "Selecting for a Police Subculture." In J. H. Skolnick and T. C. Gray (Eds.), *Police in America.* Boston: Little, Brown, 1975.

Grubb, W. N., and Lazerson, M. "Rally Round the Workplace: Continuities and Fallacies in Career Education." *Harvard Educational Review,* 1975, *45,* 451-474.

Guyot, D. "The Organization of Police Departments: Changing the Model from the Army to the Hospital." *Criminal Justice Abstracts,* 1977, *9* (2), 231-256.

Hahn, P. *The Juvenile Offender and the Law.* Cincinnati: Anderson, 1971.

Hall, G. F. Statement presented to the National Advisory Commission on Higher Education for Police Officers, John Jay College of Criminal Justice, New York City, June 20, 1977.

Harrington, F. H. *The Future of Adult Education: New Responsibilities of Colleges and Universities.* San Francisco: Jossey-Bass, 1977.

Harrington, T. F., Jr. "The Literature on the Commuter Student." *Journal of College Student Personnel,* 1972, *13* (11), 546-550.

Harris, N. C., and Grede, J. F. *Career Education in Colleges: A*

Guide for Planning Two- and Four-Year Occupational Programs. San Francisco: Jossey-Bass, 1977.

Harris, R. N. *The Police Academy.* New York: Wiley, 1973.

Harris, S. (Ed.). *Accredited Institutions of Postsecondary Education and Programs.* Washington, D.C.: American Council on Education, 1975.

Hindelang, M. J. *Criminal Victimization in Eight American Cities: A Descriptive Analysis of Common Theft and Assault.* Cambridge, Mass.: Ballinger, 1976.

Hindelang, M. J., and Gottfredson, M. R. "The Victim's Decision Not to Invoke the Criminal Justice Process." In W. McDonald (Ed.), *The Victim and the Criminal Justice System.* Beverly Hills, Calif.: Sage, 1976.

Hodge, R. W., Siegel, P. M., and Rossi, P. H. "Occupational Prestige in the United States, 1925-63." *American Journal of Sociology,* 1964, *70,* 286-302.

Hoffman, D. E., Snell, J. E., and Webb, V. J. "Insiders and Outsiders in Criminal Justice Education." *Journal of Criminal Justice,* 1976, *4,* 57-61.

Hoover, L. T. *Police Educational Characteristics and Curricula.* Washington, D.C.: U.S. Law Enforcement Assistance Administration, 1975.

Hoover, L. T., and Lund, D. W. *Guidelines for Criminal Justice Programs in Community and Junior Colleges: A Report of the Recommendations of the Criminal Justice Curriculum Institute.* Washington, D.C.: American Association of Community and Junior Colleges, 1977.

Houle, C. O. *The External Degree.* San Francisco: Jossey-Bass, 1973.

Hutchins, R. M. *The Higher Learning in America.* New Haven, Conn.: Yale University Press, 1936.

"The Hutchins View of the University." *Chronicle of Higher Education,* 1977, *14* (13), 5-6.

International Association of Chiefs of Police, Police Chief Executive Committee. *The Police Chief Executive Report.* Washington, D.C.: U.S. Government Printing Office, 1976.

Jacobs, J., and Magdovitz, S. "At LEEP's End?: A Review of the Law Enforcement Education Program." *Journal of Police Science and Administration,* 1977, *5,* 1-17.

Jacobs, J., and Magdovitz, S. *The Heights and Depths of Criminal Justice Education.* Washington, D.C.: Police Foundation, 1978.

Jencks, C., and Riesman, D. *The Academic Revolution.* New York: Doubleday, 1968.

"Jobless Rate Increases Among Young Graduates." *Chronicle of Higher Education,* January 30, 1978, p. 4.

Johnson, K. W. *New Directions in Criminal Justice Education: Training Change Agents for Entry Level Positions.* College Park: Institute of Criminal Justice and Criminology, University of Maryland, 1977.

Johnson, S. "Subcontracted Courses Stir Controversy." *New York Times,* September 11, 1977, Sec. 12, p. 15.

"Joint Commission for C. J. Higher Education Established." *ACJS Today,* 1977-78, *1* (6), 1.

Joseph, N., and Alex, N. "The Uniform: A Sociological Perspective." *American Journal of Sociology,* 1972, 77, 719-730.

Kansas City Police Department. *Kansas City Patrol Projects.* Kansas City, Mo.: Police Department, 1973.

Karabel, J. "Community Colleges and Social Stratification." *Harvard Educational Review,* 1972, *42,* 521-562.

Kaysen, C. "What Should Education Do?" *Daedalus,* Fall 1974, pp. 180-185.

Kelley, H. Address given at convocation of Immaculate Heart College, Los Angeles, February 14, 1977.

Kelling, G. L., and others. *The Kansas City Preventive Patrol Experiment: A Summary Report.* Washington, D.C.: Police Foundation, 1974.

Kerr, C. *The Uses of the University.* Cambridge, Mass.: Harvard University Press, 1964.

Kiernan, E. J. Statement presented to the National Advisory Commission on Higher Education for Police Officers, John Jay College of Criminal Justice, New York City, June 20, 1977.

King, W. "Rights Unit Says Police Misconduct Is Among South's Major Problems." *New York Times,* May 1, 1978, p. D8.

Kirkham, G. L. "From Professor to Patrolman: A Fresh Perspective on the Police." *Journal of Police Science and Administration,* 1974, 2, 127-137.

Klotsche, J. M. *The Urban University.* New York: Harper & Row, 1966.

Knapp, W., and others. *The Knapp Commission Report on Police Corruption.* New York: Braziller, 1972.

Knowles, M. S. *The Adult Learner.* Houston: Gulf Publishing, 1973.

Kobetz, R. W. *Law Enforcement and Criminal Justice Education Directory, 1975-76.* Gaithersburg, Md.: International Association of Chiefs of Police, 1975.

Kreml, F. "The Role of Colleges and Universities in Police Management." In *The Police Yearbook: 1966.* Washington, D.C.: International Association of Chiefs of Police, 1966.

Kuykendall, J. "Criminal Justice Programs in Higher Education: Course and Curriculum Orientations." *Journal of Criminal Justice,* 1977, *5,* 149-163.

Ladinsky, J. Memorandum, Department of Sociology, University of Wisconsin, February 28, 1977.

Landy, F. J. *Performance Appraisal in Police Departments.* Washington, D.C.: Police Foundation, 1977.

Lane, R. *Policing the City: Boston, 1822-1885.* Cambridge, Mass.: Harvard University Press, 1967.

Lankes, G. A. "A Profile of the Police Science Student." *Police Chief,* 1971, *38,* 60-64.

Larson, R. C. "What Happened to Patrol Operations in Kansas City? A Review of the Kansas City Preventive Patrol Experiment." *Journal of Criminal Justice,* 1975, *3,* 267-297.

Lefkowitz, J. "Industrial-Organizational Psychology and the Police." *American Psychologist,* 1977, *32,* 346-364.

Leibman, D. A., and Schwartz, J. A. "Police Programs in Domestic Crisis Intervention: A Review." In J. R. Snibbe and H. M. Snibbe (Eds.), *The Urban Policeman in Transition: A Psychological and Sociological Review.* Springfield, Ill.: Thomas, 1973.

Lejins, P. "Conference Summary." In *Proceedings of the International Conference on Doctoral Level Education in Criminal Justice and Criminology.* College Park: Institute of Criminal Justice and Criminology, University of Maryland, 1976.

Levy, R. J. "Predicting Police Failures." *Journal of Criminal Law, Criminology, and Police Science,* 1967, *58,* 265-276.

Loughrey, L. "Introduction." In M. Neary (Ed.), *Higher Education for Police.* New York: American Academy for Professional Law Enforcement, 1977.

Lynch, G. W. "The Contributions of Higher Education to Ethical Behavior in Law Enforcement." *Journal of Criminal Justice,* 1976, *4,* 285-290.

Lynch, G. W. Statement presented to the National Advisory Commission on Higher Education for Police Officers, John Jay College of Criminal Justice, New York City, June 20, 1977.

McAllister, J. A. "A Study of the Prediction and Measurement of Police Performance." *Police,* 1970, *14,* 58-64.

McGrath, E. J. *Liberal Education in the Professions.* New York: Teachers College Press, Columbia University, 1959.

McGreevy, T. J. "A Field Study of the Relationship Between the Formal Education Levels of 556 Police Officers in St. Louis, Missouri, and Their Patrol Duty Performance Records." Master's thesis, School of Public Administration and Public Safety, Michigan State University, 1964.

McHenry, D. E., and Associates. *Academic Departments: Problems, Variations, and Alternatives.* San Francisco: Jossey-Bass, 1977.

McNamara, D. E. J. "Evaluation of Higher Education for Police in Terms of Social Impact." In M. Neary (Ed.), *Higher Education for Police.* New York: American Academy for Professional Law Enforcement, 1977.

Maeroff, G. I. "General Studies Under Scrutiny as Students Seek Relevant Courses." *New York Times,* December 14, 1977, p. D15.

Magarrell, J. "Part-Time Professors on the Increase." *Chronicle of Higher Education,* 1978, *15* (18), 1.

Mann, C. R. *A Study of Engineering Education.* New York: Joint Committee on Engineering Education of the National Engineering Societies, 1918.

Manning, P. "Police Lying." *Urban Life and Culture,* 1974, *3,* 283-306.

Manning, P. "The Researcher: An Alien in the Police World." In A. Niederhoffer and A. S. Blumberg (Eds.), *The Ambivalent*

Force: Perspectives on the Police. Hinsdale, Ill.: Dryden Press, 1976.

Manning, P. *Police Work.* Cambridge, Mass.: M.I.T. Press, 1977.

Manpower Planning and Development Programs in the Law Enforcement Assistance Administration. Final Report of the Task Force on Criminal Justice Education and Training. Washington, D.C.: Office of Criminal Justice Education and Training, U.S. Law Enforcement Assistance Administration, 1976.

Markland, R. J. "A Synthesis Approach Toward Career Education for Criminal Justice Personnel." Unpublished paper, Tidewater Regional Police Academy, Old Dominion University, 1977.

Marland, S. P. *Career Education.* New York: McGraw-Hill, 1974.

Marsh, S. H. "Validating the Selection of Deputy Sheriffs." *Public Personnel Review,* 1962, *23,* 41-44.

Masini, H. "The Role of Police: Why Is a College Education Necessary?" In M. Neary (Ed.), *Higher Education for Police.* New York: American Academy for Professional Law Enforcement, 1977.

Mathias, W. J. "Higher Education and the Police." In A. Niederhoffer and A. S. Blumberg (Eds.), *The Ambivalent Force: Perspectives on the Police.* Hinsdale, Ill.: Dryden Press, 1976.

Medsker, L. L., and Tillery, D. *Breaking the Access Barriers: A Profile of Two Year Colleges.* New York: McGraw-Hill, 1971.

Medsker, L. L., and Trent, J. W. *The Influence of Different Types of Public Higher Institutions on College Attendance from Varying Socioeconomic and Ability Levels.* U.S. Department of Health, Education, and Welfare Cooperative Research Project No. 438. Berkeley: Center for the Study of Higher Education, University of California, 1965.

Meyer, P. *Awarding College Credit for Non-College Learning: A Guide to Current Practices.* San Francisco: Jossey-Bass, 1975.

Meyerson, M. "Civilizing Education: Uniting Liberal and Professional Learning." *Daedalus,* Fall 1974, pp. 173-179.

Michalak, J. "Extension Colleges Under a Cloud." *New York Times,* March 30, 1978, pp. 1, 62.

Miller, W. R. *Cops and Bobbies: Police Authority in New York and London, 1830-1870.* Chicago: University of Chicago Press, 1977.

Mills, R. B. "Implications of the Ohio Task Force Study on Law Enforcement Education." Paper presented to the Academy of Criminal Justice Sciences, San Mateo, Calif., March 1977.

Milton, C. H., and others. *Police Use of Deadly Force.* Washington, D.C.: Police Foundation, 1977.

Misner, G. "Accreditation of Criminal Justice Education Programs." *Police Chief,* 1975, *42* (8), 14-16, 78.

Misner, G. "Education for Police Service." In M. Neary (Ed.), *Higher Education for Police.* New York: American Academy for Professional Law Enforcement, 1977.

Morris, A. "The American Society of Criminology: A History, 1941-1974." *Criminology,* 1975, *13,* 123-167.

Morris, N., and Hawkins, G. *The Honest Politician's Guide to Crime Control.* Chicago: University of Chicago Press, 1970.

Muir, W. K., Jr. *Police: Streetcorner Politicians.* Chicago: University of Chicago Press, 1977.

Murchland, B. "The Eclipse of the Liberal Arts." *Change Magazine,* 1976, *8* (10), 22-26, 62.

Murphy, P. V. "Police Corruption." *Police Chief,* 1973, *40* (12), 36, 72.

Murphy, P. V., and Bloch, P. "The Beat Commander." *Police Chief,* 1970, *37* (5), 16-19.

Murphy, P. V., and Plate, T. *Commissioner: A View from the Top of American Law Enforcement.* New York: Simon & Schuster, 1977.

Myren, R. A. *Education in Criminal Justice.* Sacramento, Calif.: Coordinating Council for Higher Education, 1970.

Myren, R. A. Remarks at a conference on police education, Police Foundation, Washington, D.C., March 1976.

Myren, R. A. *State Government's Role in Criminal Justice Higher Education.* Washington, D.C.: Police Foundation, 1978.

Myren, R. A., Baridon, A., and Laskowski, P. *Programmatic Issues Arising From Administration of the Law Enforcement Education Program: Second Progress Report.* Washington,

D.C.: Center for the Administration of Justice, American University, 1978.

National Advisory Commission on Civil Disorders. *Report.* New York: Bantam Books, 1968.

National Advisory Commission on Criminal Justice Standards and Goals. *A National Strategy to Reduce Crime.* Washington, D.C.: U.S. Government Printing Office, 1973.

National Commission on Teacher Education and Professional Standards. *National Professional Accrediting Agencies: An Overview of Policies and Practices in 23 Fields.* Washington, D.C.: National Education Association, n.d.

National Planning Association, "A Nationwide Survey of Law Enforcement Criminal Justice Personnel Needs and Resources: Final Report." Unpublished manuscript. Washington, D.C.: U.S. Law Enforcement Assistance Administration, 1976.

Navasky, V., with Paster, D. "Background Paper." In Twentieth Century Fund Task Force on the Law Enforcement Assistance Administration, *Law Enforcement: The Federal Role.* New York: McGraw-Hill, 1976.

Neary, M. (Ed.). *Higher Education for Police.* New York: American Academy for Professional Law Enforcement, 1977.

"New York Policeman to Seek SJC's Master's." *The St. John's Reporter,* 1977, *4* (5), 8.

Newman, C. L., and Hunter, D. S. "Education for Careers in Law Enforcement: An Analysis of Student Output 1964-67." *Journal of Criminal Law, Criminology, and Police Science,* 1968, *59* (1), 138-143.

Newman, D. J. "Criminal Justice Education in Wisconsin: Report and Recommendations to the University of Wisconsin System." Unpublished manuscript. Albany: Graduate School of Criminal Justice, State University of New York, 1974.

Newman, D. J. *Introduction to Criminal Justice.* Philadelphia: Lippincott, 1975.

Newman, D. J. *Criminal Justice Education for Police.* Washington, D.C.: Police Foundation, 1978.

Newman, F., and others. *The Second Newman Report.* Cambridge, Mass.: M.I.T. Press, 1974.

Newman, J. H. *The Idea of a University*. New York: Longmans, Green, 1947. (Originally published 1873.)

O'Connor, G. W. *Survey of Selection Methods*. Washington, D.C.: International Association of Chiefs of Police, 1962.

O'Hara, C. *Fundamentals of Criminal Investigation*. Springfield, Ill.: Thomas, 1973. (Originally published 1956.)

O'Leary, V. "Programs of Correctional Study in Higher Education." *Crime and Delinquency*, 1976, *22* (1), 52-56.

Olscamp, P. J. "Does Our Undergraduate Curriculum Create Educated Persons?" Bellingham: Office of President, Western Washington University, 1977. (Mimeograph.)

Olson, B. T. *On the Disciplinary and Departmental Character of Criminal Justice Education for Police Officers*. Washington, D.C.: Police Foundation, 1978.

O'Neill, M. E., and Lance, J. E. "Education Versus Training: A Distinction." *Journal of California Law Enforcement*, 1970, *4*, 201-203.

Orlans, H. *Private Accreditation and Public Eligibility*. Lexington, Mass.: Heath, 1975.

Osterburg, J. A. "The Investigative Process." *Journal of Criminal Law, Criminology, and Police Science*, 1968, *9* (1), 427-433.

Ostrom, E. "Size and Performance in a Federal System." *Publius*, 1976.

Ostrom, E. *Police Department Policies Toward Education*. Washington, D.C.: Police Foundation, 1978.

O'Toole, J. *Work, Learning, and the American Future*. San Francisco: Jossey-Bass, 1977.

Pace, D. F., Stinchcomb, J. D., and Styles, J. C. *Law Enforcement Training and the Community College: Alternatives for Affiliation*. Washington, D.C.: American Association of Community and Junior Colleges, 1970.

Packer, H. *The Limits of the Criminal Sanction*. London: Oxford University Press, 1968; Stanford, Calif.: Stanford University Press, 1969.

Pearson, R., and others. *Criminal Justice Education: The End of the Beginning*. New York: Office of the Dean of Planning and Development, John Jay College of Criminal Justice, 1978.

Peirson, G. *Higher Educational Requirements and Minority Recruitment for the Police: Conflicting Goals?* Washington, D.C.: Police Foundation, 1978.

Phelps, L. "The Relationship Between the Agency and the College: The Berkeley Experience." In M. Neary (Ed.), *Higher Education for Police.* New York: American Academy for Professional Law Enforcement, 1977.

Pierson, F., and others. *The Education of American Businessmen.* New York: McGraw-Hill, 1959.

Pitchell, R. J. *Financing Part-Time Students, the New Majority in Postsecondary Education.* Washington, D.C.: American Council on Education, 1974.

Police Executive Research Forum. "Resolution on Higher Education for Police Officers." Washington, D.C.: Police Executive Research Forum, 1978.

Police Foundation. *Domestic Violence and the Police.* Washington, D.C.: Police Foundation, 1977.

Pomrenke, N. E. "Attracting and Retaining the College-Trained Officer in Law Enforcement." In *The Police Yearbook: 1966.* Washington, D.C.: International Association of Chiefs of Police, 1966.

President's Commission on Campus Unrest. *The Report of the President's Commission on Campus Unrest.* New York: Avon Books, 1971.

President's Commission on Law Enforcement and Administration of Justice. *The Challenge of Crime in a Free Society.* Washington, D.C.: U.S. Government Printing Office, 1967a.

President's Commission on Law Enforcement and Administration of Justice. *Task Force Report: The Police.* Washington, D.C.: U.S. Government Printing Office, 1967b.

Reinke, R. *Selection Through Assessment Centers: A Tool for Police Departments.* Washington, D.C.: Police Foundation, 1977.

Reiss, A. J., Jr. "Police Brutality—Answers to Key Questions." In L. Radzinowicz and M. E. Wolfgang (Eds.), *Crime and Justice.* Vol. 2: *The Criminal in the Arms of the Law.* New York: Basic Books, 1971a.

Reiss, A. J., Jr. *The Police and the Public.* New Haven, Conn.: Yale University Press, 1971b.

Reiss, A. J., Jr., and Black, D. "Interrogation and the Criminal Process." *Annals of the American Academy of Political and Social Science,* 1967, *374,* 47-57.

Reiss, A. J., Jr., and Bordua, D. J. "Environment and Organization: A Perspective on the Police." In D. J. Bordua (Ed.), *The Police: Six Sociological Essays.* New York: Wiley, 1967.

Reppetto, T. A. *Organizational Design of the Educated Police Department.* Washington, D.C.: Police Foundation, 1978.

Richardson, J. F. *The New York Police: Colonial Times to 1901.* New York: Oxford University Press, 1970.

Riddle, D. H. "Faculty and Curriculum Development in Criminal Justice Programs." Paper presented at the Conference on Key Issues in Criminal Justice Doctoral Education, University of Nebraska at Omaha, October 1975.

Riddle, D. H. "Faculty Selection." In M. Neary (Ed.), *Higher Education for Police.* New York: American Academy for Professional Law Enforcement, 1977.

Riddle, D. H. *Liberal Arts and Vocationalism in Higher Education Curricula for Police Officers.* Washington, D.C.: Police Foundation, 1978.

Riesman, D., and Jencks, C. "The Viability of the American College." In N. Sanford (Ed.), *The American College.* New York: Wiley, 1962.

Rindeau, A. J. *The Role of the Advisory Committee in Occupational Education in the Junior College.* Washington, D.C.: American Association of Community and Junior Colleges, 1967.

Rosovsky, H. "Undergraduate Education: Defining the Issues." Excerpts from *Dean's Report 1975-76.* Reprinted from *Report of the President of Harvard College and Reports of Departments, 1975-76.* Cambridge, Mass.: Harvard University Press, 1976.

Rotter, J. B., and Stein, D. K. "Public Attitudes Toward the Trustworthiness, Competence and Altruism of Twenty Selected Occupations." *Journal of Applied Social Psychology,* 1971, *1,* 334-343.

Rubinstein, J. *City Police.* New York: Farrar, Straus & Giroux, 1973.

Rudolph, F. *The American College and University: A History.* New York: Random House, 1962.

Rudolph, F. *Curriculum: A History of the American Undergraduate Course of Study Since 1636.* San Francisco: Jossey-Bass, 1977.

Salten, D. Statement presented to the National Advisory Commission on Higher Education for Police Officers, John Jay College of Criminal Justice, New York City, June 20, 1977.

Santarelli, D. "Education for Concepts—Training for Skills." *Police Chief,* 1974, *41* (8), 20, 76.

Saunders, C. *Upgrading the American Police: Education and Training for Better Law Enforcement.* Washington, D.C.: Brookings Institution, 1970.

Schembri, A. Statement presented to the National Advisory Commission on Higher Education for Police Officers, John Jay College of Criminal Justice, New York City, June 20, 1977.

Schick, R. P. *Structural and Attitudinal Barriers to Higher Education Requirements for Police Officers.* Washington, D.C.: Police Foundation, 1978.

Schrotel, S. R. "Attracting and Keeping College Trained Personnel in Law Enforcement." In *The Police Yearbook: 1966.* Washington, D.C.: International Association of Chiefs of Police, 1966.

Scott, R., and Shore, A. "Sociology and Policy Analysis." *American Sociologist,* 1974, *9,* 51-58.

Scully, M. G. "Many Colleges Reappraising Their Undergraduate Curricula." *Chronicle of Higher Education,* 1977, *13* (21), 1.

Seidman, H. "Accreditation and Federal Funding." In H. Orlans, *Private Accreditation and Public Eligibility.* Lexington, Mass.: Heath, 1975.

Selden, W. K. *Accreditation: A Struggle over Standards in Higher Education.* New York: Harper & Row, 1960.

Selden, W. K. *Accreditation and the Public Interest.* Washington, D.C.: Council on Postsecondary Accreditation, 1976.

Selznick, P. *TVA and the Grass Roots: A Study in the Sociology of Formal Organization.* Berkeley and Los Angeles: University of California Press, 1949.

Shanahan, D. "Education for Police Service: Professional or Liberal Arts." In M. Neary (Ed.), *Higher Education for Police*. New York: American Academy for Professional Law Enforcement, 1977.

Sherman, L. W. "The Breakdown of the Police Code of Silence." *Criminal Law Bulletin,* 1978a, *14,* 149-153.

Sherman, L. W. "Legal Issues in Law Enforcement." In A. W. Cohn (Ed.), *The Future of Policing.* Beverly Hills, Calif.: Sage, 1978b.

Sherman, L. W. *Scandal and Reform: Controlling Police Corruption.* Berkeley: University of California Press, 1978c.

Sherman, L. W., and McLeod, M. "Faculty Characteristics and Course Content in College Programs for Police Officers." Unpublished manuscript. School of Criminal Justice, State University of New York at Albany, 1978.

Sherman, L. W., Milton, C., and Kelley, T. *Team Policing: Seven Case Studies.* Washington, D.C.: Police Foundation, 1973.

Skolnick, J. H. *Justice Without Trial: Law Enforcement in Democratic Society.* New York: Wiley, 1966.

Skolnick, J. H. *The Politics of Protest.* New York: Simon & Schuster, 1969.

Skolnick, J. H., and Gray, T. C. (Eds.). *Police in America.* Boston: Little, Brown, 1975.

Smith, A. B., Locke, B., and Fenster, A. "Authoritarianism in Policemen Who Are College Graduates and Noncollege Police." *Journal of Criminal Law, Criminology, and Police Science,* 1970, *61,* 313-315.

Smith, A. B., Locke, B., and Walker, W. F. "Authoritarianism in College and Noncollege Oriented Police." *Journal of Criminal Law, Criminology, and Police Science,* 1967, *58,* 128-132.

Smith, A. B., Locke, B., and Walker, W. F. "Authoritarianism in Police College Students and Noncollege Students." *Journal of Criminal Law, Criminology, and Police Science,* 1968, *59,* 440-443.

Smith, D. C. "Police Professionalization and Performance: An Analysis of Public Policy from the Perspective of Police as Producers and Citizens as Consumers of Police Services." Unpublished doctoral dissertation, Indiana University, Bloomington, 1976.

Smith, D. C. *Empirical Studies of Higher Education and Police Performance.* Washington, D.C.: Police Foundation, 1978.

Smith, D. C., and Ostrom, E. "The Effects of Training and Education on Police Performance: A Preliminary Analysis." In H. Jacob (Ed.), *The Potential for Reform of Criminal Justice.* Beverly Hills, Calif.: Sage, 1974.

Solmon, L. C. "Too Many College Graduates?" In D. W. Vermilye (Ed.), *Relating Work and Education: Current Issues in Higher Education 1977.* San Francisco: Jossey-Bass, 1977.

Spaeth, J. L., and Greeley, A. M. *Recent Alumni and Higher Education.* New York: McGraw-Hill, 1970.

Spencer, G., and Nichols, R. "A Study of Chicago Police Recruits." *The Police Chief,* 1971, *38* (6), 50-55.

Spreen, J. Remarks in M. Neary (Ed.), *Higher Education for Police.* New York: American Academy for Professional Law Enforcement, 1977.

Stack, T. (U.S. Office of Management and Budget, Office of the President.) Telephone interview, April 25, 1978.

Stanley, D. T. *The History and Consequences of Federal Policies Concerning Higher Education for Police Officers.* Washington, D.C.: Police Foundation, 1978.

Stark, R. *Police Riots: Collective Violence and Law Enforcement.* Belmont, Calif.: Wadsworth, 1972.

Stead, P. J. *The Structure of Education and Police Careers in Europe and America.* Washington, D.C.: Police Foundation, 1978.

Steffens, L. *Autobiography.* New York: Harcourt Brace Jovanovich, 1931.

Stinchcomb, J. D. *Law Enforcement Technology (Police Science Technology): A Suggested Two-Year Post-High School Curriculum.* Washington, D.C.: U.S. Office of Education, 1975.

Stoddard, K. B. "Characteristics of Policemen of a County Sheriff's Office." In J. R. Snibbe and H. M. Snibbe (Eds.), *The Urban Policeman in Transition.* Springfield, Ill.: Thomas, 1973.

Streib, V. "Expanding a Traditional Criminal Justice Curriculum into an Innovative Social Control Curriculum." *Journal of Criminal Justice,* 1977, *5,* 165-169.

Swank, C. J. "Criminal Justice Education: The Dilemma of Articulation." *Journal of Criminal Justice,* 1975, *3,* 217-222.

Sykes, R. E., and Clark, J. P. "A Theory of Deference Exchange in Police-Civilian Encounters." *American Journal of Sociology,* 1975, *81* (3), 584-600.

Tamm, Q. "A Change for the Better." *Police Chief,* 1962, *32,* 5-6.

Tenney, C. W., Jr. *Higher Education Programs in Law Enforcement and Criminal Justice.* Washington, D.C.: U.S. Law Enforcement Assistance Administration, 1971.

Toch, H. *Police, Prisons, and the Problem of Violence.* Rockville, Md.: National Institute of Mental Health, 1977.

Todd, J. C. *Report of the Task Force on Law Enforcement Education.* Mentor: Ohio Council of Higher Education in Criminal Justice, Lakeland Community College, 1976.

Tolchin, M. "President Criticizes Organized Medicine." *New York Times,* May 6, 1978, p. 1.

"Training Humanists Is Goal of Engineering School." *New York Times,* January 1, 1978, p. 21.

Treiman, D. *Occupational Prestige in Comparative Perspective.* New York: Academic Press, 1977.

Trubitt, H. J. "The Hand That Holds the Baton." *Journal of Criminal Law, Criminology, and Police Science,* 1967, *58* (3), 414-417.

Twentieth Century Fund, Task Force on the Law Enforcement Assistance Administration. *Law Enforcement: The Federal Role.* New York: McGraw-Hill, 1976.

U.S. Comptroller General. *Report to the Congress: Problems in Administering Programs to Improve Law Enforcement Education.* Washington, D.C.: U.S. Government Accounting Office, 1975.

U.S. Law Enforcement Assistance Administration, Office of Regional Operations. *Guideline Manual: Law Enforcement Education Program.* Washington, D.C.: U.S. Department of Justice, May 6, 1975.

U.S. National Commission on Law Observance and Enforcement. *Report on the Police.* Washington, D.C.: U.S. National Commission on Law Observance and Enforcement, 1931.

Vaillant, G. *Adaptation to Life.* Boston: Little, Brown, 1977.

Van Maanen, J. "Working the Street: A Developmental View of Police Behavior." In H. Jacob (Ed.), *The Potential for Reform of Criminal Justice.* Beverly Hills, Calif.: Sage, 1974.

Vanagunas, S. "Police and Higher Education: A Comment on Problems and Relevancies." *Liberal Education,* March 1976, pp. 67-74.

Veblen, T. *The Higher Learning in America: A Memorandum on the Conduct of Universities by Businessmen.* New York: Sagamore Press, 1957. (Originally published 1918.)

Veysey, L. *The Emergence of the American University.* Chicago: University of Chicago Press, 1965.

Vollmer, A. "Aims and Ideals of the Police." *Journal of the American Institute of Criminal Law and Criminology,* 1922, *13,* 251-257.

Vollmer, A. *The Police and Modern Society.* Montclair, N.J.: Patterson Smith, 1971. (Originally published 1936.)

Vollmer, A., and Schneider, A. "The School for Police as Planned at Berkeley." *Journal of the American Institute of Criminal Law and Criminology,* 1917, *7,* 877-898.

von Moltke, K., and Schneevoigt, N. *Educational Leaves for Employees: European Experience for American Consideration.* San Francisco: Jossey-Bass, 1977.

Wachtel, D. "Preservice Police Academy Training: One University's Approach to Nontraditional Education." *Police Chief,* 1977, *44,* 61.

Wald, M. "Edison Offers Degrees but No Classes." *New York Times,* September 11, 1977, Sec. 12, p. 16.

Ward, D. "Report of the Section on Criminology." *ASA Footnotes,* 1978, *6* (4), 10-11.

Ward, R., and Kurz, T. *The Commuting Student: A Study of Facilities at Wayne State University.* Final Report of the Commuter Centers Project. Detroit: Michigan State University, 1969.

Watts, E. J. "Education and Career Patterns and Perceptions Among the St. Louis Police, 1947-1970." Paper presented at the annual meeting of the Academy of Criminal Justice Sciences, New Orleans, 1978.

Weber, J. K. "It Can Work for You." *Police Chief,* 1973, *40* (10), 41.

Webster, J. A. *The Realities of Police Work.* Dubuque, Iowa: Hunt, 1973.

Weiner, N. L. "The Effect of Education on Police Attitudes." *Journal of Criminal Justice,* 1974, *2;* 317-328.

Westley, W. *Violence and the Police.* Cambridge, Mass.: M.I.T. Press, 1970.

Weston, P. *The Police Traffic Control Function.* Springfield, Ill.: Thomas, 1975.

White, S. O. "A Perspective on Police Professionalization." *Law and Society Review,* 1972, *7,* 61-85.

Whitehead, A. N. *The Aims of Education and Other Essays.* New York: Free Press, 1967. (Originally published 1929.)

Whyte, W. F. *Street Corner Society: The Social Structure of an Italian Slum.* Chicago: University of Chicago Press, 1943.

Whyte, W. H. *The Organization Man.* New York: Simon & Schuster, 1956.

Williams, R. *Vice Squad.* New York: Crowell, 1973.

Wilson, J. *Police Report: A View of Law Enforcement.* Boston: Little, Brown, 1975.

Wilson, J. Q. *Varieties of Police Behavior: The Management of Law and Order in Eight Communities.* Cambridge, Mass.: Harvard University Press, 1968.

Wilson, J. Q. "Introduction to the Reprint Edition." In A. Vollmer, *The Police and Modern Society.* Montclair, N.J.: Patterson Smith, 1971.

Wilson, J. Q. *Thinking About Crime.* New York: Basic Books, 1975.

Wilson, O. W. *Police Administration.* New York: McGraw-Hill, 1963. (Originally published 1950.)

Wilson, O. W., and McLaren, R. *Police Administration.* New York: McGraw-Hill, 1972.

Zwerling, S. *Second Best: The Crisis of the Community College.* New York: McGraw-Hill, 1976.

Index